A Kenyan Adventure

Tailing the Tana: the story of a river expedition

Christopher Portway

impact books

First published in Great Britain 1993 by
Impact Books, 151 Dulwich Road, London SE24 0NG

ISBN 1 874687 15 3

Books by the same author:

Non-fiction
Journey to Dana (Kimber)
The Pregnant Unicorn (Dalton)
Corner Seat (Hale)
Double Circuit (Hale)
Journey Along the Andes (Oxford Illustrated Press/Impact Books)
The Great Railway Adventure (Oxford Illustrated Press/Coronet Books)
The Great Travelling Adventure (Oxford Illustrated Press)
Czechmate (John Murray)
Indian Odyssey (Impact Books)

Fiction
All Exits Barred (Hale)
Lost Vengeance (Hale)
The Tirana Assignment (Hale)
The Anarchy Pedlars (Hale)

Printed and bound by the Guernsey Press, Guernsey

Contents

Foreword

It was my father who first suggested a study of the Tana River back in 1974. He had been based at Garissa as a District Commissioner in the fifties and during that time had visited many parts of the river and its riverine forests. He described his journeys, often on foot and sometimes with George Adamson.

He spoke of the many peoples whose lives were influenced by this ever-changing, red-coloured river that crossed Kenya's arid equatorial savannah, bordered by a narrow but distinct belt of forest. He described the large herds of elephants, hippo and other wildlife, the great variety of birds that use the river as a 'motorway', the elusive Pel's fishing owl and the life in and around the forests. Here was a great African river with a unique diversity of life as it travelled from the tropical ice of Mount Kenya falling some 17,000 feet to the Indian Ocean.

A few days later, I wrote to Richard Leakey and others in Kenya to ask if a journey along its length to undertake a variety of studies with the National Museums of Kenya, would be welcomed. From Richard Leakey I received a positive reply – the first of many. Soon after, I wrote to a number of my student colleagues to ask if they would be interested in a source-to-sea journey down an East African river, and I was swamped with replies offering assistance and commitment. I am, to this day, astounded that so many were prepared to commit so much of their life to organising a student expedition down the Tana River in the summer of 1976.

Studying the new Life Science B.Sc. at the Polytechnic of Central London (now the University of Westminster) had its advantages. There was a group of tutors there who encouraged those on the course to undertake fieldwork overseas. With considerable help from the College and a recently formed Exploration Society, scientific expeditions had been organised to the Sahara in 1973 and down the Godare and Gilo rivers in the Illubabor Province of South-west Ethiopia in 1974. Both had produced field-data for a variety of bodies, including the Natural History Museum, the Royal Botanic Gardens, Kew and Addis Ababa University.

It was not long before a small group of us from the course met regularly in the canteen in New Cavendish Street to plan our new project. The initial team comprised fellow students Raj Patel, whose family were farmers in Kenya, Tony Pittaway, a seriously committed entomologist, Sandy Evans, who had never been overseas, Richard Matthews, the leader of the Ethiopian expedition and now a noted TV film producer, and John Axford, who was to go into the medical profession. Andrew Mitchell, a Bristol-based zoologist also joined the team. At that stage, little did we know that the team would grow to be 30 strong and involve scientists from the National Museums of Kenya and the Fisheries Department, a support team of British Army personnel, a New Zealand component comprising a Vietnam veteran nurse and a jet-boat expert, an Oxford film-maker and a stray travel writer.

At that time, the epicentre of expeditionary activities in Britain revolved around three camps. Lowther Lodge, the headquarters of the Royal Geographical Society overlooking Hyde Park was the first, with its extensive map room, its geographical library and unique collection of expedition reports. It had just appointed a new Director, John Hemming. The second was the Scientific Exploration Society, based in Room 5b in the Ministry of Defence, and headed by John Blashford-Snell (JBS), who had recently organised the great Zaire River Expedition as recounted in Richard Snailham's *A Giant Among Rivers*. JBS became a patron of the project and in so doing he kindly let us borrow his legendary address book from time to time. There was no one in Britain at the time who gave young people so much encouragement to organise projects overseas, and it is no surprise that our Tana project was influenced by John's journey down the Zaire River. The third port of call was 45 Brompton Road, the headquarters of Ian Wilson's World Expeditionary Association (WEXAS), and in particular

Penny Watts-Russell, the pioneer editor of their magazine
Expedition, the key reference for expeditioners at that time.
Among the many useful contacts Penny provided was a travel
writer to act as a chronicler for the expedition, one Christopher
Portway.

In the 18 years I have known Christopher Portway, he has not
changed one iota. His love of travel competes only with the love of
his wife Anna, whom he met behind the Iron Curtain. No one I
know has travelled in so many countries in so many ways, and this
he continues to do, having recently received a Winston Churchill
Memorial Fellowship to travel by bicycle from the Baltic port of
Tallin, Estonia to the Black Sea port of Constanta, Romania.

Here is the original independent traveller – ageless, tireless,
dedicated, and with a profound faith in all whom he meets. If there
is trouble to be found, Portway will be there. But he does so to
share the surprises with us through his many writings. Although
the Tana was Chris's first expedition as such, he was always at the
centre of adventurous mischief, as this story will relate. As a group
of students, it was a privilege to have this 'fifty-something' travel
writer join the team. His energy and vigour was a lesson to those
half his age. For me it is a pleasure to acknowledge his friendship
and his life-long support, and I treasure the times we shared a dug-
out.

Being asked to write this Foreword to Chris's new account of
the Tana River Expedition has reminded me how lucky we were to
have the opportunity to spend three months travelling the length of
this great river. Collections made now rest with the Herbarium, the
Museum and Fisheries Department in Nairobi. The counts made of
fish populations, hippo, crocodiles, birds and other wildlife
provided a benchmark. The excitement of the photographing and
filming the Pel's fishing owl for the first time by Richard
Matthews and Derek Bromhall was a particularly special moment.
There were many such tales from the slopes of Mount Kenya to
the surf of the Indian Ocean at Kipini, and I will leave the
storytelling to Chris.

However, there were also indications of a river under stress. We
witnessed the enormous pressures such a river has to bear in
providing hydroelectricity in its upper reaches and its task of

supporting a growing agricultural community along its banks. Much of the wildlife was now competing for the forests before being cut for charcoal or cleared for farmland. The Tana mangabey and red colobus monkeys were two primates having a particularly hard time. There are no easy solutions. Also we witnessed the effects of poaching and the vastly diminished elephant population. For the Government of Kenya, these issues were being tackled by the Tana River Development Authority and the Wildlife Departments. For us, it brought home the challenge of the task ahead – the need to make best use of natural resources, and the urgency of integrating conservation and development priorities in order to find sustainable solutions to a set of complex geographical problems. The enormity of the task must never stun scientists into inaction, as we are reminded by Sir Christopher Tickell, the current President of the RGS.

On a personal note, I treasure to this day the letter I received from George Adamson, inviting me to come and stay with him at his Kampi-ya-Simba near Kora rock. His love for this forgotten wilderness is now world renowned. He met me at the dusty airstrip to the east of the Kora Game Reserve in July 1975 and shared his own knowledge of this *Acacia-commiphora* bushland and his lifelong work with lions. This visit, a reconnaissance for the expedition to choose the site of the main research camp, was to be the first of many to Kora.

It was a few months before his murder in 1989 that I last visited George, with my son Philip (then four years old), to discuss the possibilities of a permanent 'field-university' in Kora for long-term training and research. When the time is right, I believe this will happen and scientists from all over the world will come to study this unique habitat. It will be a fitting memorial to George and the many years he gave to this wilderness by Kora rock, the highest inselberg near the Tana River and a natural meeting place for those living there for several thousand years.

29 March 1993

Nigel Winser, Deputy Director,
Royal Geographical Society

Introduction

There is an almost legendary affinity between the British and the great deserts and jungles of Africa. 'Doctor Livingstone, I presume' are words that epitomise the British love of inflicting discomfort upon themselves in the interests of exploration, discovery, experience and conquest. We accept the occasional Frenchman or Scandinavian upon the scene, for even other countries have their eccentrics. The inhabitants of these regions suffer simply because they happen to live there. But Peter Fleming spoke for the majority when he said that the trouble about such journeys nowadays is that they are easy to make but difficult to justify. Only a few places remain untrampled and they are those that are inaccessible on wheels.

With the spread of the package tour and ever-faster, ever-larger aircraft, the days of the explorer are numbered say the cynics. And with most of the challenges of geography overcome by intrepid pioneers, there is a certain amount of frustration creeping into the deliberations of the would-be explorer as he or she glowers perplexedly at the globe now singularly devoid of all that red which Doctor Livingstone and his kith went to such pains to daub. Thus it is becoming a case not so much of being first up or over a feature of this earth, but of finding ways to negotiate it in an original and sometimes gimmicky manner. Take Everest for example. The summit has been conquered on numerous occasions from each of its scowling faces, but there's always some bright spark waiting in the wings who can dream up a new way to suffer in the interests of conquest.

Though the fields of conquest may have diminished, the same need not be said about those of investigation. Here the choice widens dramatically. There are many regions of the world today that have been traversed by intrepid footsteps – even if few of these pioneering boots have halted long enough to scratch beneath the surface.

So when I was invited to join the Tana River Expedition, I saw myself as the new member of a band of investigators rather than explorers. My emotions were more of profound interest than surging excitement, for simple conquest will ever remain the headier potion. And, for me, Black Africa was an enigma.

I had never been there but my family had. My father commanded a battalion of the West African Frontier Force in what was then Sierra Leone in 1944. Shortly after the Second World War, my brother, a subaltern in the Essex Regiment, was stationed, I seemed to recollect, in Kenya's Mombasa. From them, in my younger and less perceptive days, I formulated a picture of Africa that had, ever after, put this great continent on the back of the queue of countries I wanted to visit. That my father enjoyed West Africa he made abundantly clear by constant repetition and patronising reference to the amusing habits of his 'boys'. My brother saw little of Kenya beyond the confines of the officers' mess; yet, for years afterwards, he endeavoured to give an impression of being knowledgeable about African affairs – injecting into every conceivable exchange some half-dozen ill-pronounced words of Swahili and sarcastic allusions to the absurdity of a life that differed from his own. These reactions, so normal for the British soldier – and I had been one, too – irked me unreasonably and kept Black Africa at arm's length. Only the brown north would subsequently claim my attention and, on some half-dozen occasions, my footsteps. A lengthy sojourn on a camel in the Sahara was one of the occasions, and though this hardly makes me a man of the desert, I felt more at home in a wilderness of sand than I thought I would in a wilderness of jungle.

It was brought home to me fequently by my contemporaries that middle age not only hardens the arteries but also one's ways, ideas and outlook. I was unable to help the arteries, but I thought I could shake up the other items. Suddenly Black Africa became a desirable place to go.

But where and what was this Tana? The first book I looked up told me it was a lake in Ethiopia. Then I discovered another to be a river in Kenya; in fact the *longest* river in Kenya. A wild, inhospitable, disease-ridden river – which cheered me up no end. Someone I met in my local who had lived some years in Nairobi casually said he knew the Tana and had crossed it once on a ferry; my dreams of discovering a 'lost river' deflated. I dug deeper and learnt that the Tana river was 650, 800 or 1,000 miles long – definitely 1,000 if every bend was taken into account. And we, paddling down the river in boats, would most emphatically be taking every bend into account. I was also given to understand that sections of its lower route had been traversed by canoe and that a century ago, the paddle-driven SS *Kenia* reached Kora in the first and last attempt to navigate a vessel upstream. Appropriately, Kora was to become the site of the expedition's first base camp, but its fame has to do with none of these occurrences. As everyone in Kenya knows, the legendary George and Terence Adamson lived below the large rock projection rising prominently above the flat scrubland, and haven't George's lions, as personified by the books and films *Born Free* and *Living Free*, caught the imagination of the world?

In the realms of science and economics the Tana could produce more down-to-earth promises than the glamourous undertones of single-minded canoeists and rehabilitated lions. More than a hundred years ago the two Denhard brothers undertook the first scientific expedition on the river. In 1892 an expedition under Captain Dundas assessed the possibility of it being the main artery of inland communication with Kipini, the future port of Kenya. An interesting speculation this, for it was a railway that lost Mombasa a capitalship and it could have been a river that neutralised its port. Half-hearted exploration continued sporadically for many years but the very inhospitability of the climate, vegetation, insects and wild game dampened enthusiasm.

However, the Tana, winding through the barren Northern Frontier District and attended by its riverine forest, was not to be ignored in spite of the miserable welcome offered to the pioneers. Like a spoilt child, it cried out for attention, and its potential as a hydroelectric power and irrigation source was noted. Today, the river is part of a vital and large-scale redevelopment programme. Dams have already been built on the upper reaches, and others are raising their concrete heads, while irrigation schemes are underway at various places along the lower Tana. But with progress comes destruction for, so often, the two walk hand-in-hand.

Progress cannot nor wants to be halted – particularly in a parched and desolate land. The Tana River Development Authority, then a new body probing its way, was resourceful enough to concern itself with arranging that human, water, animal, land and other resources be utilised to the best possible advantage. Yet there had been very little accumulation of ecological data, on account of the very inhospitability that deflected proposed development in the late 19th century. So here, on an unsympathetic river, were rewarding tasks to be performed that (if it does not sound too grandiose) could benefit mankind. An adventurous river though, that sprouts in a 17,000-foot mountain, frolics youthfully amidst untamed rapids and courses maturely through animal-infested territory remote from civilization.

Thus the challenge, a linchpin of any expedition.

A three-month scientific expedition is no overnight accomplishment. The volume of work involved in putting some two dozen adventurers and scientists into a foreign field has to be experienced to be believed. I came into the organisation in the autumn of the year before departure, but the committee and others had been hard at it for a year before that. The leader was to be Nigel Winser, then a 24-year-old student of Life Science at the Polytechnic of Central London. That his passion for running and participating in expeditions triumphed over a more mundane desire to obtain his B.Sc. was patently obvious from the start, though both achievements are fine qualifications for manhood and the business of life. For his years Nigel already had considerable expeditionary experience tucked conspicuously beneath his belt, including leadership of the PCL Sahara Expedition 1973 and membership of the PCL West Ethiopia Expedition 1974. Bearded, hairy, afflicted with a slight limp, his formidable appearance contradicts a charm and gentle force of character emerging from the heart and not just simple expediency. The limp was a legacy of polio: it severely restricted his prowess on the playing fields of

Bradford College, and to a boy such matters assume gargantuan importance. Yet, willing his good limbs to take over from a gammy one, Nigel triumphed in a public-school gymnastic tour of Denmark and went on to win a gold medal in the Duke of Edinburgh Award Scheme. There lies, often dormant, in every human soul the precious spirit of courage. In Nigel's case that spirit is far from dormant.

A resident of the country for eleven years, his eyes were fastened upon Kenya from the very start. Though not an entirely unexplored river, the remote Tana could offer, he could see, the fruit of both adventure and worthwhile investigation. With the project no more than a vague infatuation, Nigel de Northop Winser began to pick his team for his third and most ambitious exploratory undertaking.

In no way is this book a tome on how to set up and run an expedition. Such a handbook could run into multiple volumes and I, as an old new boy to the expeditionary game, would not be competent to write even a preface. But I was to learn something from the months of preparation, and knowledge is an infections acquisition.

There are, as yet, no trade union restrictions for explorers. Though each new member of the team was picked for his and her specialist knowledge and ability in a particular realm, all were expected to 'muck in' with carrying out tasks outside it. As the designated 'chronicler' of the expedition, I suppose I was flattered that somebody thought I could write; but in addition to the supplying of pre-departure features to the news media, I found myself deeply emmeshed in a world of sponsorship, publicity and public relations. The Polytechnic of Central London had an exploration society and this made a base for operations. Later, the PCL was to become the chief sponsor of the project, and their contribution to its fulfilment was a vital accoutrement. By reason of its scientific aims the expedition could raise an added dimension to that of simple exploration, which in turn added to the difficulties and complications of setting it up. Joining the team were mammalogists, ornithologists, entomologists, zoologists and an immunologist – each with his or her personal technical and/or personal problems to sort out. And though the eldest of these scientists was but twenty-five and therefore hardly of the absent-minded professor school, there had to be a back-up organisation and adventure squad. Which is how the British Army came onto the scene. With Kenya a Commonwealth country, and one of good will to boot, the British army and Royal Air Force were able to maintain a modest training 'presence' there. Thus, transport, basic food and considerable amounts of non-scientific equipment were forthcoming for the hardly burdensome cost of having a number of military personnel participating in the expedition.

All this was to involve a formidable campaign of arranging and the tying of loose ends. Month after month, between committee and general meetings in London, Nigel and the team battled with the problems, hammering at them until hard solutions were forged from the fog of indecision. Administration, finance, insurance, air transportation; liaison with High Commissions, the Royal Geographical Society, the Scientific Exploration Society, Nairobi Museum, the Tana River Development Authority, the Kenya Game Department, the British Museum, the Kenya Fishery Department and the Flying Doctor Service. Movement planning, safety, scientific programmes, trapping permits, scientific permits, fee-paying of local African members and helpers, air reconnaissance, packing and crating of equipment, customs, liaison with the Ministry of Defence, Foreign Office, Ministry of Overseas Development, Kenya Police and Army, equipment checks, vaccinations and innoculations, climbing training and contact with the Mountain Club of Kenya, brochure writing and printing, research, public relations and personal equipment discount acquisition. These were just some of the headings behind which lay a great multitude of trials, each sprouting its own tribulations like a multi-headed monster of insuperability.

A serious snag was that of getting members together – whether for a meeting or a training session. For those who were to join the expedition from Kenya itself there was, of course, no question of their coming to London; but others hailing from more distant parts of Britain had various impediments. Because of this, an ambitious scheme to hold a long weekend of training in the wilds of Scotland was reduced to a Friday-night-to-Sunday encampment on the Thames at Reading. Here some dozen members converged to play

rubber boats on England's royal river, much to the pained surprise
of nautical types in passing craft of more respectable design. Beer
flowed copiously on both nights and a collection of virtual
strangers became the nucleus of a close-knit team. A subsequent
project involving a three-day negotiation of the South Downs Way
long-distance footpath netted just two members and a crop of
painful blisters.

The question of finance always concerns and usually bedevils
budding expeditions, and that of the Tana River was no exception.
Towards the estimated total expenses, each member was asked to
contribute the cost of the airfare, London-Nairobi, plus a little
over. This, at least, had the effect of parting the wheat from the
chaff. However, it was a distinct hardship for the less prosperous
of the younger members, particularly in the knowledge that
participation would entail no income for a further three whole
months. Only the soldiers were laughing. They were *paid* to come.

So preparation for the expedition lurched on with an occasional
spurt here, a lapse there as a new member joined or an existing
one found reason for leaving. Deputy leadership was vested in an
army member since military support was expected to be
considerable. Captain Mike Rowlett of the Parachute Regiment
was forced to withdraw because of military circumstances, his
place being taken by Major Robert Williamson, a 28-year-old
Royal Green Jacket. Lower down the military hierarchy, Lance-
corporal Andy Winspear, 28, an irrepressible Brummie, took over
from a Lance-corporal Warren – whom the expedition never even
saw. A further potential military attachment was Sergeant Mike
Wortley of the Devonshire & Dorsets, who was to fill the post of
boat mechanic. He too was unable to stay the course and the post
remained unfilled. The role of documentary film producer
changed with monotonous regularity. Roger Pennington became
John Oakley, who in turn handed over to Derek Bromhall, who in
the event was able to join the expedition only some weeks after it
had set out. In addition, a handful of members were compelled for
various reasons to return home early a situation that had to be
taken into account since all had been empowered with a specific
task. A number of visitors, British and Kenyan, mostly specialists
in the scientific field though a few with more prosaic

contributions, were expected to join or become attached to the expedition for different periods, all of which was to add to the problems of logistics and administration.

At the outset, the expedition group were to be divided into three main action teams: the Mountain Team, the White Water Team and the Scientific Team – this last the largest – each with their supporting elements. In some cases, so far as the Mountain and White Water Teams were concerned, a few members were in both, which meant that events and coverage of the river had to be in chronological order. In point of fact there was some overlap, which was to put a severe strain upon transportation and supply. But the idea of negotiating the Tana from source to mouth remained, in everyone's mind, a feat to be accomplished for the simple motivation of achievement.

Not unnaturally it was the army that predominated in the adventure side of the project and the two non-scientific teams were to be headed by experts in their specific aims. Captain Harley Nott, Royal Engineers, the 28-year-old Marlborough, Christ's College Cambridge and Sandhurst-educated son of a brigadier, had amassed considerable climbing experience on the 1971 British Roraima Expedition in South America and the Blue Mountains Expedition to Jamaica in 1973-74, adequate qualification to ensure his leadership of the Mountain Team. To Captain Paul Turner, 26, of the Queen's Own Hussars, went command of the White Water Team, his membership of the famous 1974 Zaire River Expedition making him an obvious choice.

Thus the months ground by and two dozen investigators stood poised to go. Some were old hands at the expedition business; others, like myself, were no more than fervent individualists of travel, while one had never ventured further east than Calais. An ill-assorted bunch indeed to descend upon an obscure East African river.

To my wife, Anna; for all wives and loved ones left behind.

This gray spirit yearning in desire
To follow knowledge like a sinking star,
Beyond the utmost bound of human thought.

Alfred, Lord Tennyson

We carry with us the wonders we see without us;
there is all Africa and her prodigies in us.

Sir Thomas Browne

1. Musings and Meanderings on a Train

One of the loneliest places on earth is Lake Höhnel. It stands, a blue-green gem, at an altitude of 13,500 feet in an untrodden valley between walls that buttress the multiple peaks of Mount Kenya. Ranks of giant lobelia and groundsel march down from the slopes like silent robots issuing from another world, their thick trunks and filmy skirts a strange uniform of anonymity. A grin of volcanic molars makes a cockscomb to the surrounding ridges, a remnant of some glacial retreat at the birth of time. Away to the south-west, across the corrugations of lesser valleys, stand the sentinel outposts of the Aberdares, mauve with distance and haloed with cloud. Further south, directly across the silent Höhnel Valley, the stubby rampart of another of East Africa's volcanic warts, 19,000-foot Kilimanjaro, can occasionally be discerned 200 miles away, its cratered summit piercing the cotton-wool fleece that mountains are wont to draw around their barren shoulders.

From the turret of Point Joseph, commanding the crenellated rampart between the Teleki and Höhnel Valleys, it can be discerned that the lonely lake has sprouted a tadpole's tail. The mountain streams and subterranean brooks that nourish the lake are hidden beneath the fruitless earth, but the tail proclaims the beginnings of a river. Maps of this wild region give it a name: that of the Nairobi River, though its growth and stature over the miles of its course remains stunted and finally withers away. But suddenly it has become a new river with a new name: the Sagarna, and an injection of tribal growth has offered succour to the weakling babe. Other streams snake down from the heights of Mount Kenya and the Aberdares to feed lifeblood into this fevered watercourse with yet a third name: the Tana; the gathering of the fingers of a hand.

The exact source, if there is one, of Kenya's longest river remains obscure but, assuredly, its birth pangs are enacted among the country's most dramatic highlands. As I stood that day, breathless upon Point Joseph, it was difficult to visualise that, before many more days were gone, I would be living on, in and beside the Tana's turgid waters on their long tortuous journey to the sea. Soon a human relationship between a varied band of travellers from a foreign land and a remote but significant East African river would begin. Fascination, scorn, interest, love and hate would stir in the cauldron of emotions. From a tadpole's tail called the Nairobi River to an adult city that, by the diligence of its people, had become not only capital of Kenya but acknowledged chief city of East Africa is but a hundred miles. And for the investigators of the Tana River Expedition that is where the real journey began.

Our aircraft displayed a marked reluctance to leave the shores of Europe, putting down with an almost frenzied eagerness at both Frankfurt and Rome, and there lingering amongst the paraphernalia of two of the world's major airports, as if savouring their security before crossing the Mediterranean to the primitiveness of Africa. And it must be admitted that the Sahara is a drastic introduction to this mighty continent; the endless ocean of dust can be felt even in the pressurised cabin of a modern airliner. Our aircraft, *The Blue Nile* of Sudan Air, heaved and bucked as the heatwaves caught it, and I looked down from my window seat with a certain wistfulness; for the deserts of this world act as a kind of Lorelei – enticing me by a magnetic seduction. But the Sahara was not for me on this journey. Earlier, the dawn sunrise, an elongated nuclear explosion, had burst with primeval violence to terminate the long night, and its utter magnificence signified not only a desert hell but the whole untamed grandeur of Africa.

And it was to the beat of 20th-century African war drums, against a backdrop of the vicious, unpredictable violence of Black African political upheaval, that our two-dozen-strong party entered upon their quest. One hiccup in the turmoil of man's endeavour had already caused a 27-hour postponement of our flight from London. A failed coup in the Sudan against its government had closed the airport of Khartoum, an inconvenience that shrank to nothing when pitted against the sufferings of a revolution's victims. Now the airport was open again for business, though tensed beneath the shadow of civil war.

Within a minute we saw the native town of Omdurman, the shadow of our aeroplane with lowered wheels flicking across the scores of little brown courtyards and bare, unadorned mud walls of houses that looked exactly like cardboard boxes turned upside down. A glimpse of treeless streets leading straight into the swirling desert itself, and there was Khartoum.

We came in low over the housetops and saw the pattern of the city spread out, vaguely in the form of a Union Jack as Kitchener meant it to be. Today, even without its latest revolution, it is a city bewildered; divided by faiths and the conflict of ideologies. On the west bank of the Nile stands Omdurman, product of the Dervish, of Oriental-Africanised beliefs; on the east bank, Khartoum, the product of Christian or Western faith. The airport swarmed with brown men in shapeless denims with Russian – or was it American? – automatic weaponry. Anti-aircraft guns bristled from the flat roof of the terminal building like television antennas. Distrust and suspicion lay heavy on the sweltering air and it became an achievement to raise a smile out of those who had business on the tarmac and in the transit lounge. Our baggage was removed from the aircraft hold, even though we were continuing to Nairobi in the same machine, and our overweight rucksacks and absurd amounts of 'hand luggage' – tolerated and uncharged for by a sympathetic Sudan Air official at Heathrow – was scrutinised. Harley Nott, injudiciously snapping airport installations, had his camera confiscated and returned with a sharp reprimand. A final blast of humidity as we returned to our aircraft and we were off once more across two Niles that were neither blue nor white but mud-brown.

But the sky was blue, an impossible blue, as we climbed into it, and I pondered again upon the immense task of putting a small group of soldiers, scientists and others into an 'African field'. Not only the Sudan but Kenya and all Africa too were racked with crisis and political fever which could, at a stroke, invalidate the months of preparation for the expedition and wreck the carefully balanced but precarious gyroscope of logistics and communications so carefully built into it. All had culminated in a scrap of paper: form reference OP13/001/C1940/10, issued by the Office of the President of Kenya. It was the key to the expedition. In Nairobi, Doctor John Richardson, his wife Susie and their two children were our designated advance party. They had already been in the Kenyan capital for three weeks and now awaited our arrival early in July. Their task had been to oil the lock.

My eyes strayed back to the window, darting at mountains that might have been Ethiopian and an elongated lake that could have been Turkana. From 25,000 feet they looked like a papier-mâché model, unreal and impersonal. Then we began the slow descent to Kenya's capital and it came to me, idiotically, that we had only 19,000 feet to fall since Nairobi stands, already, at an altitude of 6,000 feet.

I don't know quite what I expected as I stepped out on to East African soil. The sun was shining but there was no heat. The tarmac was like that of any international airport. Everybody looked very European simply because everyone *was* European. Only the aircraft parking controller, conducting with his orange gloves, and a quartet of baggage unloaders were black – which could have been the case anywhere. The howl of our jet engines sunk to a whisper and died.

I was damned if I knew what to make of Nairobi either. And my puzzlement hardly abated with time. As a town it is pleasant and comfortable enough if you are a businessman or a tourist – or even a waiting-to-get-the-hell-out-of-it explorer. The centre of the city is a bastion of midget skyscrapers, which all African towns – and not a few elsewhere in the world – deem an indispensable badge of their devotion to progress, despite the open spaces around them. It is, of course, unworthy of the country that spreads away in all directions, but what mere city can be otherwise? One must go beyond the less impressive outer suburbs and shanty towns to climb the low hills on the horizon in order to attain the feel of the immensely exciting physical presence of Africa.

For more than a week most of us were condemned to a purgatory of urban living. There was work to be done of the type that necessitated a clean white collar, a tie and a pinstripe suit.

Authorisations to be confirmed, photograph and press agencies to be handled, PR people to be persuaded, commercial sponsors to be wheedled, receptions and press conferences to be attended. I cursed myself for not having packed my razor. Good opportunity to grow an explorer's beard I thought, quite overlooking the social razzmatazz that is, it seems, a universal pre-expedition prerequisite. Thrust into a madhouse of Bournvita, of washing powder, sweet-scented soap and Tusker Beer, my knight-errant crusade into the wilderness began to founder in a bubble bath; a vat of commercialism. I tumbled down a hundred and forty-four chocolate bars that had become my stairway to the stars. Doctor Livingstone, I realized, had survived by courtesy of the Incorporated Washer Co., while all those crates carried on the heads of Stanley's bearers could only have been full of sponsored sugar cube, treacle, foot powder and gin. 'We'll give you two hundred gallons of petrol in return for publicity in the national press' bartered the oil company with the biggest name in Kenya and, being the biggest optimists and because we wanted the petrol, we agreed. Publicity. That was the name of the game, and we wanted it too, for the more we were splashed across the pages of the *Daily Nation* and the *East African Standard*, the more we could screw out of our local benefactors. And it had been the same in Britain. Expeditions, alas, are not built upon high ideals alone. Green though I was, the fact had not escaped me, but to meet it face to face on the brink of the Great Adventure still came as a rude awakening.

Our Nairobi base, presided over by Susie Richardson with all the efficiency and earnestness of a Blackpool landlady, was the rented home of an airline pilot away on leave. A shaded suburban house in the Westlands district, surrounded by purple bougainvillaea and the inverted cream-coloured bells of the deadly poisonous angel's trumpets, it was still too small to hold the whole out-of-the-field personnel of the expedition and their multifarious kit. So the overflow was despatched to the ranch-house home of the Patels on the Kigwa Estate, some five miles out of town. Raj Patel, Indian-born, Swahili- and English-speaking, dark-skinned and petit, was the expedition's scientific leader. Like many Asians he possessed a prodigious quantity of relatives, of which he,

'Uncle Patel', was one. The rambling house, each room leading to another, held a bewildering variety of other Patels who, in sarong, djellabah and suit, smiled sweetly and bowed whenever I took a wrong turning when looking for the lavatory. Most of us, however, were billeted in a broken-down outhouse in the grounds, which was perfectly adequate for our needs.

The fact that Nigel Winser, Raj Patel and several other members of the team had lived in Kenya and retained close links with the country was to ease, very considerably, our introduction to a new environment. For some, it was almost like going home. Hardly had we arrived when a host of British residents threw open their homes to us with flamboyant gestures of hospitality. I had preconceived ideas about British expatriates living out their lives under the widening shadow of a black-dominated Africa. My first impressions tended to confirm a kind of desperate togetherness, a closing of the thinning ranks and a drink-sodden loneliness, but it was, I think, an exaggerated impression. The Africans I met in the streets of Nairobi were often unfriendly, arrogant and rude, utterly unlike the charming people I was to find outside this upstart concrete jungle. But in the cities there is an awareness that the white citizen is tolerated and not universally wanted. Both Whites and Blacks know it. So maybe the remaining Europeans of Kenya are attempting to live out a fantasy. Perhaps they pursue, in the alien setting of Africa, a dream of an English country life which has long ceased to exist even in Britain. One feels that an important part of their lives is dominated by nostalgia, as if they were obsessed with a memory which is no further use to them. Yet they soldier on, sniping at the shortcomings of the country of their birth as if the Kenyan shortcomings and restrictions – growing daily – were any the less severe.

First impressions, they say, are the ones that stick. If this is so, the ten days most of us spent in Nairobi must have had a profound effect on those, like me, who were new to and wide-eyed at the African scene. Me, I was lucky. After only three days of city-slicking I managed to escape the petty chores of sponsorship and strident demands of publicity by taking to the railway.

A word of explanation here. As a travel writer and author, my brief, rather obviously, is to observe the world and report upon it.

And to observe it one must all-too-frequently move about it. Ever since the day some woaded warrior chipped himself a wheel, the methods of transportation available to mankind have multiplied and flourished. My favourite is the lowly train, and though I do not class myself as a railway enthusiast – I know little of how the wheels go round – I have probably chalked up more train miles across the globe than most. One famous rail institution that had escaped my attention was the then East African Railway, undergoing, even as I was in Kenya, the sad process of being truncated. Already no through-trains ran to Dar-es-Salaam in Tanzania, and in the other direction, the line into Uganda was under threat. Hard-headed Kenyans with realistic views on life said 'So what?' in response to my overtures of regret; but then I was not a Kenyan taxpayer on whose shoulders fell most of the burden of financing the efficient running of the once tri-country network. With a first-class sleeper ticket given me by the excellent Tom Matsalia, publicity manager of the Railway Corporation in Nairobi – even here I was ensnared in the wicked world of commercial one-upmanship – I set off to glimpse a larger slice of Kenya.

Alone on a train one can think. It is not often that I travel first class on my trains, and on that run to Mombasa I had the compartment to myself. A friendly steward with an india-rubber face brought me a wad of bedding and I sat and watched Africa go by.

What did I know of Africa and the Africans? The facetious words of a Member of Parliament on a television panel show came to me out of the dusk. He said he thought coloured people made lousy bus conductors. And expeditionists, I reflected, could be like overland group travellers in Land Rovers. Many of them had been to evocative places; they had travelled widely in exotic lands. Yet their talk was not of the countryside they had seen nor the people they had met but of their Land Rovers and how each had behaved. They acquired a new generator in Marrakesh, needed an oil-change in Meshed and had had a 7¼-inch Whitworth stolen in front of the Taj Mahal. I hoped to be undertaking a minimum of driving on this venture but I would still be encased within this kind of air-conditioning of my fellow-countrymen and the technicalities of expeditioning, a factor that caused me unease. I had always shied away from the group conception of travel to learn how a country ticks. As a result I was sometimes lonely and often suffered hardship, but the experience laid bare the grass roots of a country. Had I now signed myself up to a *Boys' Own Paper* outing or would I, like Alice, be able to penetrate the looking glass and find the real Africa?

Far, far away in the reflection of the window pane, I saw my Brighton home against the endless Athai Plain. Our brief farewells completed, I remembered my wife trying to laugh at my clumsiness with an outsize rucksack as I set out for the station. I thought of myself, earlier, traipsing about the town on a snakes-and-ladders game of acquiring inoculations and certificates proving I had had the inoculations. And I was reminded of my neighbours appearing startled when I met them in the street, saying they thought I had already gone. Whenever I was on the threshold of a journey they said that.

Irritably, I wiped away the past and thought again, more kindly, of Nairobi. For those who are coming to Africa for the first time it serves as the perfect decompression chamber. The modern steel-and-glass shopping centre, its parking meters and traffic circling the roundabouts clockwise in the British manner, the red English post-boxes, its Wimpys, Woolworths and fish-and-chip saloons seem very homely, reassuring legacies of what one concludes to have been a beneficial British rule. Whatever *is* foreign and strange about Nairobi is not African but Indian – the minarets and the mosques, the Indian names over the arcaded shops and a dusky people neither black nor white. But unlike India I saw few beggars in the city. (I did see one crawling sideways along the pavement like a land crab. 'Jambo!' he cried, cupping his hands together in the traditional way of beggars, and because of this exception to the norm he scratched an indelible notch in my memory.) Yet there is terrible poverty to be seen behind the new boulevards of Nairobi if one cares to go and look for it. Disease and poverty are part of Africa but in Nairobi the destitute do not seem real. Everything about Nairobi seemed unreal.

Still, it is a remarkable city. Even within my father's lifetime it has grown from a malarial stretch of swamp – remembered in the name of one of its thoroughfares, Swamp Street – to a metropolis of more than three-quarters of a million; having taken over the rôle of capital from Mombasa, it has become one of the most cosmopolitan places in the world. Like New York it is constantly renewing itself. Cheek by jowl you can see all the stages of its hustling growth since it was a railway construction camp – a pioneer's town. In 1902 a wildlife authority, Colonel Meinetzhhagen, recorded in his diary: 'The only shop is a small tin hut which sells everything ... the only hotel here is a wood and tin shanty'. Today, the dazzling white mirage of Nairobi's skyscrapers rises from avenues adorned with statues and lined with great explosions of riotously coloured bougainvillaea. The suburbs, occasionally visited by lions, are alive with hibiscus, oleanders and glorious blue-flowering jacaranda trees. And it is noticeable that the main streets are still wide enough to turn a wagon and team of oxen in.

My window on Africa abruptly offered no more than a reflection of my own compartment. Here I was on one of *the* train rides of the world and they have to make it a *night* journey.

This book is no place for a detailed record of my seven days wandering on and off the tracks of the railway. But mention can legitimately be made of a few of the impressions I gathered as a newcomer to East Africa and of an experience that befell me which brought home to all members of the expedition the savage ways of African politics – the orbit into which we had placed ourselves, and which forms an intrinsic part of the story.

I often wonder if Mombasa harbours a grudge against Nairobi. Already I have alluded to Mombasa's stolen capitalship, and the salt in the wound must be the fact that it was something of an urban community way back in the 11th century, while Nairobi only received its city charter in 1950. Mombasa's original *raison d'être* was a break in the coral reef that stretches along the Kenyan coast. Ships were able to enter Kilindini – 'The Place of Deep Water' as the port is called – and landlocked Uganda could scarcely have survived without the Mombasa road and railway.

It was well past daybreak when we pulled out of Kilindini, clanked over the bridge that joins Mombasa to the mainland and pulled into the railway's eastern terminus. The station, for me, set the seal on Mombasa. Part of its scattered amenities included a row of three concrete cubicles labelled '1st class Ladies and Gentlemen's Toilets', '2nd class Ladies and Gents' and '3rd class Male & Female', in that order. Shades of the Indian Raj indeed!

And assuredly Mombasa is a slice of Asia. Here is a town embodying, in character and architecture, the mixed cultures that have come together in true unison. Arab, African and European. But the colours have run and they come out Asian.

I spent a sticky morning exploring the Old Town, its narrow streets overshadowed by tall houses with elaborately carved ornamental balconies. Itinerant Arabs sold coffee from traditional long-beaked copper pots, oriental music drifted out from the shops of goldsmiths, moneylenders, tailors, tinsmiths and makers of sweetmeats while, everywhere, there was a chatter in a multitude of tongues. At the northern corner of the Old Town stands Fort Jesus, dominating its hills, impressive in sheer mass. The walls, two and a half metres thick, rising from a coral ridge, defied undermining, and its guns still command the harbour looking out beyond English Point to the latest in a line of shipwrecks, that of the *Globestar*, which came to grief in 1973. Another set of guns grace the fort entrance, those of the warships *Koenigsburg* and *Pegasus*, each on opposing sides in 1914. All are now manned by giant iguana lizards, who scuttle about their breeches and barrels.

The charming parents of a friend of but brief acquaintance offered me hospitality for the second half of my day in Mombasa. Kelvin Patience, on leave in Britain, was the author of a book that was about to be published on the history of the East African Railway. His father Dennis and I toasted his success in quantities of good Kenyan lager and I was lucky to catch my Nairobi-bound train that night. As it was I got my sleeper mixed, which brought me face to face with two formidable English matrons. 'Sir,' they said in stern reproach, 'you seem to be in the wrong class.'

An unromantic English Electric diesel unit hauled the train through rich, dark palm groves, and thrust its buffers into a land of endless thorn trees. It was the waterless waste and red dust of the Taru Desert that assured East Africa's isolation from the world until the end of the 19th century. Even now, under a brilliant moon, it was a land of mystery, an enchanted land of Allan Quatermain. It was my first sight of the bush and gave me my first living perception of the size of Africa. Tall grass, as far as the eye could see, swayed like a vast field of ripening corn in a perpetual summer wind. There before me was a land of incidents, some dark, some light – a chequered board on which comedy and tragedy walked hand-in-hand, sometimes with mincing steps, sometimes with giant strides.

In the grey light of dawn the plains of the Masai presented one gigantic zoo. Waterbuck, gazelle, wildebeest, zebra and giraffe took little notice of the passing train and sported themselves in wild abandon. Back at Nairobi I caught the up-train to Nakuru and embarked on a very lovely journey, the track winding ever upward through green pastures to the summit of the eastern wall of the Great Rift.

The first sight of this phenomenon will remain with you for ever. Suddenly, round a bend, the forest thins and there, 2,000 feet below at the foot of a sheer escarpment, is the Rift, quite certainly the greatest valley, or, rather, set of valleys, in the world. Here the floors are tawny red in the drought, or a dusty green after the rains. Thirty miles away a further wall arose, dark purple against the sky, a procession of clouds drifting across the peaks. This colossal fault in the earth's surface is as though some gigantic thermonuclear plough had dug a furrow striking right across Africa from Lake Baikal in Siberia to the Red Sea and beyond. The geological disturbance must have convulsed half the globe in some prehistoric age to become an inland sea from which the waters have receded, leaving a succession of lakes to this day. Dozens of volcanoes erupted in the Rift and their threat still hangs in the air like the curl of smoke I could see from a herdsman's fire.

The town of Nakuru lies on the floor of the Rift and at the foot of the Menengai Mountain, the top of which is said to have subsided into some subterranean vacuum. To the south of the town is Lake Nakuru, a large expanse of shallow, saline water, the shores of which are the sacred nesting ground of ten thousand flamingoes. An acrid smell of soda rose from the lake to increase the allure of this mysterious region, while pink-white feathers in great wavering clusters made a fairy-tale snow storm reflected in the water.

Nakuru, a railway junction, makes little use of its lake, which is a pity for it has an almost alpine setting. However, I was to discover that its citizens lacked for nothing in so far as the milk of human kindness was concerned when two African ladies invited me home to tea. In swift succession I received a cup of tea, a cup of coffee, a double scotch, a hot bath and the biggest mixed grill I have ever consumed. One of the ladies had studied English near my Brighton home so we spent the evening reminiscing, in between watching Kenyan TV programmes. I was implored to stay the night but I had a train to catch.

The line divides at Nakuru, one branch continuing to Eldoret and Kampala, the other to Kisumu on Lake Victoria. Before sticking my neck out in Uganda, however, I chose to see what Kisumu had to offer and was not disappointed. No Kenyan train is exactly a paragon of high speed but the pleasant dawdling progress over the hilly countryside, with halts at innumerable wayside stations, was exactly right for a first-time observer of Africa.

Kisumu aspires to bigger things than Nakuru and makes better use of its lake – as it should since Victoria is the second largest in the world. As with many African towns, the banks were the most impressive buildings in evidence, though in spite of its port, Kisumu is something of a garden city. The place is a mixture of Africa and Asia and, being a Sunday, a conglomeration of religions were militantly competing for custom. Even the Salvation Army, beaming black faces under SA bonnets and peaked hats, was represented by a band composed entirely of percussion. The weather abruptly turned from warm to sweltering and, with a gang of African boys, I partook of a swim in the lake, in spite of warnings of crocodiles and a multitude of carnivorous evils.

Victorian crusading enterprise in East Africa was chiefly directed to Uganda, around the shore of Lake Victoria. Kenya was an afterthought. The crusade needed a railway so, with that matter-of-fact approach characteristic of the times, a railway was driven all the way from Mombasa. If the track had to rise eight or nine thousand feet and down again, what did this matter? So it was driven across hundreds of miles of bush alive with marauding wild animals, disease-carrying swamps and the lunar trough of the

Great Rift itself, to Lake Victoria. The line reached Kisumu after unbelievable human endurance and feats of engineering, and was later driven forward from Nakuru to Kampala and beyond.

I could not help but contemplate those stirring events as I continued my journey towards Kampala, though as we drew nearer the border, a certain tension began to constrict my mind. The newspapers had been screaming for weeks about the latest border tension being more serious than usual, with supposedly crack Ugandan troops massed along the frontier. Everybody had said before my departure, and now they were saying it again on the train, that I was a bloody fool to enter Ugandan territory – but I don't always believe what newspapers say. I prefer the evidence of my own eyes. More to the point, I had been unable to proceed into Tanzania by rail, which made all the more reason for carrying on to Uganda, the third constituent of the one-time East African Confederation. Gritting my teeth I determined to see things through.

The train stumbled on. Eldoret, they will tell you, was where the bank was built around its safe. Again, the railway had initiated the town, but it was because of an accident in which the big safe fell from a wagon that Eldoret came to be where it is. Found to be too heavy to move, a building was constructed over it and things grew from there. Unworried by its unscheduled beginnings, Eldoret flourishes as a busy market town, the last sizeable community before Uganda.

For this leg of my journey I had acquired a second-class compartment, and my companions were a spirited bunch of students. From the very start I was drawn into their cheerful conversation and pressed to edible delicacies from a range of newspaper packages. My neighbour was a young Ugandan law student from Nairobi University, who was returning to Kampala for a holiday with his parents. He was a most likeable chap: intelligent and witty.

It was, however, nothing short of bloody-mindedness that kept our train standing at the border station of Malaba for all of five hours; the bloody-mindedness being Ugandan-inspired, not Kenyan. Most of the delay took place during the night, and the talk going on around me was of Ugandan atrocities being perpetrated by both the rebels and the army. Currency touts selling Ugandan banknotes in thick wads stalked the corridor, though their clientele was thin on the ground since the bulk of the train's passengers had prudently alighted – and it was all I could do to desist from following suit. I stuck things out, however, and was rewarded, long after daybreak, with the precipitant jolt that heralded a resumption of the journey. We rolled solemnly across a brook shadowed by a billboard on the further bank announcing our entry into the Republic of Uganda; it put me in mind of those depressing West Berlin notices that used to emphasize one's action of leaving comparative sanity for sinister totalitarianism.

Ten minutes later we were drawing into Tororo and the train filled up once more. An immigration official treated me to an icily polite speech of welcome and, examining my passport, correctly insisted that, as a British subject, I had no need of the visa I had obtained from the Ugandan authorities in Nairobi.

Notwithstanding the many stops at wayside stations, the train did its best to make up for lost time. Each station was a colourful pageant of people, though few seemingly had any business with the railway. It was simply that the station was the community centre: the place where the action was and a potential market for bananas, nuts and anything that would sell. Simply on account of my exclusivity, I was presented with a bunch of a dozen bananas by a smiling vendor who refused to accept payment in Kenyan shillings or any other currency I possessed. Along the trackside was an assortment of exotic blossoms, bizarre shrubs and strange crops, on which my young law student offered knowledgeable commentary. At Jinja, Uganda's Sheffield, we crossed the Nile.

It was raining when we reached Kampala and I estimated that, with the lateness of the train, I would have something like four hours to see something of the city. But authority was to have other ideas. My friend escorted me up the steps to the station concourse, in the middle of which an officious-looking civilian stood by the ticket barrier eyeing the jostling crown with a quite unwarranted distaste. His gaze fell on the two of us. 'You, here,' he barked.

'You mean me?' I asked, annoyed at the man's rudeness.

My passport and that of the student were examined with a curl of the lip, as if both documents were seditious literature. To me he asked, 'Why have you and your friend come here?'

I began to sense something more ominous than immigration control. 'We're travelling companions only,' I answered. 'I've come to see a little of Kampala.' The student gave his own explanation.

'Wait here,' we were told gruffly as the man went away taking our passports. We watched him shove his way into the crowd, pushing a woman almost to the ground. People gazed at him with all the laughter gone out of their faces.

A while later he returned and led us to a bare office. Another man, smiling sardonically, lounged behind a desk. We were not invited to sit down.

The new official bombarded me with questions. Why had I come? How long did I propose to stay? Why was I staying for so short a time? What was my connection with the young Ugandan? I could appreciate a certain puzzlement over anyone mad enough to want to travel the fractured East African Railway network for no other reason than the ride. No African could be expected to understand that; maybe not all that number of Britons either. But, again, I didn't like the direction the questioning was taking, and made my answer to the last topic very plain.

'We've never met before we joined the train,' I stressed, 'and now we're going our own ways.'

In point of fact, we were both compelled to go the same way. The first official remarked that he had to go and collect some rubber stamps with which to endorse our passports and that, when he had done so, we could go. Eventually he returned, bringing a third man but no rubber stamps. We were taken out of the office, through the station concourse and pushed into the back of an antiquated black saloon car. I started to argue about my rights and the time of my Nairobi-bound train but nobody took any notice. The rain fell in buckets and the notion arose that the best way of seeing Kampala in the circumstances was by car.

Seldom have I looked upon emptier shops or a more depressing town. The rain did little to help, of course, but the shop windows were no more than eye sockets on the empty streets. Even Eastern Europe in the Stalin era could make something out of nothing so far as window-dressing was concerned, but here no effort had been made to conceal a bankruptcy of stock. The car began to cough as if starved of petrol and the driver moaned about lack of fuel coupons for even official vehicles. The engine finally died on us and we all had to clamber out into the rain and push our own prison van to the square-faced concrete building that was Kampala Police Headquarters.

Inside, a stench of sweat, rancid tobacco and an unidentifiable sweet odour permeated the bare-walled corridors. Frightened detainees, handcuffed and wild-eyed, passed us by in the charge of uniformed policemen. I noticed my young companion's face had assumed a deathly pallor, and guessed he knew more about Ugandan security police methods than I did. Within a room containing no more than a cheap desk, some hard-backed chairs, a filing cabinet and a crooked photograph of the current president of the republic, we were arrayed before a more senior member of the hierarchy. He wore civilian clothes but elicited considerable respect from our escort who, after a gabble of explanation, were dismissed with a curt wave of a hand. We were invited to sit.

Our new inquisitor was stern but not unpleasantly bad-mannered. His questioning was thorough and resulted substantially from discoveries he had made from ransacking my wallet and overnight bag. He spoke quietly and intelligently. My journalistic press card produced the first hurdle.

'How is it your passport indicates you to be a company director and this card names you as a journalist?' he asked.

To explain that I was once a company director and had retained the title in my passport in preference to the sometimes provocative 'journalist' would have complicated matters. So I told the white lie that I was a company director but a *travel* journalist in my spare time. I emphasised the type of journalism, not wishing to give the idea that I was a nosy political hack. There followed a multitude of questions about my family business which I was able to answer in simple terms (though the firm was long-since defunct).

Over the years I have learnt a thing or two about interrogation from wartime and hard postwar experience in Europe. I have suffered intensive questioning in far uglier circumstances in both Nazi and Communist prisons where, offering nothing less than the truth, I raised suspicion by giving different answers to the same repeated questions, on account of there being a choice of answers available. The key lies in keeping each answer simple and standardised, and remembering them at the subsequent bout of questioning which is sure to follow as a check on the truthfulness of the original answer.

'What school did you attend?' My answer was the one which I attended the longest. There was no need to bring up the other two.

My regimental association membership card had come up for scrutiny. 'What rank did you hold?' I was asked.

'Corporal', I replied, giving the lowest rank I had held. I could have said 'Private' but I have my pride.

'Which army?' came the startling enquiry. I had to admit that it was the British.

Of course, they found the pieces of paper in the respective wallets giving our exchanged addresses. It had been the student's idea and seemed a harmless one. But, abruptly, I was made aware how small inconsistencies can be blown up into a balloon of the deepest suspicion. 'I thought you said that you hardly knew one another,' the man remarked with withering contempt.

The disclosure was the signal for the young student's removal, together with his belongings which, like mine, were strewn about the desk. During the sort-out I quietly repacked some of my own property.

'What are you doing that for?' I was asked sharply.

'I've got a train to catch,' I told him. 'I've an expedition to join.'

The man gave me a long lingering scowl. 'What gives you the idea you'll be catching any train?' he murmured ominously. Then as an afterthought, 'What expedition?' The black face before me showed renewed interest.

So I proffered a rundown on the Tana River Expedition, its aims and role, its sponsors and its personalities. I saw no reason to mention support by the army, British or otherwise.

Thus the question and answer game continued and my life story – or as much of it as I felt like revealing – unwound. But the one bone that stuck in the throat of authority was the hoary enigma surrounding the reasons for the brevity of my visit to Uganda.

I lectured the officer on Britain being a nation not of

shopkeepers but of railway enthusiasts, but this disclosure was
contemptuously brushed aside. 'Anyway, as a travel writer I have
to travel,' I finished lamely. 'Uganda is a beautiful country. Is it a
crime to want to see even a little of it?'

Momentarily I had the initiative and made the most of it. Before
the man could ask further questions I demanded to know why I
had been arrested, what crime I was supposed to have committed
and, if they thought I was a spy, what I was supposed to be spying
on. Such counter-offensives had worked to a limited degree in
places such as the one-time Soviet Union, Czechoslovakia and
elsewhere so I couldn't see why I shouldn't give the ploy an airing
in Uganda. Running out of indignant counter-questions I fell back
on my train-catching requirement. There was not another Nairobi-
bound train for two days at best; none at all at worst.

The reply was on a more optimistic note.

'It arrived late so the departure time's been put back twenty-
four hours,' I was told. Maybe it was a lie but it seemed to me to
be a defensive lie. I felt I'd cleared the air to some extent.

Except for random notes, my questioner had not made out any
written statement. I guessed this would follow and was correct in
the assumption. Another official had entered the room and was
sitting looking out of the window as these preliminary proceedings
ended. My current questioner rose and left.

'Are you hungry?' the newcomer asked.

I said I was and meant it. Even twelve bananas could not fill the
hole in my stomach. He asked me what I wanted. Optimistic as
ever I suggested steak and chips.

'Do you want some tea?'

Thankful for even small mercies, I affirmed.

Neither steak nor tea materialised. Instead, I was marched to
another, even more basic office. No Idi Amin-type photograph
adorned the dirty wall. A table and two hard chairs were the sole
furnishings.

The ensuing interrogation was more exasperating than painful.
My proffered answers to the staccato questioning had to be
repeated at dictation speed to see if they matched the first set. I
made damn sure they did. Difficulties arose when it was found that
the space available on the form failed to fit many of my answers

but I patiently refused to be talked into varying them. I knew their game. To make matters worse the new chap was even worse at spelling than I was.By the time we had recorded my address correctly it was I who was filling in most of the form.

As I was being returned to the first office I passed my student in the passage. He was still ashen-faced and we pretended not to see one another. I was never to see him again.

A team of three was involved in the third interview and I wondered if we were playing some macabre game of musical chairs. Outside the barred window the rain fell unchecked. A church clock announced that the scheduled departure time of my train had long passed. My bag and wallet still lay on the table.

The man who had offered me tea glanced casually through the statement and repeated some of the original questions. Parrot-like I repeated the answers. My camera abruptly drew attention to itself by falling off the table. I caught it.

'What had I been filming? Had I been anywhere near Entebbe Airport? Had I taken a photograph of anything in Uganda?' All three men, simultaneously re-activated, joined in the chorus.

Truthfully, I said I had taken no picture in Uganda. The rain-clouds had made the light too poor. And excepting the time on the train I had had no opportunity anyway.

Outside it was dark but I could see no lights in the town. The isolation was unnerving. I was taken away to a cell on the floor below, where the sickly smell was overpowering. I knew what the smell was but refused to believe it, though the odour of rotting flesh is unmistakable. With no window I was unable to tell when the night ended, my wrist-watch having been removed together with my other personal effects; with no bed I could do no more than sit on the single chair that formed the cell's sole furniture, resting my head in my hands. Even the chimes of the church clock were denied me and I lost count of the passing hours.

When I was returned to the upstairs room it was daylight. My belongings still lay scattered on the table so, ever optimistic, I began packing them away into my bag. I was surprised nothing seemed to have been stolen.

The officer who had first questioned me watched but made no objection; nor did the other two men who now entered the room to stare at me. I asked the time and the officer consulted his watch. 'Eleven o'clock,' he vouchsafed. I realised it was close to the rescheduled departure hour of the Kenya-bound train.

Without warning I was told I could go. For a moment I was flabbergasted. Then, with nine minutes in hand, I grabbed my bag, together with my personal effects, and virtually propelled the two rubbernecking minions out of the door in front of me.

We rushed down the stairs, the others reluctantly entering into the spirit of the train-catching game. No longer were they my guards but the means of getting me to the station on time. Outside was another car and I sprang at it. There was some excited jabber about petrol rationing, but one of the men slid into the driving seat, the others beside me in the back. In spite of sparse traffic, every traffic light contrived to be against us and we reached the station at zero hour. Even before the car had stopped I was out and bounding through the crowded station and down the stairs. And – glory be! – the train was still there. It was very full; so full in fact that potential passengers overflowed onto the roofs and sides of the coaches. I found myself a foothold on the outer front edge of a second-class wagon and staked my claim. Rain splashed down on me from an open section of platform but, lighthearted with relief, I ignored it.

What made me believe in the allegation of the departure time I don't know, for as I could have foreseen, the train remained stationary for a further hour and a half. Equally, it could not have run at all. But at last, following a triumphal shriek, it drew out of Kampala station and wound out of the city's green suburbs towards the gradient to Seta. And here the grossly overloaded diesel unit gave up the ghost.

Up front a crowd assembled around the green-painted monster with its distinctive yellow stripe. The driver made a number of attempts to coax the motor into life against a babble of advice from a hundred tongues. Finally he succeeded. The motor caught, the wheels revolved wildly but we moved not an inch.

Everyone was dropping off the train; the men putting their shoulders to the coaches. I contemplated the idea that all this had happened before; that it was part of a cynical pantomime. The womenfolk stood about the track in the colourful wraps, clinging to babies and children – all resolutely ignoring the rain. Already I was soaked to the skin. At the third attempt the wheels gripped and we were away. Like a flash I was inside my second-class coach seconds before the mass re-entry.

It was a six-hour journey back to Tororo, and in the warm, damp atmosphere of compressed wet bodies I was dry by the time we drew into the border town. The train remained full but was slightly less packed at this final Ugandan station, and I wondered how rigidly emigration would be controlled. Another group and category of security police started pushing their way through the corridor, a posse of them making straight for me. A sergeant strung about with a machine-carbine grimaced at my passport, began asking the usual questions and, not approving of his unappreciative audience, hauled me off the train.

In the station office of the railway police – its regular inmates unceremoniously cleared out – I found myself before another officer of the security force. A stove blazed merrily in a corner of the wooden-walled room. The presidential mugshot scowled at one and all, and you could see the discolouration around it where a photograph of a previous incumbent had been.

But if the venue was a slight improvement the questions put to me were sadly unoriginal – though, initially, they showed a new angle. Why did I want to *leave* the country? Why the hurry? Had I got something to hide? Then we were back in the rut of the Kampala routine, and though I resolutely explained that these matters had already been covered, the fact made no impression. Half-way through the latest performance the train pulled out of the station and my heart sank into my boots.

With the departure of the train my new tormentor seemed to lose interest. My passport was returned to me. It was as if he *intended* me to miss the train. 'You'll have to go back to Kampala on the next one,' he ruled.

'When will that be?' I enquired wearily.

'The day after tomorrow,' came the reply and, rising to his feet, the officer carefully placed a braided khaki hat on his woolly head and left the room.

I began to think. My 'unnecessary' visa was valid for five days. But a piece of paper given me upon entry stipulated a three-day stay. This meant they could get me on a technicality. I had no Ugandan money and, at the existing rate of exchange, I didn't particularly want to acquire any. Another consideration was that I had promised Nigel Winser I would be back in Nairobi the day before the expedition's Mountain Team departure since I was to go with it. This was one day hence. It was this that clinched matters. With the border just six miles away I turned my attention to other means of leaving the country.

Though of limited use, illegal border-crossing is one of my few talents. I am no expert, but past personal experience of negotiating the well-guarded frontiers of a number of East European countries I could mention rates me higher than a mere novice. And East European borders – especially those shared by West European nations – were then assuredly more lethal than African ones. I pondered upon the matter in the fuggy room and decided to take the chance were it offered. My knowledge of how the Ugandan-Kenyan border was guarded was nil beyond the supposition that the Ugandan army was alleged to be encamped this side of it. But, if so, surely it would be on the offensive and so facing the other way; also, I was unable to believe that the regime had caught up with the finesse once practised by the East Germans, Czechs and Hungarians in their methods of discouraging illegal emigration.

My tummy rumbled with hunger. I scrounged a cup of hot, sweet tea out of the squaddies of the transport police who had been permitted to return, but their hospitality failed to run to food. I resigned myself to another sleepless and hungry night. Outside, the rain had stopped but black clouds hung in the sky.

In the event, I spent most of the night in a draughty detention room. I even managed a brief doze or two in company with some dozen occupants who gave the impression of being permanent residents. Beside me was a policeman with a rusty rifle, who I presumed to be my escort. He never spoke a word and his rôle remained unclear, but he followed me every time I went for a pee. He was curled up on the bench dead to the world when the dawn arrived so, picking up my bag, I quietly opened the door and left him to his slumbers.

Nobody was about the station, and outside it were plenty of trees to screen me. I made towards the border with the idea of keeping the railway line in sight so that it would lead me in the right direction. Back at Nairobi was my compass and all manner of Boy Scout implements I'd brought for the expedition but which I hardly thought I would need on a simple rail journey.

All went well for an hour. I crossed the track in a clearing and carried on through more trees. I was aware that the line chose a tortuous route to Malaba, but I preferred a longer walk with the track in sight to the risk of getting myself lost attempting short cuts among trees that screened distant landmarks. Foliage dripped incessantly as if it were raining again.

I bumped into the Ugandan army a moment before I became aware of its presence. Rounding a clump of bushes, I came across a military truck and a bunch of soldiers trying to make a radio transmitter work. One of the men had looked up at my approach, and to have attempted to evade them could have invited only suspicion. I guessed it was some three miles from the border – possibly more.

An NCO straightened up from the task of fiddling with the dials of his radio. As a one-time soldier myself I felt an affinity with their predicament. The bloody things never do work when you want them to. I said hello and asked if they were having trouble.

All were youngsters, probably conscripts, and they hardly looked like crack troops to me. They smiled, seemed surprised but reasonably pleased that I was British, and appeared agreeably sympathetic when I revealed my own military background. Could *I* get the thing to work asked one of them in English, indicating what my generation of soldiers knew as a No. 88 set; this was the one time in my life I wished I'd been more diligent at my training lessons.

I fiddled blindly with the dials pretending to know what I was doing. Though they had never asked, I felt obliged to explain that I had missed my train – which was no more than the truth – and so was walking to the border. After all, an Englishman hiking into a war zone needed *some* explanation. 'How far is Malaba? I enquired.

'By road about six miles,' I was told, which said little for my calculations.

I inclined my head towards the vehicle. 'Any chance of a lift?'

The soldiers looked at each other. 'We'll have to ask the officer,' said the NCO and walked off into the trees. I began to wonder if I had done the right thing.

I also became aware that the woods were full of troops. Lorries stood half-hidden among the foliage and, standing round a fire, was a group of figures. The NCO came back with a lieutenant. He was older than his men but his face was kind. He had an unopened bottle of lager in his hand, which he presented to me. 'Breakfast,' he vouchsafed. I was encouraged to believe that perhaps I *had* done the right thing.

'Do you think you could give me a lift towards Malaba?' I asked hopefully, and repeated my explanations.

'Can't take you to Malaba itself but my driver could run you close by,' came the response in English with a strong taint of the Bronx.

And so, in the petrol-reeking cab of another vintage item of British military equipment – a Bedford fifteen hundredweight – I made the border. The Tororo-Malaba road was close by; closer than I had imagined, in fact, and I was dropped off within sight of Malaba. I think the driver would have taken me right to the Ugandan border post but this was hardly fitting my scheme of things. They ask too many questions at border posts, and Ugandan authority had, so far, not exactly inspired my confidence.

Everything was falling into place which made a change. I left the road and struck across pleasant rolling country in front of a high hill for which Tororo is famous. And there was the railway again. I turned eastwards with it and came to the brook that here formed the end of Ugandan territory. Not a soul was to be seen.

I failed, by twelve inches, to jump onto dry Kenyan land but my feet were wet enough already, so what the hell.

In Malaba I boarded a bus to Eldoret. And at Eldoret, would you believe it, I caught up with my ill-fated train once more.

On the journey back to Nairobi, with more coaches attached to the train at Nakuru, I treated myself to a long, lingering luncheon in the restaurant car and, refuelled, prepared myself for transition from traveller to explorer. My new beard was thickening and I was no longer quite such a novice so far as East Africa was concerned. I had looked upon a little of its Kenyan face and borne the sting of East African politics, so now felt better prepared for adventuring in the wild.

In my profession of travel writer I cover many parts of the world into which any tourist can venture, a fact that invariably leaves me slightly deflated. It is true that not everyone would wish to go to some of the outlandish destinations I crave, but they could if they wanted. Now I was ready to go to places seldom, if ever, trodden by tourist feet; places remote, inhospitable and exciting; entirely free of what the 20th century calls 'civilisation'. I allowed the all-too-recent recollections of a lucky escape from warped authority to fade, to be replaced by the splendid anticipation of an adventure that, for me, might have had origins within the pages of the *Boy's Own Paper*, of which I was an avid reader in days gone by.

As I looked again upon the contortions of that awesome Rift the urge grew stronger. Never had I felt so gratified that I had, years before, thrown off the yoke of a secure but dull existence within the 'nine-to-five' syndrome. True, I had never been entirely shackled to an office desk, but enough to taste its bitter fruit of tedium. And yet it is a sad fact that much of the human race ties itself to tedium, struggling through this vale of tears from age sixteen to sixty-five.

'Expeditions,' says Gerald Durrell, 'are for commerce, curiosity and fun and in that order.' Putting it like that brings exploration almost back into the nine-to-five bracket. Commerce had, for us, little further to play in our expedition. Curiosity and fun most certainly had. And satisfying a curiosity surely *is* fun.

2. Mountain Ordeal

By joining the Mountain Team, as the five of us were stylishly labelled, I had, of course, so far as the initial period of the expedition was concerned, forfeited my craving to go places seldom, if ever, trodden by tourist feet. Mount Kenya, beyond all doubt, is 'wild and exciting' but it is also a national park. One saving grace was that we would be on the mountain out of season – a season, in this instance, the like of which has rarely been known before – so it was hardly likely the tourist presence, even at the lower altitudes, would reach Costa Brava proportions.

Our Nairobi base was almost deserted when I returned. The scientists and their support echelon had left for Kora two days earlier to set up a forward base camp. All that remained behind were Susie Richardson and the kids, plus my four fellow-mountaineers, who were on the point of giving me up for lost following announcements on the radio news bulletins and in the press that I had been apprehended in Uganda. I began to envy those who had gone to Kora, for *that* was a place virtually untrodden by tourist feet and a warm one into the bargain. But before the treat had to come the cold savagery of the mountain, and Harley Nott decreed the issue of arctic survival kit, which put our departure back another day so that we could draw and fit it.

Arctic conditions and Africa simply refused to come to terms in my mind. Warned that I would be part of the climbers' support group, I had taken along a polo-neck pullover and a medium-thick pair of socks to go with my safari boots but I had packed even these with a sense of absurdity. Now I was to find myself possessed of an enormous kitbag crammed with padded duvets, waterproof anoraks and over-trousers, climbing boots, gloves, balaclavas, snow-goggles, woollen over-socks and various implements designed to simulate life in a climate more suited to the North Pole.

My new companions of the team made interesting study. I was to get to know them all a lot better in the expedition, but only in a minor capacity did I have to revise my initial opinions. Harley Nott, tall, fluent, very much a ladies' man with his clipped moustache and brilliant line of patter, was a born leader. The fact that he was the only one among us who really knew anything about climbing mountains would have resulted in his leadership on that score alone. As it was he scored twice. His background coupled with a responsible role in two previous expeditions no doubt honed his flair as an organiser, but leadership is something you either have or have not. Me, I'm a 'have not' – in spite of a similar, if lesser, background. Though considerably older, I stood slightly in awe of him, his one imperfection in my eyes being a very human petulance that he sometimes displayed if things did not go the way he wanted. He had got married to a very pretty woman hardly a week before we left for Nairobi.

In some ways Robert Williamson bore similar characteristics. The same age, equally fluent, handsome almost to the point of ridicule from his crinkly black hair right the way down a lithe bronzed body, he was also intelligent and a fine organiser. Yet his qualities of leadership were such that he could take a back seat with no loss of grace. He was doing so now, in fact, for though he was deputy leader of the expedition – and militarily senior to Harley – his climbing experience was less. But nobody is perfect, and Robert could make himself utterly objectionable at times with and without reason. I personally got on well with him but others were not so fortunate.

Later, I was to observe distinct strata of differing human nature developing between the expedition's military members, its young scientists and those of professional specialist qualifications other than scientific. But it was the soldiers who differed the most. I suppose it is inevitable, but a trio of seasoned army officers abruptly immersed in the undisciplined affairs of a bunch of student scientists – and in some cases long-haired non-professionals – is only too likely to produce the occasional explosive reaction. In *my* soldiering days we looked upon ourselves as a cut above 'mere civilians', but that was in wartime. However, there is no getting away from the fact that the professional soldier of today belongs to a highly exclusive club.

But that was not where the only barrier lay. We 'mere civilians' had undertaken, at considerable financial loss and inconvenience, to run a scientific and adventure expedition along the entire length of the Tana River. Two portions of this journey, Mount Kenya and the rapids of the Middle Tana, would have to be negotiated by people who knew what they were doing – which is where the army came in. Strictly speaking, the scaling of the highest peak of Mount Kenya did not form part of the source-to-mouth aspect of the Tana journey; but because the challenge was there and because it would be good training for the military climbers the project was included. And it must be emphasized again that participation by the army was vital to the execution of the expedition. So it was not a question of just 'humouring the soldiers' but of allowing them to incorporate their specialist projects within the framework of their victualling of and providing for the whole undertaking. The one snag was that for Harley, Paul Turner the commander of the White Water Team, and to a lesser extent, Robert, their personal interests all-too clearly lay only in the adventure element. And it was the adventure teams that were to reap much of the glamour, a fact that could only but irk the workhorses of the Scientific Team carrying out their more routine investigatory chores.

To the army the project became 'Exercise Tana Osprey', and not only was their support vital but deeply appreciated. For the soldiers too the expedition was to become an exercise in liaison; to show how versatile the British armed services could be, which, in turn, would be instrumental in bringing them more recruits of the calibre they deserve.

I have, perhaps, laboured the point of 'army versus civilian' within the context of the expedition, but it made for an interesting aspect of human behaviour. Though it was occasionally felt, it rarely impinged seriously upon day-to-day expeditionary life.

Which brings me to the third military member of the Mountain Team, Doctor John Richardson, he of the advance party. If anyone could be described as a link between the military and the others it was John, for as a member of the Territorial Army Volunteer

Reserve with the rank of major, he was half-way between the two. He described his occupation as general practitioner but, at 34, was planning a return to the army. This seemed odd to me because as a doctor/medical officer he seemed to be enjoying the best of both worlds: he had been involved in at least half a dozen expeditions including, with his wife, the British Trans-Americas Expedition under Lt. Colonel John Blashford Snell. His education, via Oundle, Clare College and Barts, had left him with twenty-two letters after his name, to which he was in the process of adding another four.

I was to be thrown together with John Richardson more than with anyone else during the course of the expedition. Another highly efficient organiser, he was a calming and knowledgeable influence over the more excitable members, and his beaming face framing the inevitable pipe was as much comfort to some as the fact that he was a doctor. I did not always agree with his philosophy of life but I was mighty glad to have him with me on the mountain. Both he and I had the task of supporting the trio of climbers in their endeavours.

The fourth climber was Richard Matthews. Nothing at all was military about Richard and, at 23, he was the youngest member of the team. While he had some climbing experience (he had led the West Ethiopian Expedition in 1974), he must have felt somewhat mentally and physically ill-equipped against his older military co-climber; if so, however, he never showed it. In spite of his tender years his expedition tasks were formidable. Official stills photographer, public relations officer, a climbing stint on Mount Kenya and captain of the second boat in the White Water Team; a multiple burden for one mortal man. Yet, despite a setback up the mountain, he coped well, which speaks volumes for his spirit.

With the two of us collaborating as a two-man, non-military, non-scientific media group, Richard and I shared a common cause, though photography was his real bent. His most irritating habit was that of undertaking everything more slowly than anyone else; while this can be accepted in the field of photography it is not appreciated in the hurly-burly of expedition life. He got verbally bitten frequently, both justly and unjustly, sometimes unkindly, and more than once by myself, since I am inclined to do everything in too much of a hurry. But this seldom ruffled Richard and never altered his ways. Born in South Africa and endowed with a Bachelor of Science degree, he had yet another exasperating trait: that of removing his beard every time we became accustomed to it.!

Our last day at Base House was a busy one. Not only had we to draw and try on our climbing gear – and in the case of the climbers this meant sorting out their ropes, ice-axes, crampons and the rest of the paraphernalia of mountaineering – but also to effect the break-up of the bulk provisions. We expected to be on the mountain for at least ten days and so drew rations accordingly, but since we would be carrying much of our food, in addition to the rest of the kit, the army-issued ration packs had to be broken down to the bare essentials. In addition, a number of our sponsors had supplied 'goodies' such as sachets of Alpen cereal, packets of chocolate bars and tins of Milo and Bournvita which, being especially suited for arduous conditions, we substituted for less beneficial items. Thus, after hours of deliberating and manipulating, Harley and I produced 150 meal packets of more-or-less equal proportions plus bulk provisions of the chocolate (in addition to that which was included in the army packs) and the other heavily vitaminised 'goodies'. Even then someone was later to complain because we had removed the chewing gum! We also took one bottle of a well-known Kenyan sugar-cane-based alcoholic spirit but not, primarily, for the benefit of our health. In return for the case they donated, the firm had stipulated that we supply them with a photograph of a bottle of their precious liquor atop one of the peaks of Mount Kenya!

All items military originated from Nairobi's Kahawa Barracks 12 miles outside the city, where the British Army based its training unit and transport repair workshop. Their warehouses came in very useful for the storage of the military and sponsor-acquired goods, as well as various items of heavier equipment brought in by the Royal Air Force. The climbing gear, originating from the Scientific Expedition Society in London, and the specialised items required by the White Water Team were also stored here, whilst our four vehicles – three Land Rovers and a Bedford 3-ton lorry – were borrowed from and serviced by the extremely cooperative staff, British and African, of the workshops. Mention must be

made in particular of Lt. Colonel C.L. Lawrence, WO Tom Clark
and the cheerful WO Bob Batty, all of whom gave us their
unstinting help.

Half-way through the mountain kitting-out procedure we had a
strange visitation. In our midst appeared a venerable figure,
excitable and exuberant, sporting hockey stockings, baggy shorts,
sunburnt limbs and a long shaggy beard. It could be and was none
other than Cunningham van Someren, the world-famous
ornithologist, who was to make similar appearances out of the
bush on many occasions during the expedition. Known
affectionately as 'Chum', he was to become a valuable friend to
the scientists because of his influence in the Nairobi National
Museum, presided over by another famous figure, Richard Leakey
(who himself had pledged full support).

In the morning we left Base House and turned our Land Rover
wheels northwards, away from Nairobi, on the fine two-
carriageway motorway that petered out beyond Thika. We were
tightly packed into the vehicle together with our bulging kitbags
and rucksacks, with Richard and I at the back, behind the wire
mesh of its thief-proof cage. Harley and Robert drove between
them and the former, taking a rut at 60 m.p.h., caused a wicked
blow against the cage roof, giving me a bloodied temple and a
splitting headache for the rest of the day.

We spent the night at the Nanyuki home of the Allens, friends
of John Richardson, at the foot of the towering colossus of Mount
Kenya. The mountain had buried its multiple heads in a dirty froth
of rain-cloud, so we could see nothing of the fine peaks as we
strolled round Ann Allen's garden, dined in pre-departure
splendour and drunk pints of Nanyuki Sports Club beer, but the
sombre giant made its presence felt. And in the morning there it
was for all to see.

It is impossible to do justice to the serene splendour of this
mountain set where no mountain has a right to be. The twin peaks
of Bation and Nelion shone white above the glistening glaciers. A
belt of ever-drifting snow, like weft on a loom of mist, spread
downward to a region of giant groundsel and lobelia and, lower
still, to forests of strange gnarled trees, the home of elephant and
leopard. To add delight to this ethereal sight the sun shone

warmly, to offer an impression of a soaring land of milk and
honey. And to the Kikuyu people, of course, it was more: for was
not Mount Kenya a sacred treasure, more precious than all the
gold in Christendom?

The highest summits, including Bation (17,058 feet) and Nelion
(17,022 feet), which are separated by the icy gash of the Gate of
the Mists, are hard rock cores exposed by the erosion of the
volcanic crater. At the mountain's prime, perhaps a million years
ago, the peak stood at nearer 19,000 feet. This began to decrease
about 15,000 years ago, a process that continued until the early
19th century, when the glaciers could have been smaller than they
are even now. But the renewed advance of the ice, occurring over
a period of 50 years, was succeeded by a further general retreat
which is continuing to the present day. It is interesting, if sad, to
reflect upon the possibility of Mount Kenya being bare of ice
within a century – though another reversal of the climatic trend
could, in opposite fashion, take place to preserve and even extend
the glaciers.

We left after breakfast, full of optimism at the prospect of
warm, day-long sunshine and cool velvet nights. Our approach to
the mountain was by the Naro Moru route via a road that turned
into a track at the entrance to the Mount Kenya National Park. The
track wound through the girth of forest the mountain wears like a
kilt, with a tartan composed of European elder bearing large flat
clusters of white-pink flowers that turn to purple fruits. These
elder trees were mixed with tall cedars, bamboo thickets and a
type of yellow wood tree with a massive twisted trunk. Palm and
bamboo form distinct crescents at certain altitudes with sporrans of
dense *Alchemilla* and curious 'old man's beard' hanging ghostlike
from outstretched limbs. Within this fertile jungle are buffalo,
black rhinoceros, leopard, antelope and elephant. We watched for
a fleeting glimpse of movement within the skein of trees that was,
for some of us, a first encounter with wild forest.

I found it intriguing to reflect upon the fact that the birds and
animals inhabiting these regions, as well as the plants growing out
of them, though identical at the same altitude on different
mountains of East Africa, can no longer migrate from one to the
other. Mount Kenya, Kilimanjaro, Mount Meru and Ngurdoto are

islands rising out of a plain, their fauna and flora cut off as if by hundreds of miles of ocean with, between the 'islands', virtually nothing to sustain their particular lives. Here was a zoological park placed by nature in an alien environment.

As we rose from the warm savannah country and the plains below spread away into the haze of distance, the temperature fell and belts of cloud, dark and angry, spat raindrops at us. The track had turned to mud and the Land Rover slid from side to side as Harley fought with the wheel. Our earlier optimism fled. We crossed Percival's Bridge then climbed more steeply to a bog at 9,000 feet that defied further ascent by motor-power. Parking the vehicle with its bonnet pushed deep into a bamboo thicket, we struggled into the harnesses of our immense rucksacks and tottered up the last 1,000 feet from 'swamp corner' to the meteorological station at a nice, round 10,000 feet.

Seven porters were awaiting us. So we were not to be human pack horses after all – which was just as well since I could barely *lift* my load, let alone carry it. They were smiling fellows, garrulous and swathed in old British Army greatcoats. Harley, full of military zeal, called an 'orders group', gave out his instructions for the next morning and called it a day.

The night was spent in quite delightful circumstances. The 'Met Station' camp was composed of well-built, well-equipped timber cabins with foam-rubber based bunks, And, glory be, hot water came out of the taps! Our efforts at camp-cooking were less spectacular however, and for this a newly-acquired pressure-cooker was the prime cause. Finally having assembled the thing, we raised a lot of pressure but apparently not much heat, for the contents of the tins remained stone cold. But practice make perfect, and following a more successful reheating operation we were rewarded with a stew consisting of baked beans, corned beef, instant potato mash and chocolate pudding!

Leaving camp shortly after dawn we made reasonable progress, with lightened loads, along a steep winding track, our porters bounding ahead carrying our main rucksacks. The forest thinned to herald a region of open parkland studded with small trees bearing leaf rosettes at the tips of their branches; they, in turn, led to another floral zone, clearly defined and entirely distinctive.

This, the heather zone, is exuberantly characterised by the presence of giant heathers of almost tree-like proportions and, of lesser attraction, it was where the bog started. This lies in open country and the texture of the marshy ground is governed by the rainfall. And since Mount Kenya's rainfall all-time records had been broken that very year we were in for severe punishment. The 'Vertical Bog', as the area is named, had become a steeply climbing sea of clinging, slippery, sucking mud, to produce the toughest and most exhausting of uphill trekking.

It was young Richard Matthews who made the heaviest going of a route that, after all, is basically no more than a well-trodden track. At first we were puzzled, for as the third climber we knew he had to do better than that. Then John Richardson discovered that he was suffering from some sort of allergy brought on and aggravated by the altitude. I myself was experiencing a shortage of breath which worsened with every step, but managed to keep going. Our porters, leaping over the sticky terrain with their incredible loads, ensured – as nothing else could – that none of the team would admit to our European shortcomings.

Gradually we squelched our way up and over each false summit and crest, the fitness of the army telling its own story. Harley and Robert were nearly a mile ahead at one point with the altitude-stricken Richard, escorted by John, far behind me. We rested awhile at a trig point marker but cold and damp cloud drove us on. Giant groundsel, 20 feet high, swollen, silky lobelia and miles of tussocky grass marked the beginning of the alpine zone – though the lowering temperature had already made this clear. An oblique descent from 13,000 feet into the Teleki Valley brought us to the Naro Moru River, boulder-strewn and icy cold, where some of us had an involuntary paddle while crossing.

The Teleki Refuge Hut provided an excuse for another rest, and inside we found a half-frozen young man who had reached his limit of endurance. He was now awaiting his hardier companion who had gone ahead on his own. The youngster seemed genuinely amazed that anyone as ancient as I should have got so far under the present conditions, an opinion I accepted with a mixture of indignation and encouragement. I pushed on before my aching limbs stiffened and, painful hours later, was rewarded with arrival at the Teleki Valley floor, directly beneath Mount Kenya's clutch of peaks, a plateau known as Mackinders Camp.

And a camp it is, comprising three rows of permanently erected two-person bivouacs plus a couple of larger mess tents. It was something of a comedown from the luxurious accommodation and temperate environment of the 'Met Station' and it marked the first night of at least eight that we all went to bed fully clothed. It was here too that we made the acquaintance of the Mount Kenya rock hyrax, a friendly rabbit-sized animal, resembling the alpine marmot and entirely ignorant of the spiteful ways of humans. Living among the rocks, they emerged in scores to greet us and scrounge for food, which they would steal given the slightest chance. They were joined in this pursuit by tiny mountain birds that hopped inside our tents to sit on discarded boots and regard us quizzically. It is an interesting fact that the hyrax – the 'coney' of the Bible – has as its closest relative the mighty elephant, to which it is akin in many structural details, particularly the hoof-like feet.

We dined on the eternal stew and hard-tack biscuits that had changed little from my own World War Two military days. The night was cold with flurries of snow, and we lay listening to the curious high-pitched chattering of the hyrax. But it was the unaccustomed altitude of 13,000 feet and its effect that reduced my sleep to a minimum.

The trio of the highest summits of Mount Kenya drenched in dawn sunshine is a sight of sheer magnificence, the orange hues striking diamonds out of the frozen snow. To me, Bation and Nelion looked the more dramatic in the knowledge that they were the private domain of experienced climbers only; the likes of me could only grovel in awe at their feet. Gazing at them reminded me of the Kikuyu legend whereby their god Mogai, maker and distributor of the universe, created Kere-Nyaga – 'Mountain of Brightness' – as a sign of his miracles and as a resting place for himself. Mogai took the man Kikuyu, founder of the race, onto the top of the mountain and showed him the beautiful land he had created for him. Before dismissing him, he told Kikuyu that whenever he needed help, he must hold up his hand and he, Mogai, would come to his aid. Surreptitiously I raised my own hand half-expecting something to happen. But cloud now masked the summit and the magic was gone.

The sun moved perceptibly higher in the sky to bathe the camp in warm brilliance, encouragement enough for us to dab our faces and hands with icy water from the stream that gurgled past the tents. Richard Mathews, slightly better, insisted upon joining us for the double climb and descent to Lake Höhnel.

To reach the lake meant a stiff climb up and over the southern wall of the Teleki Valley and it was here my lack of acclimatisation really made itself felt. Richard suffered more but gamely stuck it out. At the top, the wall was crowned by age-worn pinnacles of the strangest shapes. The highest was Point Joseph. Below was the emerald-green tarn, its polished surface calm and unruffled. And, beyond, all Africa lay at our feet ...

We descended to the water's edge and performed an 'arrival at the source' scene for the cameras. Source of the Tana or not, I would have been very content to put the mountain behind me and follow down, through the forest, the infant river. But there was no turning back; we had mountain climbers with us and their eyes had seen Bation.

Atop Point Joseph once more, we paused to gaze for the last time at the lonely tarn.

Harley was thoughtful. 'You know, there were buffalo droppings on the shore', he remarked. The others too had noticed them. Thirteen thousand feet is high for buffalo but not for elephant who, moving with extreme delicacy, are fine mountaineers. Hannibal knew what he was doing when he chose elephants with which to cross the Alps.

Back at Mackinders Camp, the afternoon sun was warm enough for basking and for drying wet boots. A visit from the park warden and famous international climber, Phil Snyder, interrupted this pleasant interlude. A man not much younger than myself, he had a girl companion and they chatted briefly with us before continuing to Mackinders ranger station a mile ahead. We were to meet them again.

The moment the sun dropped behind the hill the cold leapt upon us, and such were our appetites that there was some good-natured squabbling over who deserved the more popular but limited steak-and-kidney puddings for supper. There were problems too with the spaghetti, its length and springiness not making it ultra-suitable raw material with which to stuff a petulant pressure cooker.

Yet another early morning start saw us on the way to Top Hut, at 15,720 feet, and a steep uphill grind that had me gasping for breath at ever-decreasing intervals. Richard remained behind in the care of an English dentist and an American climber also in temporary residence at Mackinders, the three of them to make their own way to Two Tarn Hut where we would join them the following day. In the meantime the four of us would conquer Point Lenana, 16,300 feet, the third highest peak.

Put like this, the 'conquest of Lenana' sounds a formidable undertaking. In normal circumstances this is far from the case, for anyone with a sturdy pair of legs and lungs can 'conquer' it. But the severe weather conditions and freezing snow had added a sprinkling of peril to the climb. Nevertheless, John and I were determined to have a go at it since the other two main peaks were not for us.

Merely attaining Top Hut means that one is higher than the summit of Mont Blanc, and it feels like it too. The wind cut through our clothes, stung ears and faces and spun iced particles of snow into eddies about us. The white bulk of Lenana rose behind the hut, and I was all for dashing up and down it and getting the agony over. But the fact that mountaineering is a more precise sort of game was made abundantly clear by Harley and Robert who stipulated an ascent in proper order the next day. All except two of our porters had been dismissed and, of the two remaining, one had been despatched direct to Two Tarn Hut while the other was to stay with us for the climb. Peter was his name: a garrulous fellow made the more self-centred by a degree of education, and whom we made the mistake of treating as an equal.

Top Hut is composed of three compartments each sparsely furnished with a few bunks and a lot of debris. We made ourselves as comfortable as we could in the substantially built cabin and, with no water, were forced to collect snow-covered ice hacked from the nearby Lewis Glacier for melting down in the pressure cooker. In the other compartments were a party of Germans and a party of Japanese; all the ingredients necessary, vouchsafed Robert, to reignite the Second World War. In the event everyone was extremely amiable – even sociable – the status of society rising to the heights with the arrival of the Swiss ambassador and his wife, followed by Phil Snyder and his young companion. I felt sorry for the girl. She was shivering with cold, inadequately shod, and looked downright miserable. While the climbers were engaged in heavy mountaineering discussion I fed the lady with discoloured chocolate bars, and some Spangles which she seemed to appreciate. She was American, lived in both New York and Massachusetts, knew my hometown on account of having been to the opera at nearby Glyndebourne and thought the British – as well as their Spangles – 'cute'. Speculation was rife as to who she was until, later, Phil Snyder revealed the lady to be none other than Caroline Kennedy, daughter of the late United States president. Quite a party developed, which broke up with the dusk, the search for candles and when our beloved pressure cooker, in an excess of enthusiasm, blew jets of boiling soup around the room.

The night was nothing if not chaotic. Most of us slept on the floor, and in our compartment there was a period of what I can only describe as mass claustrophobia brought on by our confined space and lack of air. Thereafter, the door of the room remained open in spite of the cold. But hardly had we fallen asleep when Harley's alarm clock shrilled to spill us out of our cocoons. Then it was discovered that the clock had gone off two hours early, though it took most of those two hours to transform our glacial ice into water for hot tea. It was still barely light when, slightly punch-drunk, we set out for Lenana's summit.

With the help of steps worn into the hard snow by the footprints of previous climbers, the steep ascent was not so difficult. I suffer very mildly, in certain circumstances, from vertigo and so kept my eyes straight ahead for much of the time. One slip and you could slither down a slope that ended with a drop into a crevasse of the Lewis Glacier, and the idea of my refrigerated corpse emerging at the bottom of the mountain sometime in the 22nd century failed to appeal. Poor John suffered far worse from the same scourge but stuck it out to the rocky crags at the summit.

Here the cold was bitter; the view of the twin peaks and across to the Aberdares between wisps of cloud the stuff of poetry. That we had to fumble about taking pictures of a sponsor's bottle of hooch bordered upon blasphemy but, without doubt, the contents were to find appreciative throats later.

We made a roped descent; hardly necessary but it offered practice for Harley and Robert and comfort for John. The bottle descended more rapidly on its own, the rope, tautening suddenly, ejecting it from my anorak pocket. We watched in agony as it rolled madly towards the void, to stop at the very edge.

Top Hut stands at an altitude of 15,720 feet; that of Two Tarn Hut, 14,730 feet. But the difference of 990 feet involved a sharp descent to 13,700 feet and a rise of similar proportions the other side of the valley, which turns the simple subtraction and addition into something of an exhausting equation. At the bottom of the cleft the cold, clear glacial water of a tinkling stream was nectar to thirsty throats. We wore snow goggles on the strict orders of Harley, for the risk of snow blindness in the bright sunlight was very real.

We found a much-improved Richard Matthews in residence at the refuge that was to become our home for a week. Two Tarn Hut can hardly be described as a mountain Hilton. A corrugated iron shack something on the lines of a Second World War Anderson air-raid shelter might give older readers the picture. It leaked, had tattered plastic sheeting in lieu of window panes and was infested by a particularly fearless brand of rat. But there was water. One of the two tarns hereabouts lay just below the hut, though its grey waters held a minimum of attraction.

Then arose the problem of fitting seven bodies into space that had optimistically been designed for five. A raised shelf represented the sleeping quarters; some four tattered foam rubber pads constituted the beds (someone had removed the fifth). Everything was filthy and muck-strewn, so our first task was that of a major spring-clean. My teeth chattering with cold, I viewed these preparations for a prolonged sojourn with the deepest misgiving. Kora, with its day-long African sun, became an even more desirable place to be.

The two extra bodies were those of Alister, the English dentist, and Ram, an American. Neither had booked themselves into the hut in advance but, in the circumstances, we could hardly throw them out. They settled in with us well and donated some welcome fresh tomatoes and other vegetables, as well as bread, to our tinned creations, which in spite of John's undoubted culinary expertise were fast becoming monotonous. Our new companions were bearded youngsters working the wanderlust out of their systems and had been on the road in many countries for months. What they thought of our semi-military group I was to glean from Ram's personal diary, an entry of which started thus: 'Coming up Mt. K, freelance as usual, meet an ultra-organised British Army group eating inedible shit out of small cans'.

If the night was cold we never felt it. Not only did we wear everything except our boots but, compressed together, the heat generated was considerable. And it was as well we had our boots to hand since they made useful missiles against the food-seeking rats that were soon scurrying amongst us in droves. A physical phenomenon that affected me more that it did the others was a distressing and incessant necessity to break wind, though in the confined space the distress was more theirs than mine.

In spite of deteriorating weather conditions, Harley was fully determined to accomplish the ultimate climb and had instigated a series of practice ascents in preparation for the main event, the scaling of Bation. The first scaling exercise involved the conquest of the huge, unfriendly-looking pyramid of rock that loomed above us from across the tarn. At 16,100 feet, Point Piggott was fourth in the Mount Kenya hierarchy and a very different kettle of fish to Lenana.

Accordingly, we all rose at the bid of his infernal alarm clock early next morning and bustled about in preparation for getting two pairs of climbers onto Piggott. Because of Harley's insistence on ropework in pairs an even number of climbers were to make the ascent. The chosen few were to be himself and Robert together with Alister and Ram, whose disapproval of our life-style was, apparently, not strong enough to prevent them wanting to share Piggott with us.

The morning was fine and clear, but as the four figures, muffled and swathed in ropes, ice-axes and crampons, strode off round the edge of the tarn, I felt no envy. I did, however, feel depressed, and I wasn't alone. For John, Richard and I the prospect of being confined to a rat-infested tin hut for days on end was not an enviable one.

Throughout the morning we were to catch glimpses of the quartet as they made slow progress up the granite walls of Piggott. The sunshine failed to last; we hardly expected it to. A pattern of weather was beginning to emerge, with the best of it invariably at the start of the day. John read his medical journals, of which he had brought an endless supply, and Richard polished and repolished his camera lenses – activities occasionally interrupted by dismembered voices issuing from mist-shrouded rock high in the air. The odd rat, boldly venturing out in the daytime, was put to flight; innumerable mugs of tea or coffee were made on a new toy, a temperamental petrol cooker, the lighting of which was an exercise in Russian roulette. Our main baggage had been brought to Two Tarn Hut by our dismissed homeward-bound porters, and this had been the first opportunity we had of unpacking the bulging rucksacks.

At midday we were joined by a trio of Japanese climbers, part of the party we had seen at Top Hut. The social whirl on Mount Kenya revolved in a somewhat repetitive cycle and we began to wonder how the amenities of Two Tarn Hut could be stretched to embrace the German contingent. The Japanese, however, had made their booking, so had as much right as us to use the hut, though this said little for the booking authority. Resigning themselves to the prospect of occupying an already overflowing communal bed, the new arrivals straightaway went to work on the mass production of chapatis, full of herbs and tantalising smells. The operation ended with a bowing session before sitting themselves cross-legged on the floor for an orgy of consumption that turned Two Tarn Hut into a Mount Kenya equivalent of the Teahouse of the August Moon.

But there was nothing afternoon tea-like about what was happening outside. A thin veil of snow had turned to a blizzard, with low cloud obscuring not only Piggott but even the far shore of the tarn. And as dusk brought an ugly darkness to the sombre scene, a nagging worry developed into stark crisis.

We held a brisk council of war to decide upon the action we would take in an emergency that was already upon us. No-one had read the mountaineer's book of rules but we assumed that to stay put was the only action we could take until we were at least certain that things *had* gone wrong. And for a climber with no torch to attempt the descent of a mountain in darkness would be folly. What could the most sophisticated rescue service do at night even if it were to be contacted? I volunteered to descend to Mackinders Rangers Station at first light next morning – if it came to it – while John, with his emergency medical supplies, and Richard made efforts to get as close as possible to the trapped climbers. In the meantime we could only play the waiting game and try to get as close as we could to the base of Piggot to make verbal contact.

Togged up in every item of clothing we could lay our hands on, we set out into the blizzard. I felt a little like Captain Oates emerging heroically from his North Pole bivouac but, in this instance, it wasn't me doing the dying. This woeful privilege was reserved for the four men out there somewhere in the hell of rock, cold and darkness. The Japanese group, though understanding little English, had caught the whiff of tragedy and came with us into the hostile night. And there, by the side of that evil little lake, we waved our torches and attempted communication. To indicate that they were not quite alone in their distress seemed to us a worthwhile point to transmit across the snow-swept ether.

One by one we cupped our hands to our mouths and yelled futile questions: Are you OK? Do you require help? Is anyone hurt? At first our words were whipped away by the howling gale, but by moving to the windward side of the tarn we eventually succeeded in getting a message across the void. Faintly, well-nigh inaudibly, came words that might have been a ploy of the wind or trick of our ears, but by constant repetitions resolved themselves into the basic answers to our shouted questions. 'Are you OK?' 'No.' 'Do you require help?' 'Yes.' 'Is anyone hurt?' 'No.' At least this last reply raised a hope that our four friends had a chance of remaining alive through the coming hours.

That night was a long one. Guiltily we consumed their supper of onion soup and overcooked spaghetti, which one of the Japanese had tenderly prepared, nearly incinerating himself in the process. And in bed, warm but unhappy, we lay listening to the wind and, through a freak of acoustics, fragments of ghostlike voices that, to our tortured minds, were pleas for help. In the window the tiny flame of the candle both epitomised our hope and frightened away the rats.

Excerpt from Robert's diary:

16.30. Finally free rope and prepare for a further descent which might bring us back onto our original route. I feel certain at this stage that we are destined to spend the night on the mountain. A dismal and rather frightening prospect. This last abseil brought Harley and me down to a small ledge a hundred below Alister and Ram. Here disaster struck. The two of us, in fading light, unable to flick [the rope] within reach of the two above. 19.15, and we all realise we are here for the night. Harley made a brave but futile effort to climb in almost total darkness. Alister and Ram began shouting that something had to be done, [for] with some justification, they rate their chances of surviving the night as slim. It has dawned on us that from being a five-hour training climb we are now involved in a possible life-and-death situation. Thought of exposure, frostbite, hypothermia, etc. spring to mind. Alister and Ram are convinced they will not survive the night belayed, as they are, on a small ledge with virtually no room to move. But we know it is suicidal to attempt to climb in the dark. Harley and I occupy a narrow sloping ledge [of which] the only available protection consists of the end of the rope and an ice axe with a sling. The ledge allows only for two narrow footsteps, which means we are not able to do much more than move on the spot to keep warm. We wear every available garment and discuss ways of staying alive. Sleep out of the question and we have to keep up constant movement to prevent frostbite. We also shout to the two above periodically to maintain their and our [own] morale. Probably we have overrated the severity of the conditions for the low cloud ensures the temperature does not sink much below freezing. But we are worried about Alister and Ram because of their lighter clothing and more exposed situation. After the first three hours we know we can survive relatively unscathed. Harley and I do all we can to remain warm and awake, telling each other stories and executing shadow punches at our rucksacks. The [shouts] from John, Christopher and Richard from below are a good morale booster. Alister keeps repeating that his leg is dead. The hours seem interminable and from 02.30 onwards it becomes increasingly difficult to remain awake. Our stories, jokes and singing become less effective and we look pretty ridiculous standing bolt upright side by side solemnly asking each other 'Are you awake?'

At last dawn begins to suffuse the mountain. It also begins to snow hard little pellets of ice. Harley dons his crampons and inches his way up towards the ledge above. Through breaks in the mist I can see a candle burning in the window of Two Tarn Hut...

The alarm clock trilled at four in the morning, though its summons was hardly necessary. Two Tarn Hut was at once a hive of activity, with its British and Japanese occupiers donning climbing boots, over-trousers and duvets with enthusiastic deliberation. At last we could now do something useful.

It was pitch dark outside but snow no longer fell. The wind, too, had dropped. With John and Richard making ready to scale the base of Piggott and re-establish contact with the climbers I made my stumbling way up and over the crest of the ridge. One of the Japanese was with me, an earnest young fellow who spoke very limited English. We carried torches, but the whiteness of the snow and our eyes accustoming to the darkness muted the blackness of the night. The first streaks of dawn showed as we commenced the treacherous descent of the 900-foot escarpment, the snow now becoming a hindrance on account of its concealment of the pitfalls and slippery patches of rock. Sometimes on my buttocks, occasionally with a helping hand from my companion, skidding and careering down scree, we reached the floor of the valley. Here bog was our only impediment, its veneer of ice fragmenting as we floundered through; cold water was sluicing around the inside of my boots. A track led by the low wooden cabin with its sprouting antennae and, such was our haste, we almost missed it. I completed the journey on all fours, crawling up to the door in a state of utter exhaustion.

Within very few minutes a squad of African rangers, equipped with walkie-talkie radios, were leaping up the escarpment like chamois. I followed in my own time, my task at an end.

It was broad daylight when I regained the top of the ridge. The young Japanese had gone on ahead of me to impart the news to John and Richard that professional help was on the way. Snow was falling again and cloud once more wrapped the silent peaks in their deep embrace. The only occupant of the hut was one of the other Japanese engaged upon the preparation of a mammoth breakfast in celebration of what we all hoped would be a deliverance. From the direction of the rocky bulwarks of Piggott came the buzz and crackle of voices.

Halting a moment to regain my breath, I made my way along the edge of the tarn to rejoin the rescuers. Low cloud eclipsed any possibilities of a helicopter lift-off but John and Richard, together with little Itsui the third Japanese, had managed to attain a point from which communication with the climbers was easier. They could even see them descending under their own steam through rents in the cloud. The lower sections of Piggott had become an ants' nest of muffled figures in old army greatcoats, and before long the four weary survivors were safely amongst us.

Dragging the loads off their backs, John and Richard wrapped the quartet in sleeping bags and shepherded them down to the hut. A swift examination revealed no damage and, within the hour, all of us were consuming vast helpings of tea, soup and porridge. One-by-one the African rangers departed and life in Two Tarn Hut reverted to normal. With no source of heat available we went to bed, the climbers to sleep, the rest of us to thaw out our frozen feet.

True climbers are not easily beaten. That Harley and Robert as well as Alister and Ram could have joined the victims of previous mishaps, whose silent graves overlooked the Lewis Glacier, had them not in the slightest concerned. Hardly had they awoken from their overdue slumber than Harley and Robert were discussing ways and means of completing their mission. But the weather remained fickle to the last: tempting in the early morning, downright vicious thereafter. And it was on those early mornings that Bation beckoned the loudest, for it was then that the spectral rags of mist parted from her face and flashes of frozen snow on the summit signalled its challenge.

However, the fact that the twin peaks would hardly be in a fit state for climbing even were the weather to improve that very moment had to be taken into account in Harley's deliberations. A cautious reconnaissance onto the glacier confirmed the worst and, since we had but a limited time at our disposal, he declared the intention of abandoning the mountain. Me, I couldn't get off it fast enough.

Minus porters, our individual loads for the main descent were of gargantuan proportions. Dividing everything into five equal portions we distributed equipment, clothing and the remaining rations into our big army rucksacks, and what couldn't be put in

them was tied to the sides. The weight was prodigious; each bag
could hardly have weighed less than seventy pounds, which had
the most serious and disturbing effect on balance. We staggered
about like drunken sailors attempting to accustom ourselves to the
sensation, fell over, rolled over trying to rise and had to be helped
to our feet by those of us still upright.

What had been snow above 14,000 feet was water below it, and
the Teleki Valley was awash. Often up to our calves in the watery
mud of the 'Vertical Bog', we made agonisingly slow progress
even though the gradient was downward. It was all-too easy to
break a leg or twist an ankle in the slime hidden beneath the waist-
high grass, while a fall could even result in drowning, the weight
on one's shoulders being such as to hold a man down beneath the
water level. Somewhere over to the left the infant Tana made less
burdensome progress on its way off the mountain.

To each his own pace. Spread out over a mile, the five of us
fought our own battles. I keeled over a dozen times to find myself
gazing at the sky in the manner of a capsized beetle. But, like the
beetle, I found methods of righting myself, squirming around
grunting with exertion. Thus we progressed to the jungle belt,
through which we marched on legs that threatened to buckle at
every step. A flock of parakeets on a tree screeched with maniacal
laughter at my muddied appearance. Elephant droppings littered
the path. And around the hundredth corner was our Land Rover.

At the boundary of the National Park we were met by Phil
Snynder, who invited us to his house for tea. His African man-
servant had his work cut out replenishing our cups as we sat
overlooking the 'lawn' of his fine country residence – kept in trim,
he told us, by passing rhinos, one of which had killed his gardener
the week before. Back at Nanyuki we celebrated we knew not
what with three huge helpings each of sausages, eggs and chips at
the local transport cafe. Simple fare, but it was what we all craved.
Anyway, we deserved no better.

In a real bed that night I totted up the score. We had failed in
the bid to conquer Mount Kenya; instead we had lived with and
experienced the ruthless spawning ground of the river which we
had come so far to explore. And there is nothing like beginning at
the beginning.

3. Kora

In retrospect I am inclined to dispute the assertion, stoutly
maintained by the Scientific Team and its supporting elements,
that Kora was the best camp of all. Of course, I was not a fit
subject to judge since I was there for only very few days against
the three weeks of the others. On the other hand, coming from the
cold of the mountain to the idyllic warmth of Kora I had every
reason to praise its amenities which, without doubt, were the finest
of the six base camps to be established from Kora to the mouth of
the Tana. Subsequent camps were to be of no more than a week's
duration, which gave less time for improvement.

If there was a village called Kora I never saw it. There was
Kora Rock, an immense granite boil on the face of the flat bush-
country that was an eye-catcher for twenty miles in all directions.
And there was Kora Rapids, a section of angry Tana water not far
away. But for most of us Kora camp was an introduction to the
real Africa. Situated in a remote north-eastern province, it marked
the Tana's half-way mark and the point at which our scientific
survey began. In all respects, Kora was ideal. As both a terminal
and a terminus it signalled the end of Tana's youthful tantrums and
the beginning of serene adult progress through the life-giving
riverine forests.

Lions, elephants, rhinos, basilisks and unicorns dwell in East
Africa according to historians of medieval times, intermingling
fact and legend. The Queen of Sheba was an Ethiopian ancestress
of the late Emperor. King Solomon's mines, supplying the queen's
mythical wealth, were said to lie in its snow-capped Mountains of
the Moon. Dotted around the endless territory were giants and
pygmies and incredibly rich African potentates. East Africa was
an altogether wondrous land.

Today it still is. Granted, no unicorn has yet appeared on hunters' trophy lists; neither has anyone been known lately to have come face to face with a basilisk and been instantly transformed into granite. But all the other creatures that have excited travellers since Ptolemy compiled his famous map are there. Alas, some are on the verge of extinction due to the poachers' greed, but many have become wise to man's hostility and managed to survive. It is just that, outside the game parks, one has to go and find them.

So Kora, for most of us, reaped the distinction of being the place where we actually saw our first wild animals. By the time the five of us of the Mountain Team had rejoined our companions at Kora the others had seen their first hippo, crocodile, baboon, monkey, wart hog, bushbuck and snake and were fast becoming blasé about it. Mount Kenya had produced only the undramatic hyrax, though I attempted to keep my end up by pressing my sightings earlier of giraffe and zebra from the train and elsewhere. And it is a fact of life that to see a wild animal outside of a zoo for the first time is an experience in itself. Sir Julian Huxley puts it most aptly: 'To see large animals going about their natural business in their own natural ways, safe and unafraid, is one of the most exciting and moving experiences in the world'.

To the scientists Kora will be remembered as the camp where it all started. Animals were more numerous and exciting further down river, but the magic of living in the African wild, of seeing strange creatures and sleeping directly under an African sky for the first time gave the place a special significance. Remote, all but unattainable and, yes, ethereal, Kora was a landmark not only for the expedition itself but in our lives. Even after two days the so-called civilised world seemed not only non-existent but nearly impossible to envisage. Life's usual mundane preoccupations had been completely replaced by the most sensitive attention to noises and movement. We too had become creatures of awareness, attentiveness, quietness and not a little fear.

From Nairobi, Kora lies directly north-east at a distance, I suppose, of some 250 miles. Two days in the Kenyan capital to brush the snow off our boots was quite long enough, and the shackles of a brief moment of civilisation departed with the last of the tarmac on the Garissa road.

And with the dust comes the new world. When you move along African roads, you feel that all Africa must be on foot, for there is a continuous patient procession of women carrying tremendous burdens, women with babies in slings on their backs, old men with a goat or a cow on a string, young people on bicycles, children running. At the bus stops are more people busily doing nothing, a pastime repeated in every little dusty village. Nowhere in the world has the art of doing nothing – and enjoying it – been practised with such aptitude as in Africa.

Sprawled in the back of our 3-ton Bedford lorry, Richard and I suffered a frosty ride until the sun was up. As the vehicle hit the bumps and raised the dust, a trio of giraffe feeding off the top of a tree took to their heels, moving in that strange imperfectly co-ordinated fashion with neck and head floating along on top of a cantering body. We watched the motion rippling down the reddish manes until all three had vanished from view. Only our driver, Lance-Corporal Andy Winspeare, feigned indifference, being an old hand of Kora.

A resourceful and useful chap to have around was Andy. Aged 23, he knew his trade as vehicle mechanic long before he joined the Royal Electrical and Mechanical Engineers. His cheerful Birmingham accent and a repartee that never sagged even with extreme exhaustion was a tonic for us all when times were hard. He was to drive for thousands of miles over the impossible roads, tracks and open country of the Kenyan outback with a skill and a pace that had me both envious and alarmed on many an occasion.

After Mwingi the road deteriorated further until we were bouncing and lurching along a track cut by deep wadis and bounded by thick bush that did its utmost to sweep us off the back of the vehicle. Known as Boundary Road, the route was one of several such tracks surveyed and brought into being by Terence Adamson, brother of the more famous George, with whom, half an hour short of our destination, we stopped for late afternoon tea.

Stripped to the waist, red dust plastered about our sweaty bodies, we made improbable guests of the Adamsons at their ever-open, straw-thatched encampment home at Kora Rock. Yet the Adamsons must have been equally improbable hosts; George and

Terence then living alone with their lions and their guinea fowl, with beady-eyed chameleons darting about the furniture. A younger man, Tony Fitzjohn, helped George with his tasks, and we dutifully did the rounds – to be rewarded by sight of two wild lion cubs, the only lions I was to see in East Africa during the entire expedition. Offspring of the renowned Elsa, they were wild, it is true, but a semi-tameness and the necessity of seeing them fed behind a fence robbed the moment of its magic.

George had little to say. More accustomed to royalty or celebrities flying in by helicopter, he seemed slightly taken aback by our unscheduled arrival in a dirt-encrusted lorry via one of his brother's roads. But Terence enjoyed seeing us. A small, battered, weathered man with nervous mannerisms, great endurance and undaunted courage, he had been farmer, prospector, professional hunter, road-, dam- and bridge-builder, soldier, water-diviner and hotel-keeper throughout his sixty-nine years. His roads are as legendary in Kenya as George's lions are to the world – though each professed complete lack of interest in the other's life work. We drank copious cups of tea, expressed the hope we would see them both at our camp, and left.

We received a great welcome from the scientists. Fresh faces, even those of recent acquaintance, at remote camps invariably made the day a red-letter one. I was singled out for special treatment – my Ugandan ordeal having been inflated in its transmission to the outback. Arrival at the camps of a vehicle from rear base also meant the chance of mail from home, plus an injection of new tastes into our uninspiring meals. This visitation was no exception.

The camp had been erected on a spit of sand where the Tana curves to such an extent as to make a virtual island of the site. So low was the water that the 'causeway' was dry, but I was assured that, whenever irrigation requirements allowed it, the river rose high enough to permit a trickle to creep in behind us. Within the taped boundary four 6-person bivouacs had been erected down one side, while a marquee – which we never saw again – doubled as mess tent and laboratory at the other. Such was the warmth most of the inmates slept outside, thus adding to the storage facilities – which were further extended by a lean-to larder and

kitchen. A generator provided electric light, and tastefully hidden
by the nearby jungle foliage were the hessian screens of the camp
bathroom and toilets. To round off this outpost of empire there
rose, from the centre of a little England in a foreign field, a flag-
pole bearing the expedition's pennant of a hippo's head on a green
background.

Everyone wore the minimum of clothing and was abnormally
brown. I had been reasonably tanned myself – a legacy mainly of
Brighton beach – but had lost some of it over the last ten days.
Mary, Alison and Mona, three females of the expeditionary
species, sported a natty line in bikinis, and I began to wonder why
I had left Brighton beach, which could produce, right on my own
doorstep, an equally attractive human panorama.

But the Sussex Downs could never quite rise to the occasion of
a first night in an African wilderness. After a substantial evening
meal, far superior to anything we had been able to rustle up on
Mount Kenya, two of us were invited by our young zoologist,
Andrew Mitchell, to partake of a night observation walk. I
accepted with alacrity and we left about nine. With us we took one
of a pair of image intensifiers loaned to the expedition by Rank
Pullin Control Ltd. and the Ministry of Defence. These expensive
items of equipment were originally developed for military
purposes, to assist vision at night without the use of artificial light.
The telescope-like instruments gather all available light from the
moon and stars (to which the human eye is insensitive) and
transform it into light images that the eye can see. These images
are projected onto a phosphorous screen in the form of a greeny
glowing picture, the power source being no more than ordinary
Mercury 1.5 volt batteries.

We also carried head-torches, ordinary torches but with the
bulb and reflector attached to the forehead by a harness. With
these probing the dark ahead, we moved off parallel to the trees
towards the further extremity of our 'island'. As we walked,
Andrew quietly related his adventures while on previous nocturnal
prowls. On one occasion he had come face to face with a hippo at
point blank range, and scared the living daylights out of both
himself and the hippo. And he had manoeuvred himself very close
to crocodiles languishing on sandbanks; he had been able to

observe them there for minutes on end before vague suspicions that all was not as it should be sent the creatures sliding back into the water. But on *my* first night observation, nothing, absolutely nothing, came into my straining vision, unless you count tiny spiders' eyes, like glow-worms, twinkling from beneath small rocks in the wet sand. But at least I got a whiff of stalking the African wilderness by night, and it is exciting, heady stuff. Every noise was laced with menace, every shadow edged with terror. The lights of the camp were never more welcome, and to cross the flimsy boundary tape was like returning to the barbed wire coils of one's own lines after a wartime night patrol into enemy territory.

I lay awake in my sleeping bag looking at the sky ablaze with a myriad stars. Is it only for Africa that the heavens can produce such magnificence? And when I snuggled down to sleep I found myself listening to the unexplained noises of the living jungle, so that when I slept my dreams were but a continuation of those wonders of the darkness. In the small hours I awoke to make my way to the boundary tapes to surreptitiously relieve myself, and nearly jumped out of my skin when our African *askari* (guard) crept up to flash his torch upon me. But if the African night is a period of mysticism, so is the African dawn. Never would I have believed that light could fashion so much beauty anywhere on earth. It was the birth of the very first day; a radiance and a richness streaming over golden sand and intangible trees that shimmered as molten wire.

Gradually the camp came alive. The *askaris* had kept the fire alight and the duty cooks distributed mugs of tea. It was a case of first come first served in the 'bathroom' – particularly if you wanted a shower, which consisted of an erratic contraption dribbling cold water from a makeshift tank (if somebody had remembered to fill it first). While having mine, I noticed some logs in the mirror-calm Tana, but they suddenly moved and I perceived they were hippos. The river looked peaceful and inviting in the early morning but, as with Africa in general, things are not always what they seem. At Kora the water was not badly contaminated, though we were instructed to have as little physical contact with it as possible. In the weeks to come even our washing water taken from the Tana had to be treated, a task that offered a near full-time job for one of the support members.

Breakfast was a feast. Alpen cereal with dried or condensed milk, fried bacon roll and as much tea or coffee as one wanted. Where I got the idea that expeditioning had to be an exercise in spartan living I don't know. We had not exactly starved on Mount Kenya either. Anything lacking there had been simply due to a more limited choice of basic materials.

And then everyone moved off to execute their various tasks. It was a bit like 'going to the office'. Had there been a railway station nearby I'm damned if we would not have become a group of commuters. Instead, it was a short walk to the jungle or, nearer still, the laboratory tent. I felt I ought to clock in somewhere, or at least carry a millboard around with me as an indication of employment. Instead, I made it my task to do the rounds and find out what had been going on during my absence.

A couple of days before the five of us had started out for the mountain, the Scientific Team had left Nairobi. They had taken two days to reach the camp site, spending the night at the township of Garissa, on the Tana. They put up at the town's only hotel which, seemingly, was also the local whore shop. A party developed and Tusker beer flowed copiously to celebrate the entry into the wilderness, but thereafter reports become somewhat vague and my informers reticent. Only one, rather diffidently, came out with a story of waking up in the morning to find a Black woman beside him in the big, old-fashioned double bed. They bade each other a polite 'good morning' and promptly returned to sleep. At least, that was the man's story and the teller shall remain nameless. Later, I too was to spend some time in Garissa, so could appreciate the fact that hotel accommodation was, indeed, limited and its amenities somewhat original.

It took two days to set up camp, during which came a visitation by 'Chum' van Someren and a couple of companions, who pitched their caravan camp nearby. George and Terence Adamson and Tony Fitzjohn breezed in on several occasions to see how everybody was settling down. Superficially things were all very civilised.

Local residents were few and far between, for we were in an area devoid of any static communities. What other humans there were consisted of roving Somalis, and for days on end we were to see these scowling nomads, with their endless herds of camels and goats grazing their way past our camp. It was hard to say whether these sour-looking men, without the happy smile of the Kenyan, were those of the province, or whether they were part of the 'peaceful invasion' from Somalia itself. Many may have been *shifta**, for the north-east corner of Kenya had long been a breeding ground of trouble. Inter-tribal banditry was rife, and terrorism arising from and aggravated by political tension between Somalia, Somaliland and the Kenyan government, a constant threat. Ethnically this area of the country was Somali by right, but politics have a habit of going their own ugly way.

Somalis have been living in the north-east of the country ever since the territory was part of Somalia. The Somali Youth League was introduced by the Allied Military Government during World War Two, mainly through its officers being hoodwinked by the Somalis' undeniable charm. What was thought to be a cross between the Boy Scouts and the Primrose League turned out to be a nest of vipers. By methods all-too familiar in this day and age the SYL became a powerful left-wing political party, declared illegal following its attempt to set up an independent state in what was once known as Northern Frontier Province. But, as is invariably the case, driving the party underground only increased its activities – even glamourising them – and it remained the political mouthpiece of the largest grouping of the Somali tribes. It was the governments of Britain, France, Ethiopia, Italy and Kenya which, unwittingly no doubt, caused this unhappy situation by the enforced division of the Somalis. The people of Somalia are now theoretically united, but their eyes are on the former NFP, containing an overwhelming majority of their fellows in what was originally their territory anyway. It was obvious from the start that an independent SYL government in Mogadishu would be an irresistible attraction for NFP Somalis, who would hardly be impressed by the alternative appeal of 'Uhuru' in Kenya. This, to them, simply meant rule by politicians representing tribes which they had always, if unjustly, regarded as 'dirty black fellows with crinkly hair and foreskins' – to put it in the words of the writer Charles Chenevix Trench.

*It was the *Shifta* who ultimately murdered George Adamson at Kora.

Hence therefore this 'peaceful invasion' westwards. Whether these surly men, with their great herds of beast slowly grazing their way forward like locusts, were *shifta*-disguised soldiers, or simply homeless Somalian citizens 'encouraged' by a government to occupy their former land nobody knew, but many had guns barely concealed beneath their dress. We uneasily watched them pass, for they went their way as enemy and spurned our gestures of friendship. In one instance a kid was born to a labouring goat close to the camp and some of us approached in interest and sympathy. The nomad keeper snatched both animals away and the message in his eyes was that of hate.

The Kenyan Somali attitude was equally plain. He was impervious to reason. To him it was against the law of nature for a nobler race to be rule by a rabble of former slaves. The future of the province – now known as North-Eastern Province – was being decided by power politics clothed in the holy armour of anticolonisation. Vicious clashes between Kenyan police and Somalis, who may have been Kenyan or Somalian, were occurring all-too frequently, though the fact was rarely reported. The government of Somalia would nourish an armed rebellion, as it did the silent invasion, but were restrained from excesses by fear of the Ethiopian army, who in spite of their recent commitments in Eritrea, had the power and mounting enthusiasm for a drive on Mogadishu. An Ethiopian army and a Somali army, both of them lavishly equipped by the Americans and the former Soviet Union respectively, made for a recipe for conflict that had a depressing sameness about it. As I lay in my sleeping bag looking at the stars, it was, if the truth be known, not only for wild animals that I listened.

But this sinister background failed to dampen the enthusiasm of the scientists and the enjoyment of life by us all. I began to pry into the doings of our young investigators and to accompany them on their business in the forests. At first I was somewhat nonplussed. Taken individually the tasks seemed insignificant, childish in their simplicity. How could the collection, examination and occasional dissection of a little furry creature or delicate butterfly help mankind to delve into the complex and massive problems of the development and harnessing of a great river.

I watched Gail, our one-and-only woman scientist, lay out her traps – small wooden boxes with spring-lids that caught their prey unharmed – on the (to me) invisible runs of the tiny mammals of the forest. And in the morning I would accompany Lorio, our African taxidermist and skinner, to collect the catches and reset the traps. Frequently we caught nothing, but every now and again we would return triumphant with a brand of rat or squirrel. And I well remember the excitement at the capture of a civet-cat, a long-bodied, wiry-coated animal as large as a medium-sized dog but with a very unsociable bent. Some of the smaller mammals were put to sleep to become specimens for dissection or for preservation in the Nairobi Museum and the British Natural History Museum in London. Others were held simply for observation and photography, then released.

The butterflies caught were not so lucky. Tony Pittaway, 23-year-old Bachelor of Science, was our entomologist, and he lived in his own world of butterflies, moths, insects, bugs and creepy-crawlies. That he loved his subject was plain to all, his career having commenced from the moment a poisonous caterpillar painfully crossed his path during school javelin practice. Rapid-speaking, tall and bronzed, he remained an aloof figure, preferring the intimate company of his bugs to close human companionship. During the weeks of Kora he collected over seventy butterflies, including a number exclusive to the Tana, whose ever-beautiful forms filled his showcase alongside those of less attractively endowed creatures.

His methods of capture were by the use of a butterfly net slightly larger than the ones I had used as a child, together with a fine net stretched between trees across what he considered to be nocturnal and daytime 'flight paths', and special net traps baited by a smelly concoction of fermented banana soaked in Guinness. Butterflies by day; moths by night – and the nocturnal wanderings of many a moth ended in a plastic cone containing an ultra-violet light bulb.

Through Tony's drum-fire narrative and catching the germ of his enthusiasm, I learnt more about butterflies and moths than I ever thought possible. He talked of butterfly migrations, million upon untold million arriving from some source unknown and travelling to an equally mysterious destination. And in the sun-pierced jungle I could clearly discern how the ancestral development of the butterfly and the moth led back through a million years, how their patterns had reason as well as intricacy, and why their colours meant life and death as well as beauty. At night, as I watched moths being drawn to our jungle lantern, a latent dread of nocturnal predators turned to a sensation akin to horror as a rabble of moths became an enormous, amorphous super-organisation piled up in fluttering droves, pressed against the lantern glass, manacled by the unreasoning drawing power of light. It occurred to me that what the sun, moon and stars do is performed by a single hundred-watt bulb.

One particularly colourful specimen fell on its side, its wings stretched back and the body curved into an unpleasant hairy caterpillar, or so it appeared. Upon the insect a trance had settled which neither shaking nor dropping disturbed. If I were a hungry bird or lizard I should have nothing to do with such an unpleasant object, and this is exactly what this unconsciously induced display was trying to effect. We humans are not so clever, nor are our eyes so unconfused. We see a butterfly and marvel at the beauty of its wings, but shudder at the caterpillar whose metamorphic body lies between those wings.

The wonder of the lowly insect world became apparent too. At Kora and elsewhere I saw many a bug, beetle or fly similar to our own, except in size and sometimes colour. But everything was bigger and better, and this included the bite or sting in the tail. Here at Kora I saw scorpions, big brown and black specimens crawling in the sand, loathsome but fascinating. Here too were wasps that were not wasps, beetles that were moths, centipedes as big as slow-worms, moths with wings rolled tight as maps. And here too, all but invisible, were craneflies dancing up and down on bended knees for no reason that our poor brains could fathom.

Birds of the forest and the river came into Sandy Evan's domain. Sandy, at 22, was the youngest full member of the expedition, but his knowledge of ornithology was considerable, a knowledge that had resulted in an award of a B.Sc. degree. An inveterate smoker and a lover of rugby, as well as the bawdy songs its players are wont to render, he would go around reciting dubious

limericks from a paperback of equally dubious source. His thirst
for adventure was partly quenched by his curiosity about birds and
animals, and on the bird side, he had an ally in Kenneth Campbell
who joined the expedition from his Nairobi home towards the end
of our Kora sojourn. A serious young man of 23, another B.Sc.,
and with an ambition to be a zoologist in Malawi, the expedition
was to rub the raw edges off Ken – as it did few other members.

The catching of birds was effected by mist nets erected at
strategic points in the jungle, and sometimes by the more drastic
method emanating from the barrel of a gun. (The expedition's only
weapons were an aged small-bore shotgun and a .22 rifle, both lent
to us by the Nairobi Museum, while our protection from man or
beast was entrusted to a Kenyan police Mark 4 rifle. In all cases
ammunition was severely limited. While in the jungle or on the
river we also carried a number of pyrotechnical devices known as
'thunderflashes' which, when ignited and thrown, exploded with
considerable violence. They are supposed to be non-lethal, but an
ex-army friend of mine goes about one-handed to this day to prove
how wrong you can be.) However, it was the mist net that claimed
the bulk of our winged specimens – especially bats – which were
collected at dawn and dusk by Joseph, our second dark-skinned
taxidermist and skinner, and from which a selection were dissected
or preserved for study.

The expedition's chief zoologist was Andrew Mitchell,
mentioned earlier. Another 23-year-old B.Sc., a native of Jersey,
Andrew had already packed into his life more than many people
manage by the age of eighty. Travel in Europe, Central America
and North Africa, three months game-counting in the Tsavo
National Park, ship-crewing in the Mediterranean, his interests
ranged over wildlife conservation, sailing, surfing, skiing, skin-
diving, photography and exploration. Surprisingly, acting was not
amongst the list, for he was a fine mimic; he could act the fool
with considerable skill, and though it was half-hidden by a
golliwog head of hair and massive beard, he possessed a face alive
with character and intelligence. In many ways his tasks overlapped
with those of Sandy and Ken, but the hippo and crocodile count to
be executed down the river was specifically Andrew's baby.

Many geographical authors refer to the Tana as a faunal barrier.

This we hoped to prove or disprove. Quite plainly the river was the largest single factor contributing to the presence and survival of the various tribes we would be meeting on our journey along its tortuous course. The communities living on its banks obviously depended heavily upon its water for much of their livelihood. Just how much, again, we had to learn. Much of the old nomadic way of life was being abandoned – even by the tribes whose way of life had rested on the need and habit of constant movement. It was not adopted by choice in the first place but of necessity: they are nomadic because of the grazing facilities available to their animals. But the Tana provided a good reason for not indulging in constant moving and, as a result, tribal villages along the lower Tana were growing and becoming more permanent. Here at remote Kora there were only nomadic Somalis, and *their* movement was, ominously, more for strategic reasons than any other.

Yet both man and beast of Tana country were approaching the crossroads. Already we had noted the daily change in the level of the water as the few existing upstream dams controlled or released its flow. It was almost like a tidal river, yet Kora was hundreds of miles from the nearest sea. But what was happening at Kinderuma – where the initial series of dams were situated – would, over the next decade, be repeated in the Hola area down-river, for the lower Tana Hydroelectric Scheme was Kenya's most ambitious infrastructural project. The long-term venture was to cost in the region of £40 million; its intention was not only to spread the benefits of electricity to much of the country, but also to replace a water supply then dependent upon a highly unreliable source. At that time Kenya was importing power from the Owen Falls power station in Uganda, which had put a political lever in the hands of that unstable country. The Tana River Scheme was intended to make Kenya self-sufficient not only for her existing needs but also for industrial expansion. This alone might not have made the project worthwhile – self-sufficiency can be bought at too high a price. But the fact that the Tana also flowed through a large area of near-desert, lacking only water to become highly fertile since the soil itself was known to be good, gave a new dimension to the programme. Opportunity there was, vast opportunity; but nothing in this world is quite what it seems, and progress could also bring destruction in its wake. The lives and ways of the Tana people, the big game that could provide new injections of funds from increased tourism, the river itself. Little was known about the mud-brown Tana, but knowledge stems from small beginnings. Hence the examination, in life and sometimes death, of little furry creatures and delicate butterflies which signalled the start of our much-needed survey. Our mission, in fact, was that of bringing tiny chinks of light where before there was darkness; small beginnings where there had been next to nothing.

My third afternoon I sat idly on the river bank ostensibly writing my notes but, in reality, reflecting upon a 12-foot-long crocodile basking on a rock. After the drama of the mountain I found the knowledgeable doings of the scientists slightly tedious. Like our soldiers, they belonged to an exclusive club, and I was an outsider – an ignorant one at that – who didn't know a bug from a beetle, a croc from an alligator. Their private findings were all being jotted down in exclusive books in an exclusive language that all seemed very inconclusive to me.

Scientific Team leader Raj Patel sat in his canvas laboratory, lord of a paraphernalia of microscopes, textbooks, unpleasant-looking instruments, and small opened-up bodies of fur and feather. Small himself, his dark face with its sharp eyes, white teeth and neat beard had an air of distinction. We were all very fond of him but he never quite belonged, a fact that had nothing at all to do with the colour of his skin. Almost desperately, it seemed, he projected his 'belongingness' at the local Africans we were to meet and whose language he spoke. Yet, because of his Asian parentage, his entry into Kenya had been the most difficult to effect, and I had the feeling that he never quite belonged in Black Africa either. Alas, this could be the story of many an exiled Asian's life.

It was this afternoon that we lost a scientist. Gail Magrath could be with us only a month and her time was up. I had seen little of her petite form and smiling face but was as sorry as anyone to see her go. Richard Matthews was most sorrowful of all, for she was his girlfriend. For the uninterrupted continuance of the small mammal programme it was Raj who stepped into her shoes.

Even in the jungle our sponsorship undertakings crept up on us. The last day at Kora, in between the striking of camp and the loading of the vehicles, we had to perform before Richard's camera some striking poses, on land and in the river, holding aloft a variety of branded goods donated by our sponsors. Already our Bedford lorry, two Land Rovers and inflatable dinghies were sandwich-boards for commercial stickers. The hippos and crocodiles we were likely to encounter on our impending voyage down the Tana would remain in no doubt as to whose oil, petrol and washing powder we were using.

The shallowness of the river was to have a disappointing effect on one of our more flamboyant of craft, the jet boat. There had been rumblings of discontent about permitting what initially seemed like a noisy gimmick to blight the expedition's aura of earnest endeavour. But its alleged usefulness as a reconnaissance boat was vigorously expounded by its owner, Ralph Brown, who – dare it be said – was an agent of the Hamilton Jet Boat Company of New Zealand. However, it was Ralph himself who, by his likeable character, won us over; any remaining doubters fell to the charms of Ralph's Swedish wife Mona, who possessed every physical endowment for which Swedish girls are famous.

At 50, Ralph was the second oldest member of the expedition. He was a Californian but had homes around the world, including New Zealand and Andorra. His was a lifetime of boats and water and methods by which each could take advantage of the other. Ten years in the United States Navy as a deck officer, he continued his absorption with boats on a number of expeditions, including the 1974 Zaire River Expedition as a member of their jet boat team. Sailing, ski-racing, Colorado river-running, surf-rescue, airlifting boats over waterfalls, white water negotiation – there can hardly be a water activity in which he had never been involved. His craggy, bronzed face, invariably wreathed in smiles, made him something of a Rock of Gibraltar of dependability.

Mona, in her early 30s, made a perfect foil. She was, of course, blonde. Born a Gothenburger, she could speak English, German and Spanish in addition to her native tongue. On top of these attributes she was a warm-hearted person who never looked put out, fatigued or unkempt, whatever disaster was to have the rest of us in turmoil.

I do declare that I had no idea what a jet boat was until I joined the expedition. I had read somewhere of their usefulness on the Zaire River Expedition, where such a craft could operate in ankle-deep waters and over sandbars and shoals, but now, at Kora, I was to learn more. Newton's Third Law: 'For every force there is an equal but opposite force of reaction' explains the principle upon which the outboard jet is based. Water is drawn into the unit through an intake grill by means of an impeller driven directly by the engine's drive-shaft. This water is then forced at high pressure and volume through a nozzle directed astern of the boat. The velocity imparted to the mass of water creates an opposite force and drives the boat forward. Directly the boat reaches planing speed the jet discharges freely into the air and only the skimming intake grill touches the water. QED. Archimedes even comes into it with his theory regarding the screw, which is supposed to have signified the birth of jet propulsion.

But things went sadly wrong, and the days of attempts by Ralph and another jet boat enthusiast, Chris Metchette, who brought along his bigger vessel, to get things moving failed. It was not just the 'state of the tide' that fouled operations. The muddy waters of the Tana and its sandy bed were contributory factors, as well as a number of technical malfunctions and misfortunes. Yet there were moments when the craft spluttered into life and the two of them went tearing up the river in twin plumes of spray.

At this point, mention must be made of the remaining members of its personnel, for the expedition's administrative tail had their vital tasks to perform. Perhaps the hardest worker in the field of welfare was Mary Garner, expeditionary secretary, treasurer, nurse and, later, supervisor of water treatment. New Zealand-born, Mary's itchy feet had taken her to North America, India and the Far East where, as a nurse, she had served in the Vietnam War. Her cheerful good nature was, just occasionally, broken by short spells of depression which she diagnosed as culture shock. For one of her tender years too much work and responsibility were laid upon those slender shoulders, but she was a person who would rarely allow others to take over some of her burden.

Though with the expedition almost from the start, Alison Izatt was never officially a member of it. She had pleaded to be allowed to come along, and Nigel had relented on the strength of her qualifications. Like Mary, she was an SRN and was prepared to take on anything in the domestic managerial field. She also purported to be something of a zoologist, and the six years she had worked with the World Wildlife Fund must have given her an insight into the ways of birds and animals. Another New Zealander, she had spent many years in Italy where she had dabbled in modelling, acting, public relations, interpreting and translating. One of the most decorative among us, she never quite managed the tough explorer image – but for sheer good nature I have never met anyone like her. She was teased unmercifully, though more often than not, she laid herself wide open to it. Her most famous gaffe came prior to the first visit to Kora camp from George Adamson. His assistant, Tony Fitzjohn, arrived first and Alison, starry-eyed, bounded forward to shake his hand. In an earnest Kiwi accent she poured out her admiration, and until the real and more elderly George arrived, Tony, with our connivance, was able to bathe happily in his new-found glory.

In all there were four African members of the expedition. Already I have alluded to Lorio and Joseph. Also there was Charles Odvol, B.Sc., who in the scientific team was our fish expert, and Samuel Kibus, botanist, who was to join us later. Lorio, Joseph and Charles were great characters, of whom we were inordinately fond. They lived, slept and ate with us on completely equal terms, the only times inequality intruded being when there were unscheduled jobs to be carried out. Seldom would any of them lift a finger to help unless it formed part of their expedition contract. I hold this negative attitude not so much against them in person but more against Africa as a whole.

As the tents fell and the scientific chests were loaded onto the Bedford, there was a distinct feeling in the air akin to the last day of the holiday. Three weeks at Kora and the team had established themselves in this tranquil and beautiful place more than it cared to admit. Moving off into the unknown produced something of a threat. In the remains of the laboratory Raj was supervising the packing of books and I thumbed through the *Kora Animal Record* notebook, full of entries in different handwriting giving dates and details of birds and animals seen in the vicinity of the camp. 'Fish eagle, bateleur eagle, baboon, vervet monkey, wart hog, water buck, hippo, albino bushback, mamba, Sykes monkey, crocodile, impala, spotted genet, dik-dik, jackal, lesser kudu, camel, gerenuk, African hare, civet-cat, wildebeest, giraffe, osprey, bohor reedbuck, monitor lizard, steinbok, galagos and goat'. Not perhaps the most thrilling bunch of animals that Africa could offer but not bad as an introduction.

To go with the *Kora Animal Record* was the *Kora Quote Record*, a somewhat less serious tome. Started, I believe, by Andrew Mitchell, it was full of alleged utterances by members of the team, taken out of context and thought worthy of recording for posterity. If nothing else it showed how Kora had made for knitting the scientists and supporters together into the cohesive force they had become. Extracts I took note of were: 'Alison's got a nice pear.' [Andrew]; 'I couldn't eat *my* Testicles.' [Mary]; 'I'm a big girl and I *need* it.' [Mary]; and 'Alison's just pulled something out of Sandy's trousers.' [Gail].

Yet the security and cosiness of Kora was, in some ways, a false one. The Somali threat remained. And that very evening an ailing cow was despatched by a lion just a hundred yards from the site. Chum, George and Terence, attending our farewell 'mess-tin' dinner, spoke of the risks. 'They – the Somalis – now know your habits. It's time you moved on'.

It was Nigel who gave us the pre-departure briefing and outlined the possible hazards – natural, human and animal – likely to be met. We were reminded to stay alert for *shifta*, keeping our one rifle and its meagre supply of ammunition dry, clean, protected and out of sight. The chief animal menace would be, of course, the crocodile; the likely danger here arose from land or water, for though timid creatures, when ashore they lunge for deep water at the approach of alien craft and woe betide anybody or anything in the way. The river itself held less obvious danger, that of the disease bilharzia being the nastiest. Already we had been banned from unnecessary swimming, though the risks were minimal – at least this side of Garissa, the first major human habitation.

Our boats were a 15-foot Avon Professional and two Avon 12-foot Redshanks, as well as the out-of-action jet boat to be crewed by Ralph and Mona. My boat was *East Midlander*, one of the Redshanks, captained by John Richardson with Alison as my fellow crewperson. With the jet boat as 'pathfinder', the Professional *Habari* (Swahili for 'greeting') was to follow carrying the bulk of the scientists, under Sandy Evans. *Charity*, the other Redshank, was to take up the rear. We were given a lesson in boat drill and methods of communication between boats and told, cryptically, that the only method of relieving oneself *en route* was to stick whatever extremity we chose to use over the side.

The vehicle support party, composed of Andy, Raj and Tony in the first instance, were to meet up with us at the river's edge at Saki, a village some 50 miles distant and close to the next designated camp site. Optimistically, the rendezvous was set for two days hence.

As darkness fell I sat listening to the gurgle of camels on the evening air. The camp fire was poked into a cheerful blaze. This was now to become our sole source of illumination, for luxuries like generators and oil lamps had been packed away. I felt at ease with the world. Tomorrow perhaps I would at last find out what exploring was all about.

4.   White Water, Blue Funk

For me, the ascent of Mount Kenya was something of a diversion.
Lake Höhnel had shown me the birth of a great river; now I was
eager to pick up the thread of this new life.

The Tana is put to work, like many of its peoples, at any early
age. When still a child and meandering through Kikuyu country it
becomes, prosaically, a drainage source for the mud and straw
villages along the way. From the base of the virgin forest clothing
the shoulders of the mountain we followed it as best we could. The
scenery changed to that of sparse trees and brown bush that
choked all efforts by other plants to grow. The lush grass banks
gave way to sand, soft and powdery. Like an old beggar woman
the countryside grew poorer and poorer as if it had donned a
ragged coat. The young face of the Tana had been transformed to
one deeply lined with dried-out streams and pimples of rock to
disfigure it still further. Even as I looked at it in its youthful dotage
at Sagana Bridge I had sorrow in my heart.

The river was dark, dank and bubbled with infection. Here and
there it increased pace and made small clattering noises while
rushing over ledges of rock, as if objecting to the countryside
around it. But out beyond Sagana, the noisy little township through
which beautifully ancient locomotives hauled ramshackle wagons
along the freight-only line to Nanyuki, the Tana kicks itself free of
its torment and roams, idyllically, through the lonely bushland.

Something happens when you enter northern Kenya. The land
opens up, the distances brim over to engulf you and the rest of the
world seems hardly to exist. But together with the physical change,
a psychological metamorphosis takes place as well. Things swing
into proportion, values shuffle themselves like a pack of cards and
there is a new sense of harmony. All stems from that special sense

of freedom that arises with the remoteness of the bush or the vastness of the desert. As we moved along Kenya's equivalent of the Great North Road, a line of barren hills on our left emphasized the infinity of the plains on our right. But however barren and dry the African earth, the play of light upon it appears to make it glow with shifting colours as if it were opal, not dust, so that the hills unrolled past us in constantly delicately changing splendour.

We were still in the country of the Kikuyu, a farming tribe who cultivate every square foot of hill or valley with maize, coffee, bananas and vegetables. They pasture their cattle along the sides of the roads, so that the verges are close-cut, brilliant-green grass, all tracked through with paths.

Already we had passed through Fort Hall (or Muranga, as it is called locally), away from the Tana but one of the earliest settlements and now a market centre for African farmers. Known as the Garden of Eden of the Kikuyu, it is reputed to be the site of Gikuyu and Mumbi which, they believe, were their Agikuyu ancestors, who were sent by God to live on the hilltop and bore nine daughters. As directed by God, Gikuyu sacrificed a lamb here, whereupon nine youths appeared and helped his daughters found the nine Kikuyu clans. Today, with family and clan ties strong, their two million or so descendants are East Africa's most numerous and influential group, with the late President Kenyatta their most distinguished son. While I was there, a Saturday market was in full swing with cheerful people and overcrowded taxis and lorries competing dangerously for priority in its high street. While partaking of an iced Coke at a stall I watched a cripple, with leather pads where his feet and hands should have been, thread his way through the mêlée, angrily refusing offers of assistance.

Sprawling candelabra cactus rose spiky from the red-earth embankments and then, out beyond Kinderuma, we were back in the bush and among the baobab trees, a phenomenon of the vegetable world. Huge, fat trunks with a few squiggles of bare branches coming out at the top, they look like upside-down Brussels sprout plants with their roots at the top. Soft bark and warm pink tones offered an illusion of melting wax running down the side of a bottle.

For the Tana, its freedom and old abandon through the embryo bush is short-lived. At Kinderuma the dam complex deflects it into slavery. The Tana seems to understand and emerges from this indignity a different river. Gone is the placid stream following a meandering, aimless course through a thick bush that scorns it. Now a sullen waterway, dark with anger, drives into a harsh territory of solid rock. Sandy banks become chasms, mudflats are transformed to barriers of boulders, and quiet ripples build into restless waves flaked with madness. The battle of water against rock begins and the Tana lowers its head for the charge.

Naturally, we had a team set to conquer it. Our White Water squad was, if anything, even less experienced than its mountain-fighting predecessor had seemed to me. But we were an enthusiastic bunch, blithely ignorant of what we were in for. At such times ignorance emphatically can be bliss.

To negotiate the rapids of the Middle Tana we had the two 13-foot Avon Adventurer inflatables, *Adamson* and *Thesiger*, each with a crew of four. The lead-boat was to be *Adamson*, commanded by Captain Paul Turner who, in view of his alleged white water experience on the Zaire River, was team leader. Joining him would be Harley Nott, Marcus Keane and myself. In *Thesiger* there was to be Richard Matthews as captain, Robert Williamson – again taking a back seat – Peter Gilfillan and Derek Bromhill. *Thesiger* had been designated the photographic boat and had been rigged out with a Meccano-like frame to which various cameras could be affixed to record for posterity the antics or deeds of daring to be performed.

Another word here about the unintroduced members of the team. Paul Turner, had he not chosen the army, would, to my mind, have made a fine diplomat. In the ensuing days he was to pour much oil on the troubled waters of a rebellious team. He was quiet-spoken, remarkably intelligent, and behaved in a manner well in advance of his 26 years. Though born in Germany, he was undeniably British and was 'something in advertising' before becoming a soldier. I never observed him in uniform but, again, I was of the opinion that the bowler hat of a 'city gent' would have fitted him better than an army beret. We saw little of him on the expedition outside of its white water section.

Derek Bromhall arrived late to the expedition; barely had he flown into Nairobi than he was whipped off to record the doings of the second adventure team. For Derek was our documentary film-maker and not only had he his own skin to look after but several thousand pounds-worth of delicate equipment. But if anyone had the capabilities of doing so it was Derek. Staffordshire-born, 47 years of age, a Ph.D., his life to date was the most varied of us all. National Service in the Ordnance Corps; Balliol College, Oxford; Chief Scientific Officer, University of Hong Kong; Director of Fisheries at the Hong Kong Research Station; oyster and pearl culture research; oceanography; Director of Tropical Fish Culture Research in Malacca, Malaysia; frequent flits around the world to represent Britain at United Nations meetings: these were just some of the milestones of his life. A love of underwater photography triumphed over all else and had blossomed into the field of documentary photography, from whence he had opted to pursue a highly insecure vocation as a freelance. Already he had had one qualified success, an exploratory documentary on television out of three expeditions in South America, Jamaica and Kenya in which he had participated. He was married too, and I was to meet his delightful wife, Julia, and 14-year-old son Clive, who possessed all the assurance of his father.

The other two members of the team were classed as 'attached personnel'. Peter Gilfillan was a photographer of some standing, joining the team as assistant to Derek. Resourceful and knowledgeable, he could turn on the charm like a tap, thus being in the fortunate position of being able to get anything out of anybody. Resourceful too was young Marcus Keane who, like Peter, lived in Kenya. Son of Ann Allen of Nanyuki, he bribed his way into the White Water Team by offering his Toyota Land Cruiser for our exclusive use. It was a fine bargain; not only the Toyota but 19-year-old Marcus himself, who chain-smoked his way through disaster after disaster with an agility and ability that defied his tender years. I felt he would go far, that young man, and the army – on which he had set his sights – would have no difficulty in making something very beneficial out of him.

In addition to the complement of the boats, we had a vehicle support group. This was composed of Peter Tilbury and Andrew

Mitchell who, although his zoological duties put him squarely in the Scientific Team, was able to delegate them temporarily. Peter Tilbury and his wife Ann lived in Nairobi; though strictly speaking not members of the expedition, they were twin towers of strength in the administrative field. At Base House, Ann had virtually become my secretary, typing and sending our various reports and press releases, while at the same time helping with the thousand-and-one tasks that fell to Susie Richardson as the rear link. And Peter, like Marcus, had put *his* Toyota Land Cruiser at our disposal, also while playing truant from his Nairobi business. Along with Andrew, he joined us to act as team-vehicle and radio support. Plump and ever-beaming, he looked a man who enjoyed life and lived it to the full. His catchy laugh and devastating comments were a tonic to us all, even though he was hardly cast in the exploratory mould.

We had chosen as our start point a bend in the Tana close to a hill called Kaumuthai, below Kamburu Bridge. These were the only two land-marks on the map for miles around, though close by was a tiny hamlet of *manyattas* – little thatched huts – these ones on stilts. Everywhere was the bush, formidable in its sense of eternity.

Our two well-loaded Land Cruisers fought their way through thickets reinforced with baobab trees until we came to the river, there to be welcomed by the dismaying shriek of the 'go-away bird', the real name of which I cannot recall. Ignoring the note of entreaty in its call, we prepared our overnight camp and inflated the boats. The river looked deceptively tranquil, though a faint roar heralded tantrums to come. Lying under the stars that night I pondered, for the first time, upon what I had once more let myself in for.

We were up and about with the sunrise, loading the boats and, on Paul's instructions, lashing everything down. Into *Adamson* went all our personal kit doubly sealed into thick plastic bags, cooking gear and rations for three days (though we expected to be away from the main supplies on the vehicles for only two), an Evinrude engine together with a five gallon container of petrol which we planned to utilise on the longer stretches of calm water, the .303 rifle with its ammunition carefully wrapped in plastic, and an assortment of canvas baler buckets, bellows, paddles, life-jackets and crash helmets, all anchored to the boats with lengths of cord. *Thesiger*, being the filming boat, we loaded less heavily, and though Paul stipulated a nine o'clock start it was nearer eleven before his motley crews of cantankerous individualists had untangled themselves from various unaccustomed chores. Paul himself hardly shone his brightest by accidentally slashing his own inflatable with a penknife while cutting a length of cord.

One false start for the benefit of Derek and his movie cameras and we were away, bobbing down-river in a remorseless current that was very much stronger than it was at Kora. High banks hemmed it in and the water was dark and petulant.

We planned to meet up with Andrew and Peter two days hence and some forty miles on, as inspired a piece of over-optimism as ever I have come across. But, a rank amateur at the white water game, it was not for me to raise objections. We possessed a military transmitting set; the support group had a transmitting set. If both sets and operators did better than those of the Ugandan army I could assume we were in clover.

Five hundred yards and an island on, we came upon the first obstacle. Paul Turner stood up in the boat with a professional air to survey the thundering water ahead. The current gripped us but we veered to the island, hugging the bank, to give the captain a prolonged view.

'No problem. It's quite a small one,' he muttered, referring to the cataract ahead. 'We'll take the middle tongue, keeping the prow to the front and avoiding that rock on the left. Now when I say "paddle", push hard on the right to midstream, then straight for it. Is that clear?' It wasn't, but again I felt it not my place to argue. Paul signalled *Thesiger* to follow when we were through, and we pushed off, accelerating in the current.

Gazing forlornly at the frenzy of water before us and at the sharp drop into it that, to my startled eyes, offered a reasonable imitation of the Aswan Dam, all previous enthusiasm I might have had for white water negotiation began to drain away very swiftly indeed. *Adamson* now lay firmly in midstream.

I glanced at Paul anxiously. 'Aren't we supposed to wear those?' I enquired, indicating the crash helmets and life-jackets adorning the inflated walls of the boat.

He bit his lip. 'Good point,' he replied, 'of course we should. I forgot, but it's too late now. HOLD ON!'

The prow approached the slipway of water that Paul called a tongue. Even though I was sitting on the stern of the vessel I could see the yawning drop and a cauldron of spray at the bottom. I held my breath, anchored my feet securely beneath the thwart and fixed my eyes on calm water beyond the maelstrom wishing to hell I was there.

The boat up-ended, fell prow-first, pierced the raging waters and was jostled madly.

'Paddle!' screamed Paul, and we were galvanised into action. The boat had all but disappeared under the foam, to emerge miraculously with all on board yelling like dervishes. I was pleased to note that I was not the only one on board that had been terrified out of his skin.

Now it was *Thesiger*'s turn, and I was smugly glad to be in *Adamson*. We beached the craft on a sandspit, started to bale out the water sloshing about the rubber floor, then turned to watch how our colleagues fared.

Richard Matthews was not entirely devoid of white water experience, having apparently shot rapids on the Omo River in Ethiopia, but his crew were older than him and more experienced in most matters. I felt a pang of anxiety for him, which was entirely misplaced because *Thesiger* took the obstacle with illogical ease.

'That's the advantage of a light load,' observed Paul drily. Told by the two experts that we had done well, that we were in full control of our craft and that the shoot was a polished performance was astonishing news to me.

Baling is a thankless task in the knowledge that, with most of the water out of the boat, it will be full again at the next rapid. With a more-or-less dry floor we continued on our way, making good progress before the ominous sound of more angry water impinged on our ears. I stared uneasily ahead. On both banks of the river the iniquitous bush was devoid of pity.

Again Paul struck his Horatio Nelson pose, standing at the prow of the boat and assessing the turmoil of water that lay before us.

Encouraged no doubt by our earlier feat, he came to a swift decision. 'We'll take it,' he affirmed. 'Don life-jackets and helmets. It's a bigger one than before.'

He wasn't kidding. The lip of the fall hid what was beneath it, but a fog of spray told its own story. Ahead of the actual fall the storm of white-flecked water tumbled headlong through a pinboard of granite dragon's teeth, to seethe joyously onward round a curve. Somewhere in the bush the 'go-away bird' squawked its message and I would have been happy to oblige.

We approached the new hazard with caution, resisting the strong tug of the current. Yards short of the point of no return we halted, anchoring the boat by clinging to overhead foliage beside the bank. Paul's eyes flicked over the course he proposed to take.

'We'll make it the right-hand tongue, keeping left of that rock on the edge. At the bottom, that boulder that's bang in our path will have to be avoided. We'll go to the right of it and down that chute over there.' He sounded to me as if he was designating a route through a golf course.

At least we started in the right manner and hurtled, prow first, down the correct tongue. In the swirl of water we hit a submerged rock, then another which buffeted us from beneath and knocked us off course so that we were moving crabwise.

'Paddle left!' screamed Paul, and Harley, on the left side of the boat, back-paddled for all he was worth while I, opposite, frantically forward-paddled. But to little avail. The craft gyrated, smashed into rocks, shook itself free of one cauldron and was flung into another. My feet, firmly planted under the rubber thwart, alone held me from being flung overboard as wave after wave boiled over us with pile-driving force.

There was no let-up. First the prow reared, then the stern. I could only be amazed to still count three heads as we emerged from one sledge-hammer wave that came in unaccountably from the opposite direction.

Abruptly, the storm subsided, and looking over my shoulder, I perceived *Thesiger* under fire; saw the black neoprene of her underside as the vessel stood on end like some torpedoed destroyer on its death-dive.

I suppose the whole storm had lasted no more than a hundred

seconds but it seemed a lifetime. Then we were clear, both boats none the worse for their battering. Neither crew could raise the breath to cheer, though exhilaration edged our crazed laughter. Both boats were beached and baling carried out. Cargoes were floating about in the trapped water like flotsam from a shipwreck.

For the next couple of hours we were content to let the current carry us. A hill strained upward from the flat bushland, and we attempted, without success, to pinpoint our position. A further couple of rapids we shot with little fuss, for they were mere playthings invested with a minimum of anger.

In all we managed about 15 miles that first day, and could have improved on this had not *Thesiger* lagged behind, her photographically minded crew indulging in taking close-ups of strange water birds and long-legged beasties. Satisfied with progress and none-too keen to acquaint ourselves with the source of a thundering that emanated from round the next bend, we beached on an island and prepared camp for the night, first attempting to raise the support group on the radio but without success.

That the island belonged to a colony of crocodiles was clear the moment of our arrival. Several long, scaly forms slid reluctantly into the river from the warm sand. And they had not been the only tenants. Before realizing it, we had floated over a group of hippos who had taken crash action upon our approach. Now, indignant at our acquisition of what was plainly their pad, they proceeded to blow angrily at us as we spread out damp sleeping-bags to catch the last rays of the sun.

Over a fire we cooked a scanty supper. Long after the meal we kept the logs ablaze to hold at bay the former occupiers of the island, and round the comforting flames we lay down to sleep in troughs of scooped-out sand. Our shadows danced all night, for when the flames died a brilliant moon-light took over the manipulation of the strings.

With 25 miles estimated to the rendezvous, an early morning start was deemed essential. We had at least five miles to make up and heaven knows what watery horrors lay in wait. We washed hastily to a reveille of hippo snorts and endeavoured to improve upon yesterday's boat packing timings.

The thunder up front resolved itself into another set of rapids – different in that they were preceded by a general widening of the river and a stretch of shallows. A maze of tree-covered islands and rocky islets were drawn across our path. There was nothing for it but to get into the water and push the boats, for, even crewless, our flat-bottomed craft struck the stone-strewn bed. The operation was made the more difficult by virtue of the very unevenness and sharpness of the bed, where one leg could be thigh-deep in water with the other unable to locate any footing whatsoever – and when it did the terra firma was slippery and as piercing as a razor. This made the going excruciatingly slow and highly erratic. At times it became necessary to lift the boats, cargo and all, out of the water, which at least made good material for Derek filming our struggling, cursing figures.

The Tana had impulsively put on a new face, pretending to go all Amazonian, its banks overgrown with lush greenery liberally strewn with thick hanging creepers. Those islands bare of trees were carpeted by a tough, cutting grass, over which some of us clambered to reconnoitre the rapids beyond.

These Paul pronounced as child's play, and I felt almost pleased at the prospect of floating again, however unserenely, down-river. With Derek grimacing behind his shoulder-supported camera we took off into the grasping current. 'Keep away from that rock!' reiterated Paul, but such was the pressure we smashed straight into it, spun and went backwards over the one portion of the fall we had decided to avoid at all costs. *Adamson* immediately tipped onto her stern, and went over the edge with us clinging for dear life to any fixture within reach. We flopped squarely into the massive turbulence. Water gushed everywhere in an exuberant cascade hiding everything from view, and when we emerged from this convulsion the vessel was flung onwards, to collide madly with rock after rock – those you could see and those you couldn't. And then we were out of the storm, and the silence was sepulchral. But not for long.

We continued to surge forward, only to realise we were being swept swiftly towards a second cataract. There was simply nothing we could do about it. A worried Paul briefly surveyed the fast-approaching maelstrom and, in a voice weary with resignation, observed: 'We're committed, chaps. That left-hand tongue's the only way.'

In we went again, to be assailed, buffeted, hurled against rocks and overwhelmed by water. Once we were projected clean into the air and our 70lb. engine and 5-gallon petrol can were, for a fragment of time, suspended in space. Their descent could all too easily have broken an arm or a leg.

Free of the river's fury, we beached the battered craft and set to making it shipshape once more. We kept an eye open for *Thesiger* following in our wake. There was nothing we could have done to warn her of the second rapid.

The second crew were surprisingly chirpy when they reached us. Much of it was relief, and the reason quickly became apparent. Richard had been thrown bodily out of the boat, the waters carrying him forward ahead of it. He managed to climb onto a rock island and as the vessel slewed by had simply thrown himself back into it.

A stretch of calm water gave us the opportunity to make some headway and we made the best of it. But again the photographers on *Thesiger* found subjects for their camera and so lost valuable time. This resulted in friction between the 'let's-move-while-we-can' faction and those of the 'must-get-that-bird' brigade. Anger – human anger this time – flared as taut nerves snapped.

The subsequent set of rapids showed not the slightest desire to humour us. Instead, it rejected our efforts to move into a chosen tongue and deflected *Adamson* up a backwater and cul-de-sac. We fought the unaccountable side motion but to no avail. Hoping the subsidiary route of the river would return us to the main course, we allowed the current to carry us for several hundred yards until we found ourselves nearing the head of an unnavigable waterfall. The tributary was not actually a cul-de-sac but it was 'road closed' as far as we were concerned.

There was nothing to do but return the way we had come, which was easier said than done against the vicious flow. *Thesiger* had prudently remained to await the outcome of our enforced side excursion, so we made haste to rejoin her before she too made the same mistake.

We attached ropes to *Adamson* and attempted to haul her

upstream from the bank, but trees and other obstacles kept getting in the way. Marcus, the strongest swimmer among us, was prevailed upon to swim across to the opposite bank and so instigate a hauling operation from a position only slightly less entangled by undergrowth. In this manner, slowly and painfully, we proceeded against the current until our strength gave out and the riverine foliage confounded our efforts.

But reinforcements were at hand with the appearance of the *Thesiger* crew, who meanwhile had come by land to investigate the situation. However, even with the help of the extra manpower we were unable to get far.

Thus began the 'Day of the Portages'. The dictionary defines the word 'portage' as 'the act of carrying; a journey over which boats have to be dragged or carried overland'. It omits to add that it is the most dispiriting of occupations, with everything having to be painstakingly untied, unloaded, reloaded and retied. And in our case this whole business was to occur again and again.

This first portage of the day was not the worst of them. Across boulder-strewn, uneven grassland, by way of prickly entanglements of foliage, up and over bulwarks of granite, and through a mud-pool reeking of bilharzia to a position close to *Thesiger* and well clear of the spot in the main river which had sucked us so ignominiously into our predicament. This was our way out of it, and its execution took all of four heart-breaking hours.

Upon completion we rewarded ourselves with lunch of two and a half hard-tack biscuits apiece and a tube of greengage jam between the eight of us. The biscuits had been engulfed by water and so had to be dried out on a rock. We were only too aware that we were not going to make the rendezvous by nightfall, and the conservation of our frugal rations had become of paramount importance.

Pushing off into the river, we managed, this time, to hold course and overcome the reluctance of the rapids to accept us. Successfully, if not skilfully, we smashed through them, *Thesiger* at our heels.

The subsequent obstacle introduced itself with a fantail, the river dividing into a kind of delta. We investigated each rivulet but, without exception, all led to another waterfall of 'they shall not pass' dimensions; at least 20-foot drops with ugly rocks at the bottom. It was not good; there was no way through.

So, another portage. This one took us staggering over a plateau of stone and down its near-vertical face into ruffled water the far side of the mainstream fall. The plateau, riddled with concealed fissures, became an exercise in how easy it is to break a leg. It has to be said that carrying a double-skinned Adventurer, even utilising the services of six persons, is no light undertaking at the best of times, not only because of the weight but also through difficulty in synchronising one's direction and footsteps. Even so, the undertaking was accomplished with no casualties and the cargo – including the wretched engine and its petrol – restowed. If nothing else, we were becoming highly proficient packers and our timings were inspired. As usual, *Thesiger* (requiring a more intricate packing procedure) lagged in this respect, and further flashes of resentment were ignited when the crew of *Adamson* were requested to go to her aid. Fatigue was wearing us down, draining away the milk of human kindness.

We reckoned upon having put only five miles behind us this second day – and that was an optimistic reckoning. Half-way to the rendezvous; a further 20 miles to go, two punch-drunk crews and – if we spun things out – infinitesimal rations for one more day. It was a more thoughtful team that hauled their boats onto the mudflats and prepared camp that nightfall. Everything in my 'waterproof' bag was soaked and had to be draped around the smokey campfire – and sleeping bags are the very devil to dry. Tea, with the last of the milk powder and sugar, helped fill the gaps our frugal supper failed to plug. Again we were unsuccessful in our efforts to contact Andrew and Peter, in spite of repeated and prolonged attempts made throughout the evening and into the night.

A small but unfriendly looking crocodile slid into the water from a pool nearby, to awaken recollection of another menace. Strange how the mind cancels out one danger when confronted by another. We sat and discussed the day's events, not without some acrimony, and resolved to undergo no further unreconnoitred shooting of rapids, even if the pre-shooting survey sacrificed our precious time. But time, too, was running out and – God forbid – tomorrow was Friday the thirteenth!

It couldn't have been anything else. If yesterday was the 'Day of the Portage', today was the 'Day of Disasters'. The first of the new day's portages had sapped our sleep-revitalized strength and resilience, so when *Adamson* was pinned against a large rock and overwhelmed in mid-cauldron we were too occupied in saving our own skins and chattels to warn *Thesiger* against taking the same route through the umpteenth rapid. And, sure enough, down she came, tossing and twisting in the maw of the tempest. Stone walls restricted the channel to a deep and powerful conveyor belt of water and there was really no alternative path other than that dictated by a ruthless flow. *Thesiger* performed a mirror-image repetition of our own gyrations and to our horror we watched as, in spite of the frantic paddling of her crew, the craft smashed into the self-same rock, to disappear beneath a wall of water.

Derek and Peter Gilfillan were swept out of the overwhelmed boat but grimly held onto the outboard life ropes. We managed to throw our lifeline to Richard and Robert – their own was already floating away downstream – who secured the craft and hastily began throwing items of cargo ashore. Derek, abruptly discovering that an expensive piece of his equipment had gone to the bottom, went berserk and had to be physically restrained from a suicidal exploration of the rocky depths. Evacuation of both boats and their contents was hastily effected onto a shore that was a skating rink of such slippery stone that, Derek's loss notwithstanding, it was a miracle so much cargo was recovered.

The portage that followed was quite the worst of all. Already that day we had carried out a major overland detour to skirt another waterfall. In fact, right from the start it had been Friday the thirteenth with a vengeance – commencing, soon after dawn, with a momentary threat from a new quarter.

Hardly had we risen from our sleeping bags when we became aware of a straggling line of near-naked tribesmen moving stealthily along our front on the opposite side of the river. They were armed with bows and arrows, and we knew those arrows to be tipped with a deadly poison. Poachers or *shifta*? The question lay uneasily on our minds, and more than one pair of eyes wandered to our solitary rifle. Obviously we had been spotted, and though they made no attempt to cross the Tana in our sight we envisaged an idea that a more strategically convenient fording place might exist further upstream. There must have been at least forty in the party.

To add to the possibility of an attack, Peter, on a foraging mission, had come across a poacher's cache of food – mostly barrels of honey. The resourceful Peter, ever ready to augment depleted food supplies, was anxious to annex a few items; but there is a law of the bush that stipulates an eye for an eye, and we had nothing worthwhile to leave in their place. Yet this was not the point. The cache could be another reason the tribal warriors across the river might want to come over to our side. Hastily we loaded our vessels, spread over the sandbank like stranded whales, and pushed off.

A set of rapids that looked worse than they were offered hope for a better rate of progress, and we did indeed cover several miles in the cool of the morning. But our new-found optimism was not to last. Round a bend we were confronted with another fantail, each channel terminating in a sheer drop of unnavigable severity.

Two portages carried out through the hottest part of the day, three sets of rapids that might be described as of medium negotiability and the day was well into the afternoon. The second portage, made under a blazing midday sun, involved a quarter-mile haul along an almost vertical cliff face that formed one wall of a minor gorge. It was a hard enough traverse even empty-handed, but encumbered with items of kit, the engine and a share of an empty inflatable so light and manageable on water but a deadweight on land, it was a different story. Each of us must have made at least half a dozen return journeys along this hellish traverse.

'We'll get out of this canyon and then have lunch,' announced Paul with exaggerated relish. But even two and a half biscuits and a squeeze of jam hold a certain attraction when there's nothing else.

We moved off nervously, suspicious of a current that saved us the effort of paddling. We were all desperately tired and the hot sun had scoured our backs. I must have fallen asleep where I sat, for all at once we were in creamy water and being tossed unmercifully. Presumably Paul had investigated the new peril: for I heard him say it looked worse than it probably was and that our proposed way through seemed thankfully rock-free. It was a supposition with a familiar – and hollow – ring.

The tongue was a steep one and so fast that we lost control at the onset. Spiralling towards the vortex of the storm of water, I heard Paul yelling 'Bale! Bale! Faster! Faster! Paddle! Paddle!' as *Adamson* caught four huge waves, was engulfed, filled, and became uncontrollable. Like automatons we acted as best we could upon the staccato instructions, but you can't bale *and* paddle at the same time, and the boat refused to respond to anything we did anyway. We were in midstream paddling desperately, fighting with every ounce of our combined strength, our eyes wide with fright. The boiling cauldron was all around us and we were being sucked sideways straight towards the huge stopper: a reverse wave that loomed towards us. I watched it mounting over us in a kind of slow motion inevitability of doom. Then it hit us, knocked us round in a complete circle, and threw everyone into the middle of the boat in a whirl of arms, legs and paddles before slamming us into the only rock in sight. This slewed us round again and sent the craft into the second towering reverse wave, even bigger than the one before.

We all saw it, guessed what it could do to us and cowered down into the flooded boat. For one fleeting second I saw *Adamson* as if it were another vessel, prow uppermost, vertical in the air. I clung to a rope, but the force of the water that hit me tore it from my grasp. I performed what seemed a double somersault and felt myself being sucked down into the depths, gently revolving as I went. Everything went quiet; the water turned from brown to grey and there was a great peace everywhere. I experienced no panic. Instead I was able to calmly assess the situation and marvel at the ease of the process of drowning. I remember thinking of my notes; I always thought of my notes in moments of crisis, for they were the reason for my being on the expedition. Richard had his camera, Derek had his movie apparatus, I had my notes. On this leg of the journey I had been crafty. My notes remained safely with the other boat in a specially designed waterproof pocket, so that even if *Thesiger* rolled upside-down in the river no harm could come to them. A rushing in my ears produced a new sensation but I could not tell if I were still going down or coming up. I was wearing a life-jacket so maybe it was upwards, and anyway the water was becoming lighter in colour – though maybe the suction-power of the whirlpool was greater than that produced by the buoyancy of the jacket. My thoughts were clogging, my brain clouding up. Sleep. That's what it was. Drowning was no more than going to sleep...

The antics of my mind were rudely shattered. Suddenly I was at the surface amongst utter confusion and the thunder of wild water. Instinctively I struck out for a mass of rocks that had to be the shore. The current fought me but I was abruptly desperate to live and desperation manufactures strength. I missed the clump of rocks I'd been aiming for, made for another and, gasping, hauled myself out of the water.

I looked around. Paul was already ashore and running towards me. Far downstream I perceived Harley and Marcus had beached the boat and were struggling to turn it right side up. It took me some time to regain my breath and rejoin the others.

'God, I thought we were gonners then', exclaimed Paul with feeling. We exchanged our individual misadventures. Paul, it appeared, had been luckier with the stretch of river into which he had been pitched. In spite of the overturning of the boat, Harley and Marcus had hung grimly on, managing to climb onto its bottom and guide it shorewards, picking up Paul on the way. The miracle was that we had lost very little. A gym shoe, a belt and a few other personal belongings: that was all.

A while later we were joined by *Thesiger*, whose crew, witness to our debacle, had portaged her round the offending rapids. Smugly I retrieved my notes from their bone-dry cubby hole. With them were a spare camera, a pair of binoculars and the radio battery for our so-far useless transmitting set. Everything was fine except that the paper in my notebook had begun flaking away, and I discovered it to have been liberally sprinkled with battery acid. In this game you just can't win.

Nineteen miles down river Andrew and Peter Tilbury lay in the shadow of one of the Toyotas. Three days they had waited; two and a half to be exact, for it had taken them hours of track and bush driving to get themselves from the start point into position at the rendezvous point. Until the previous night the waiting had been no more than a boring but not unpleasant chore and the fact that no word had come through on the radio from Paul was, initially, of no great concern. After all, distance and hills would make communication difficult. But today the silent radio and empty river aroused nagging fears. Peter checked and re-checked the set, transmitting Paul's call sign again and again, and preparing to receive incoming messages long before and long after the designated times. The third day dragged on towards its end and the fears grew. Below them the river smiled, serene and innocent, the banks shimmering in the heat. Dusk clothed the low, bush-clad hills in a cloak of an abruptly menacing darkness.

Back in Nairobi the rear link would be expecting a report. Peter gave it another ten minutes, searched the quietly chortling, phosphorescent river one last time and raised Base House on the radio-telephone to spell out two emotive words: 'Disaster Action'.

I was, frankly, amazed, Here we were, a group of supposedly responsible adults, three of us officers of Her Majesty's Army, and we were behaving like a group of kids. Both crews were sprawled around a well-fuelled fire on a sandy inlet where a bank and some scraggy trees formed an arbour. The evening meal had exhausted our remaining stock of food except for tea, milkless and sugarless. This unpalatable, overbrewed beverage we sipped now, at dusk, as we held a council of war.

Paul had firmly stipulated a halt; a permanent halt. Not only was *Adamson* torn beyond rudimentary repair, but ahead lay the Kiambere Gorge, a deep cleft through which the Tana hurled itself and which offered an impasse to any type of vessel. This impassable section of river had been designated a portaging undertaking, but nobody, it seemed, had properly investigated the difficulties this would have offered, in spite of an aerial reconnaissance Paul had made before we had set out. The section was several miles long, and even had the carrying of boats and cargo overland been possible it would certainly have taken still more time, a commodity already exhausted.

But now that we could make no further progress on our own came the question of what action we *should* take. At once we split into two factions again; this time it was the let's-bash-on-boatless group and the let's-stay-put group. However, it was the spectre of starvation that sent everyone into a tizzy and brought the let's-bash-ons to heel. Paul, playing the role of diplomat, drew the factions together by pronouncing that, at daybreak, two foraging parties would fan out into the countryside in search of succour, while the remaining personnel would stay behind and attempt to entice fish out of the quieter backwaters of the Tana. This would ensure a live camp-site in existence should anyone take it into their head to come and look for us. In spite of this, to me, very sensible plan of action, the prophets of doom had to have their say: 'There's absolutely no human habitation within miles,' bemoaned one who should have known better. 'The ammunition's gone to the bottom so we can't shoot anything even if there *was* anything,' lamented another, and the council broke up with acrimonious dissension and a certain amount of petty reproach.

I mostly kept out of the argument since I had my notes to rewrite. I just could not believe that no human community existed near a major waterway coursing through the near-desert of the bush, whatever the pundits said. I just couldn't feel the slightest concern about our situation, even though I probably possessed the least knowledge of Africa of anyone.

Next morning we duly divided into scavenging parties. Marcus and I were designated an area of search downstream, Harley and Peter Gilfillan were to cover an upstream location. None of us had slept well, the sand of our encampment being inhabited by unsociable stinging ants bolstered by a sprinkling of baby scorpions. Even before the scavengers had left, the fishermen of the group were drawing barbel out of the Tana with hooks and lines taken from our survival kits. So much for the prophets of starvation.

Marcus and I carried between us a compass, a knife, money, a water bottle and a powerful catapult. I observed, with a mixture of optimism and foreboding, that the path we took alongside the river

could only have been made by man or beast. Occasionally Marcus
let fly with his catapult at some inoffensive bird, and we had put
about a mile between us and the camp when we came upon our
first fellow-creature. There, poling himself across the river in a
square box of a boat, was a tousle-haired African. Even while we
looked, three more Africans appeared, and we noted that they
were waiting to be transported across the Tana. Not only had we
stumbled on a likely source of succour but also an artery of
communication and transportation, to wit, a ferry. Yet for a
moment we held back. The three were Wakamba hunters, just like
those we had seen in force the previous morning. And these too
were armed with bows and arrows – probably poisoned arrows.
Shrugging away our instinctive caution we approached the group
waving a greeting.

They stared at us blankly. White men were obviously a rarity in
this neck of the woods. Marcus spoke to them in Swahili and they
responded with nervous grins, ceasing to finger their bows. Yes,
there was a village a mile or two into the bush the other side of the
river. There was also another upstream but more distant. Yes,
quite certainly the Kiambere was impassable for any kind of boat.
Yes, there were provisions and a shop in the village across the
river.

The Wakamba hunters made a picturesque trio. Small men, they
had fierce faces and wore next to nothing. Jet black, their skin
shone with vigour, while their bare feet were balls of hard cracked
skin, tougher than the leather of any sandal. As we were talking
another man approached. He was attired in Western dress and
belonged to a different tribe, for he possessed none of the striking
features of his fellows. But he was going to the village across the
river and would be happy to lead us there. What's more he spoke
very reasonable English.

We negotiated a party-fare with the ferryman, and squatting –
hardly daring to breathe for fear of upsetting the keelless boat –
crossed to the further bank. Up-river a couple of hippos sported,
blowing thin plumes of spray into the air.

The 'mile or two' extended to something nearer five, mostly
uphill and at a killing pace. A network of paths criss-crossed the
thorny bush and, had we been alone, heaven knows where we

would have got to. Our guide, it transpired, was the local Christian lay reader. He spent his time touring the villages of the region imparting the word of God, in addition to the negotiation of more earthly transactions. From this he made a living and, if his surprisingly smart suit was anything to go by, a lucrative one too. Everyone knew him in the village when we eventually reached it and were solemnly introduced to the elders congregated in the communal charhouse.

The name of the village was Katheni. Its centre consisted of a single row of mud-and-wattle huts and a 'bush supermarket' guarded by a heavily-padlocked door beneath which any child could have crawled. The villagers were unashamedly curious about us, as well they might be, and flocked into the charhouse or stood poking their heads in at the entrance as Marcus and I poured mug after mug of hot, sickly-sweet tea down our parched throats. The village was surrounded by a thorn stockade, or *boma*, embracing about three acres of bush.

Over a charcoal fire the hindquarters of a goat were roasted and, joined by His Reverence, we consumed this hungrily, together with a sweet of chapatis liberally sprinkled with gritty, off-white sugar. Between mouthfuls of goat, Marcus bargained for supplies to be delivered to our encampment without delay, our own fast-dissipating appetites pricking his conscience. As we knocked back the rest of the tea, the sound of a low-flying aeroplane brought us to our feet and out of the hut.

Diving out of an azure-blue sky came a light Beaver monoplane, its pilot and passenger staring down at the community of huts. We waved our arms wildly and, skimming low, the aircraft performed a circuit and returned to drop a weighted message as it roared overhead. Upon retrieval, the message was found to read: 'If unable to reach you by 15.00 tomorrow will return to drop food. Others informed. Nigel'.

The very fact of having aeroplanes out looking for us increased our stature in the eyes of the villagers – as well as notching up the price of the proffered goods and services. The salesmen of Katheni had all of a sudden heard of the expedition; weren't we the famous Tana Survey team known throughout all Africa, and the most compelling occurrence since *Msee* Jomo Kenyatta. The literal translation of 'msee' is 'elderly and respected', and I was henceforth thrust into the bargaining when things reached stalemate. Only old men wear beards among the tribes of Africa, 'old' being anything over forty. My beard was by now a startling ginger, more bristly than flowing, but with my age thus arbitrarily increased by ten years, I managed to wield a sobering influence over the more zealous merchants. The bargaining committee consisted of a wizened little man with a multi-coloured woollen tea cosy for a hat, a younger, more plausible character wearing a Dunlop sports cap, and a woman of indeterminate age whose breasts kept bursting out of a torn blouse to romp amongst the potatoes she was trying to sell at an exorbitant price.

Accompanied by half a dozen villagers loaded with portions of goat, bags of flour, potatoes and tinned milk we returned the way we had come. At the ferry our trio of warriors were still to be seen but had fallen asleep in the shade of a bush, though they roused themselves long enough to allow us to handle their weapons and dolefully admire the black plasticine poison daubed on the barbs of the arrows. So strong were the bows that none of us could dent their tautness, yet these little men can bring down an elephant at a hundred yards.

Back at camp everyone had indulged in a surfeit of fish, which the pressure cooker had turned into a brand of *bouillabaisse*, so our fresh offerings were hardly received with the enthusiasm of starving men. As the fireflies flickered and drew sparks on the glittering surface of the Tana, the evening discussion this time revolved around how we were to be recovered. Once again we split into factions: the stay-puts and the move-to-Katheni brigade. It made sense to stay where we were since Nigel now knew of our location; he had seen the battered boats by the river's edge, read the 'no casualties' counter-message scratched in the sand, and would, presumably, this very moment be working out ways to reach us. However, having also seen our scavenging party at Katheni, he would probably surmise that the village would make a more appropriate rendezvous point for the whole party. A further strong argument for the Katheni move was the existence of a track from the village, leading eventually to a road, and the practicalities of geography were not to be ignored.

So loading everything, including the deflated *Adamson*, into *Thesiger* we floated down to the ferry point, to find an array of donkeys and women porters awaiting us on the further shore in anticipation of our return to their village.

Thus we effected the transfer of the White Water Team to the urban iniquities of Katheni, and it was at this little village on the hill that we were united with Nigel and our support group.

Andrew was to tell me later about the support group's journey, made together with Nigel from the designated rendezvous to Katheni. Just nineteen miles it may have been as the crow flies, but to approach the village by vehicle involved a gruelling hundred-and-fifty. Like knights of old they hurled themselves to the rescue of what may have been starving, despairing men. No damsel in distress could have demanded more. Nothing stopped them. The thicker the bush, the faster was the plunging through; the wider the ditches, the more shattering the gear changes. 'It was impossible,' Nigel reported, 'but that vehicle accomplished the impossible.'

For our night in Katheni we were offered the luxury of the village 'guesthouse', with open framework walls and a thatched roof. The rest of the day had been given over to repairing our ravaged persons and kit, as well as attendance at a thanksgiving service organised by His Reverence. His sermon was so long and involved that we had to kick one another in order to prevent our going to sleep and falling off the log upon which we were seated. I personally had a singularly pressing reason for playing truant from some of it: the affliction of a violent bout of diarrhoea that sent me, cross-legged, into the bush.

Our preparation of the evening meal and the tantrums of that arch-enemy of the Mountain Team – the pressure-cooker – made a treat for village eyes. It was accomplished within a tight circle of awed children, amused women, scornful men and indifferent dogs, cats, goats and cows. In the place of port and walnuts we were offered a dessert of 'fun girls' by none other than His Reverence, who acted as their pimp!

It was not until the following midday that, joined by the second Toyota, we finally got away. To a barrage of fond farewells we left Katheni, heading in the direction of Usueni where, it was alleged, the vehicle ferry was operating. Of course it wasn't. A night in the bare bush and we entered Usueni, made wretched for us by the sight of a dealer engaged upon cramming baby crocodiles and frightened dik-diks into crates. The spectacle of this ugly enclave of 20th-century commercialism left a bitter taste in our mouths as we sped along atrocious roads towards Kora.

And it was Kora Rapids, some dozen miles above the now abandoned scientist's base camp site, that held the key to a triumph so badly needed to avenge what can only be described as a second ignominious defeat. Kora Rapids had never been shot before. They were considered extremely dangerous and it was easy to see why. Less than 30 feet wide, the river had, over the centuries, forced its way through a plateau of solid rock. Now, concentrated waters lunged at horrifying speed into the deep gash they had worn. The river bed dropped perceptibly, some 30–40 feet, forming a series of vicious flumes of water among the grotesque shapes of gigantic boulders. The twisting turmoil of water plunged downwards and onwards to a point where the banks softened and opened out once more to abate the anger. Driftwood lay trapped against granite pillars or rocking gently in pools and crevices close to the shore.

The awful deluge by its very presence provided a provocation. Nothing, surely, could survive in that tumult; but as we gazed in awe, each of us bent a fertile imagination to the possibilities of conquest. Combining our theories of ways and means of carrying this out, we set up a camp overlooking the lower, quieter sections of the gorge at a spot shaded by stunted trees and, for a whole day, closely investigated the obstacle. The water was treacherously low, revealing a hefty rock in the very centre of the main flow that could kill any crew foolhardy enough to swept into it.

The second day we shot and reshot some of the upper rapids in *Thesiger* for the benefit of Derek's camera perched high atop the pinnacle of the gorge. The shooting also made a baptism of fire for Andrew Mitchell, who transferred to the team for the last days. Of particular interest to him was the school of hippos enjoying ruffled waters at the far end of the trough, though they added yet further danger to the proposed run.

On the third day we shot the growling torrents to the very edge of the fall, as if to steel ourselves for an ordeal we knew we could not evade. Again we inspected the eye of the cyclone against a background of restlessness and indecision, and to test for hidden treachery, put the patched-up *Adamson* empty through the falls, with Harley and Andrew below holding a lifeline across the gorge to retrieve it. The boat came through, riding the storm like a thoroughbred, even missing the lethal rock of its own accord. Paul thereupon nominated his crew for the climactic contest, taking into consideration skill, experience and, of course, acceptance of the risks involved. Joining him in *Thesiger* were to be Robert and Peter. Only one three-man crew was to make the shoot.

As if determined to give the trio a good run for their money, *Thesiger* sped like an avenger for the tongue, dropped down the first chute, gave a boulder a glancing blow and, out of control, was lost in the maelstrom. Emerging momentarily, the vessel hit a huge wave but, made sluggish by amount of shipped water, punched through it, taking more on board in the process and then rearing up, though lacking her earlier bounce. Slipping and sliding through peaks and troughs, *Thesiger* entirely disappeared from sight again, only to reappear a little further downstream, completely at the mercy of the water, her occupants hanging on for life. Crash-helmeted heads and orange life-jacketed torsos emerged occasionally into view as the boat swept on, safely passing the larger boulder, to plunge down the further step while nearly overturning in the process. Encased in a spume of foam, Peter was lifted bodily overboard; grimly he hung to the exterior line, his survival dependent upon it, and gradually managed, with the tenacity of fear, to pull himself back. And then it was all over, with the crew whooping with relief and victory as *Thesiger* glided into smooth waters, a record broken.

On the fourth day we continued downstream to the site of the Kora camp, closing the twelve-mile gap. Our tasks were at an end and we could relax for a day. Lion and leopard prowled our open-air encampment that night but they held no terrors.

Against a sunset – a memory of which Kora had bequeathed us for evermore – and a hideous chattering of baboons, we toasted our success and our endeavours with a long-concealed bottle of sponsored whisky, and offered silent gratitude for our deliverance.

5.   The Voyage to Mulanjo

The merging of the 'adventurists' with the scientists for the long voyage down the middle and lower Tana could be described as a high-water mark of the expedition. It was a moment when individual talents could be utilised for the benefit of the expedition as a whole and not simply for one small portion of it. Henceforth, 'the team' meant all two dozen of us, not just a group of five or eight. Yet there were those of the 'adventurists' who prophesied an anticlimax upon reversion to the role of explorer, a notion to which, as already intimated, the army chiefly subscribed. On the other side of the coin, one or two of the scientists were beginning to chafe at the bit, finding three static weeks of Kora – beautiful though somewhat devoid of the subjects of their survey – quite long enough to be hanging around while others were performing feats of daring. Only Andrew had managed a stint with the drama-makers, and though not all the scientists were cast in his mould, there were others for whom adventure held undeniable attraction.

Of the ex-members of the White Water Team, a number, like old soldiers, simply faded away. Harley Nott's time was up, and who could deny him the pull of a newlywed and beautiful young wife. Paul Turner returned to Nairobi to involve himself in sundry administrative, PR and personal duties. And Peter Gilfillan and Marcus Keane had never intended to become part of the main expedition anyway. However, about this time we received an injection of fresh blood in the guise of John Axford and Sue Hall of the Tana Pox Group (of which more later) as well as Karen Ross, an English resident of Kenya. Our one remaining commissioned soldier, Robert Williamson, was at last to be able to carry out his designated task as expedition deputy leader and quartermaster, though for an initial week or two these duties lay back at Base House.

Our departure from Kora was effected to a degree by the dictates of the documentary camera, and, with a cast of exceedingly amateur actors, was something of a slapstick performance. Crews wielded paddles and punt poles – to which they were entirely unaccustomed – with the air of having done it all before, which meant that some of the boats promptly vanished into thick, prickly undergrowth, swiftly transforming stiff upper lips into squeals of pain.

In my boat John Richardson was the only crew member with the remotest poling experience, but even this failed to compensate for the fact that my paddling was stronger than that of Alison Izatt. Each vessel carried its crew, personal kit, camp-beds and boat equipment. We wore whatever we chose according to the sensitivity of our skins. I sported the absolute minimum of swimming trunks and a toggle rope which, with a whistle on a string around the neck,was compulsory attire. We were not equipped with crash helmets or life-jackets, which I thought a pity, for the latter made good pillows.

The Tana was the colour of Windsor soup, and much debris – mainly fallen trees – muddled the edges. It swept round eternal corners in wide curves with a certain grandeur, dimpling and gurgling in its shallow sections and leaving the deep channels to surge ponderously forward. The current was not strong – nothing like that of the upper middle reaches – yet it provided enough impetus to allow occasional respites from constant paddling.

We were as happy as sandboys. For many, to move down a river was a new and exciting experience after the restrictive activities of Kora. To sit and watch the lush banks go by, knowing that it was only a matter of time before an assortment of fascinating wildlife would appear on nature's wide screen, riveted our eyes to every tree and clump of thicket. The birdlife caught our attention almost immediately, as a vividly coloured malachite kingfisher, a small enamelled statuette, came to life to catch a fish from the river's surface. Standing defiantly in the water, a great white egret, with compact snow-white plumage and sleek, torpedo-smooth body, minced with appalling deliberateness after frogs and minnows. In the tangled creepers tiny bee-eaters perched close together, darting straight upwards to snatch a moth or bug.

The bush had drawn closer to the river again, and the bank here and there showed a touch of generosity to enterprising trees and bushes, allowing them to wear green leaves – which was a wonderful and welcome relief from the brown deadly rocks of the gorges and the sand of Kora. That the river offered life as well as death was re-emphasized with the sight of buck coming down to its edges to drink. They made a beautiful sight: so gentle and delicate, yet so aware of the close proximity of attack from their predators.

With Ralph and Mona Brown in the hand-propelled jet boat leading the way and locating the most advantageous currents and channels – a rôle that had originally been assigned to it – we advanced upon our first hippo herd in the full knowledge of their presence. Previously, those of us in the White Water Team had sallied over and past them before we knew they were there – so making all the difference to our peace of mind. Now came another clash of interests. The scientists and photographers, congregated in the big inflatable, wanted to get as near as possible to observe and film the animals. Not so keen on close-ups and brinkmanship were the others, who were quite prepared to live and let live.

The hippopotamus – *kiboko* in Swahili, and the original Greek meaning 'horse of the river' – is actually a member of the even-toed pig family. To sustain their two or more tons they require a nightly 45 kilos of grass and they live for an average of 80 years. With huge tusks and jaws, these stumpy-legged, pink-grey leviathans can outrun a man and kill lions and crocodiles.

We could see their low foreheads and protruding eyes above the water level some distance away, so had ample warning of their presence. We moved quietly, for hippo are shy creatures – unless you get between them and their young or cut off their escape to the water, in which case they can be viciously dangerous. Assured that we constituted no great threat, these ones continued their frisking and cavorting in the water, sometimes disappearing beneath the surface for a couple of minutes at a time. Hippo can remain submerged for as long as four minutes, and they take pleasure in blowing water from their nostrils in fine jets. Despite their thick skins, they are subject to sunburn if they stay away from water too long; equally surprising, however, is the fact that beneath the water their hides do not protect them from attacks by bloodthirsty leeches. Contrary to popular belief hippo are agile swimmers.

As we neared the group the blowing gave an impression of anger as, one by one, the heads submerged; being ignorant of the ways of hippo, we imagined them to be approaching us in the manner of hostile submariners. This fallacy was given impetus by the optical illusion created by a twig or static item of debris sticking out of the river creating a furrow of water, a tiny bow wave that looked as if it were approaching the boat. But when we were well beyond the group, out of the water would pop their heads, all eyes upon us in curiosity and mild distrust.

The river meandered in an aimless fashion, often doubling back on itself to follow a course of four miles, which could have been one had it run in a straight line. It was easy to understand the wide diversity of the estimates for the length of the Tana, while to complicate matters still further, it sometimes split into two seemingly equal-sized arteries which met up again on the other side of an island. And it was not always clever to take what appeared to be a short cut. We found this out by hard experience when grounding on shoals and sandbanks just below the water line. The trick was to follow the deep-water channel, and with his considerable river experience Ralph saved us many a time-consuming grounding.

All large but basically shallow rivers possess a deep-flowing channel, and this has a distressing habit of following the outer curve of any and every bend – which precludes even the possibility of cutting any corners. Gradually we all developed a sixth sense as to where the deep channel lay, and in this Sandy Evans was to become a master. Faint ripples on the surface usually proclaimed shallows to be avoided, though the Tana wind – more regular even than France's *mistral* – not only blew us off course but ruffled the water's surface to deceive our eyes and senses.

Grounding produced a drill which became second nature to us. Our flat-bottomed craft displaced very few inches of water when unladen, but considerably more when loaded with three or more hefty humans. Thus it hardly needed the flotilla leader's order of 'All out' for the crews to be over the side, pushing or pulling the craft to deeper water. At first some of us wore no shoes for this job, but the Tana had some sharp surprises for tender feet, which meant another lesson learnt. In the bush, sandals are recommended. They let in the dust, gravel and, occasionally, thorns, but they also let them out again; bare feet in sandals seldom sweat or blister.

It was surprising, too, how soon we came to terms with the crocodile menace. Yet the threat still mesmerised us. It was always our secret fear, mainly on account of the experience of previous Tana explorers, and possibly because it represented the main danger in the minds of our families, friends and the general public. The greatest number of crocodiles we saw were small ones of about eight feet in length, though larger specimens were more in evidence further down river. Crocodiles are despised animals, yet their very unpleasantness is respected. Heavily armoured, they are accountable for more human deaths than any other African beast, in spite of their shyness. Once frightened they stay submerged for hours, and the ones we saw were, more often than not, those asleep in the sun or feeding at night. As soon as they saw us they would slip into the water very silently, a mere ripple in an ever-widening circle betraying their entry.

Though the water itself was another hazard we had been warned about earlier, there was little likelihood of picking up the dreaded water disease bilharzia, prevalent in the lower reaches and in semi-static water, where snails are the carriers. However, John Richardson played things on the side of safety by forbidding any unnecessary swimming or immersion – a measure that irritated some of us immensely. Yet one usually managed to take a ducking either accidentally or with a little help from providence during the boat-pushing procedures, since the river had a practice of deepening without warning. Once, when about to disembark, I made a flying leap from *East Midlander* to the shore and grabbed at a tree stump, whereupon the stump plus a large chunk of bank descended with me into deep water.

Hippo concentrations became increasingly numerous, with Andrew's hippo and crocodile tally book filling rapidly. To bypass them we sometimes had to press close against the bank, our inexperienced boat-handling projecting us painfully amongst thick overhanging bushes that, being African, are plentifully endowed with thorns. The hippos, of course, disappeared from view, leaving us to envisage their reappearance beneath our respective boats.

We covered a good 20 miles that first day, and as dusk descended, made camp beside the river on a plateau of cut-down trees. Away from the sand 'platforms' so beloved of the crocodiles, we were nevertheless conscious of being on a hippo track, and thus slept close against tree trunks to minimise the slight possibility of being trampled on in the night. The chores of making camp were to be repeated over and over again on our way down the river; being no more than overnight encampments, these were simple in the extreme. Following the unloading of boats, we divided ourselves into parties with tasks varying from wood-collection through fire-making to cooking. Sandy regularly chose to sleep in the bottom of his inflatable, both as a measure to discourage theft by marauding Africans and, more to the point, because it made a softer pad than the hard ground. On account of his culinary expertise John became chief cook, and a very fine job he made of it. With a little imagination much can be made from the simplest ingredients.

It was extraordinary how soon and how completely we took African vicissitudes in our stride, particularly at night. There were occasions when one's hair ought rightly to have stood on end. Familiarity must have had something to do with immunity to alarm; mosquito-netting – which we were to use on the Lower Tana – gave a sense of security which was a complete illusion.

I awoke the camp the first morning by literally blowing everyone out of their sleeping bags. Each boat was equipped with an aerosol-operated hand siren, for use should hippo attack a boat or, later, elephants threaten a camp. The noise these small 'toys' made was prodigious, and on this occasion my intended quick toot turned into a mournful blast expanding to a crescendo when the trigger stuck. To make amends I offered to cook breakfast, which resulted in burnt porridge for all.

Barely had we moved off when we saw our first buffalo, on the opposite bank. Enormous, head down, the beast stood preparing to drink before he spotted us. Come upon unexpectedly, the buffalo is exceptionally dangerous, for it has alert, sharp senses and is exceedingly crafty. This old bull was probably cantankerous as well. I was not aware at the time of the fact that they are looked upon as the cruellest and most feared of all big-game animals, and this one gave no indication of his reputation by loping off into the forest. As if it were an exaggerated echo there came a thunder of multiple hooves; the source was hidden from view, but it was not hard to imagine since buffalo always move in herds.

The river scenery changed little, though every corner produced a new view of it. Yet we were aware that the scenery was unique to the river and that within a few hundred yards of the lush forest clothing both banks the ubiquitous bush spread away to an infinity of dry plain.

Ken Campbell was our bird man. Whenever a great Flying Fortress-like monstrosity or a tiny ball of fluff came into our vision Ken would unhesitatingly expound upon its vital statistics and habits. At first I thought he was putting on an act, but then realized that Ken really knew his birds. All manner of winged things we saw those early days, for as yet we were still seeing the wood for the trees. Later, familiarity dulled our interest, though to some of us birds will ever remain a fascinating study. In Africa the variety is bewildering. Some are ugly – like the vulture and the marabou stork; some are tiny and brilliantly coloured – like the sunbirds; and some are predatory – like the hawks and eagles. Ken's bird record of those first two days alone gave the cold facts: water thick-knee, grey heron, hardaba hybis, African dart, Egyptian goose, grey-headed kingfisher, fish eagle, wood sandpiper (rare for the Middle Tana at that time), spurwing plover, pied kingfisher, malachite kingfisher, open-billed stork, yellow-billed stork, great white eaglet, little eaglet, common sandpiper, tawney eagle, African kite, sacred ibis, Wahlburg eagle, hooded vulture, Garba goshawk, woolly-necked stork, Goliath heron, green-backed heron, spoonbill, bateleur eagle, night heron, marabou stork, hammer cap, pale chanting goshawk, Ruppell griffin vulture, Woodford owl...

The second afternoon we had a mild encounter with a crocodile. I was dangling my legs in the water while John was gently poling when suddenly, quite close to my left foot, I saw a twelve-footer gliding along just ahead of the boat. Alison gave a lady-like gasp as we all watched, riveted by the reptile, which swung round, bared its teeth and dived. Only then did I remember to withdraw my feet from the water.

We were supposed to have met our vehicle support group below the village of Sarka and raise the second base camp close by, but the rendezvous failed to materialise owing to the vehicle being unable to reach the river. At Sarka, however, we were back among people. The village was a big one so we halted to investigate the possibility of acquiring the fresh food we all craved. The original village, or what was left of it, lay close to the river, behind a belt of trees, and consisted of a row of ruined houses of surprisingly solid construction. Word gets around quickly of strangers – particularly white strangers – in the vicinity, and in Sarka there was good reason for the speed of that word. The place had been raided by *shifta*, who had not only destroyed many of the dwellings but murdered the inmates as well. These grim facts were excitedly relayed to us by the growing crowd of villagers who had come to stare at us and lead the way to the new village site half a mile from the old.

Its general layout was typical of others we were to see. We entered through one of several openings in the protective *boma* – at least six feet thick and consisting of two fences of saplings driven into the ground, the space between liberally filled with brush. Right across the entrance lay a frame of branches which was dragged across it at night to wall in both villagers and cattle. The herds were out with their herdsmen, so the compound was now nearly deserted. Here the dwellings, likewise, were finely constructed; plastered with dried dung on the inside, backed by a stuffing of grass and finished on the outside by upright sticks bound together with some kind of tough reed. The roofs – also of dung – were dry and firm, like thick felt.

The village shop could produce no fresh provisions of any kind but was good for a prolonged chat with the elders, who appeared to use it as a council chamber. The rotund 'chief' was a merry little man who must have owned the shop, judging by the persuasive manner in which he unloaded much of his stock of cigarettes and matches onto the smokers of our party. Incongruously, a new Ford tractor stood in the compound.

On our way back to the river we glimpsed in the distance another 'convoy' of Somali nomads making their slow, relentless progress south. I could guess what the citizens of Sarka must have thought of these hostile wanderers. Nor would I have been surprised to see, on this twilit, sinister path, a line of slaves yoked neck-to-neck, driven on by Arabs and Somalis with whips and long muzzle-loaders. Surely a scene of Africa as Livingstone saw it.

The ferry crossing, which offered the reason for the existence of Sarka, was marked on the map, even though no vehicle-carrying craft existed. Instead, the long, heavy, expertly manipulated dugout canoes criss-crossed the river, their landing points offering further meeting places for those men of the village with nothing to do. Women were present too in considerable numbers; attractive, often strikingly so in their colourful *kangas*, they scrubbed and beat their loads of washing in the murky Tana.

Amongst the crowd we suddenly perceived Raj Patel and Andy Winspeare, so drew in and learned of their inability to locate a base camp site hereabouts. Nigel thereupon decided to continue downstream to the nearest point at which the equipment could be brought down to the river, even if this entailed another couple of days' voyaging.

In the event it was to be nearly three days before we were to reach countryside that relented enough to allow passage of the Land Rover and the Bedford. It was as well we were unaware of such a lengthy extension to this leg of the voyage, for constant poling, paddling, pushing and hauling of boats becomes a wearisome business without a break.

That night we raised camp on top of a steep bank among scrub and a light green vegetation bearing luscious-looking fruits of deadly poison. Below, on the damp spit of sand, crocodile eyes shone as brightly as the stars that formed our ceiling. We had earned the copious mugs of tea we consumed late into the night, and the fire remained alight for as long as someone could stay awake to replenish it.

I have already alluded to the fact that my fellow-paddler, Alison, was not exactly made of the stuff of African explorers – and the Tana hippos quite plainly put the fear of God into her. So it was ironic that next morning, as we continued on our way, *East Midlander* found itself among a whole herd of the species, with the boat between the parents and their young – just the situation to avoid in a boat of its fragile nature.

'Paddle like hell,' growled John, suddenly aware of the danger.

I hardly needed the instruction, and plunged my blade through the water with all the strength at my disposal. But Alison, paralysed with fright, made no such move – with the result that the boat simply veered in a tight circle towards the nearest hippo family, into whose eyes had appeared an aggressive light. John, the great helmsman, occupied with removing the igniter from a thunderflash, made no move to correct the manoeuvre.

Low squawks of fear emerged from Alison but my grated 'For Christ's sake *do* something' sent her paddle back into the water, and we slowly swung the other way.

All this must have been very confusing to one male hippo, for he abruptly lunged at us, and a line of bubbles that was definitely not an illusion made a beeline for the boat from the spot where he had crash-dived. I raised my paddle with the idea of giving him a crack about the ears should he appear at the side of the boat, but nothing more happened. Considerably shaken, we made the fastest progress of the day.

'Why didn't you sound your foghorn?' Nigel had asked afterwards, referring to our siren. Why not indeed? We would remember it next time.

This day was also notable for the sighting of more game. Baboons screamed and barked at us from the bank and hyenas wailed like sirens. Tiny dik-dik shyly stared out of huge mouse-eyes ringed in white; these little creatures are among the smallest of the antelopes, only some fourteen inches high at the shoulder, with delicate two-inch horns standing erect. We spotted wart hog, too, cropping grass and digging for roots with their villainous tusks.

Herds of waterbuck, a larger member of the antelope fraternity, watched us quizzically before bounding off into the trees, frightening some tailcoated marabou storks – solemn and pompous on the ground but so graceful in flight. With them were sharp-faced vultures, peering at us evilly from their huddled witch capes.

The trees beside the river were alive with Sykes monkeys leaping spectacularly from branch to branch. They are similar to the blue monkey except for the pronounced white gorget round the throat and sides of the neck, the so-called blue monkey having blue-grey and black forelimbs. Again Ken was the fount of this knowledge, even though birds were his domain. We lunched on biscuits and fish paste on the edge of a clearing – the frugality of the meal dictated by both the time and rations at our immediate disposal – and from this sheltered position we watched wildebeest approaching a favoured watering place in docile line. They seem to have an orderly system of drinking, these substantial animals: no crowding, yet when finished, they retire hastily but calmly. Gazelles, too, we saw on a similar errand. We witnessed few attacks by predators at water holes: could there be some form of truce among drinkers of the wild?

Another night was spent on a sandbank unmistakably used by denizens of the river. We congregated close to the fire, laying out our bedding in a tight circle around it, for it is the straggler, human or otherwise, that falls easy prey to the crocodile. Poor Joseph took things too literally and had to be rolled in the sand when his sleeping bag – with him in it – caught light.

Our precautions were not overdone either. In the morning we discovered fresh spore in the sand only yards from our circle of bodies. However, our African trio, Joseph, Charles and Lorio, raised a cacophonous symphony which, when the fire had died, undoubtedly contributed to keeping hostile elements at bay. There had been moments of wakefulness, it must be said, when I would have preferred the hostile elements, which at least go about their business quietly.

Another morning was to pass before the tangle of undergrowth along the banks showed any signs of thinning; we began to feel the imminence of the vehicle support party, not to mention the draw of another base camp with its little additional comforts of semi-permanency. All of a sudden the delicious prospect of a whole week of relative languor as an alternative to the incessant hand-propelling of boats had us straining our eyes for a tell-tale marker. We humans are funny creatures. Only a few days earlier we had been itching to be on the move, and now we could hardly wait for a return to camp life. But, again, nothing is ever quite what it seems in this world.

Every bend in the river was deemed to be the last, as we paddled and poled – sometimes against a head wind, always the long way around the outer curve where the deep channel lay – following orange banks topped by brushwood that carried an awful sameness about them. With every new prospect we scanned the new scene presented to us, a scene no different from the one before except that the sun shone down on it from another position.

Occasionally we loosed off a clarion call from our miniature sirens, but no answering howl echoed back across the ether.

And then suddenly, half-way through the midday swelter – when only mad dogs and Englishmen would be toiling at so negative a task – a red disc showed against the distant bank. Our eyes, glazed with sweat, were surely playing tricks, but no, this mirage refused to evaporate. We had arrived at Mulanjo camp.

Raj, Andy and Tony Pattaway had done us proud. The camp, erected and ready for occupation, lay like an oasis beneath a cluster of trees. Tony had excelled himself by laboriously cutting steps into the high bank that barred us from our new home. We mounted this stairway to the stars and gazed with critical eyes at the result of the support group's handiwork. We had broken camp at Kora nostalgic at leaving a site we had come to know. Now we were being hypercritical on arrival at the new one. Yet it takes much less than we think to make a place one's own.

A large stew lay ready and steaming on a trestle table. Stew again. Hardly the most exotic concoction in the culinary field, but hunger turns beggars into kings.

Most of us spurned the tents, since comfort does not have to mean everything that civilisation has to offer: nor would we be denied the sights of our eyes. By the time the dawn came to the forest in a blaze of scarlet and gold, most of the nocturnal animals had retreated to holes in trees and caves and the diurnal animals taken over. There was a great echoing burst of bird-song and, in the morning dew, the cicadas started zithering experimentally, with long pauses as if aware they were out of tune. Then the forest promptly rang with its more characteristic noise – the wild exuberant cries of the baboons.

These dawns were, to me, one of Africa's greatest gifts and could only, occasionally, be equalled by an African dusk. 'Kora dawns' we called them, for the eastward sky at Kora was also bare of foliage. In other respects too Mulanjo was very similar to Kora, and camp life at Mulanjo was to start where it had terminated at Kora.

Though the straggling village of Mulanjo was but a mile into the bush and a number of its more impulsive souls came to visit us daily, the pattern of observation of tribal life and customs never took coherent shape at our second base camp. Thirty miles downstream was Garissa, a township on the east bank of the river with a road bridge to boot, one of the very few on the Tana. And not until below Garissa would our enquiring minds delve into the ways of the Tana peoples. From the point of view of wildlife Mulanjo was, perhaps, only a slight improvement upon Kora. To the visitors' book of animals we were able to add an alleged sighting of three elephants by Joseph, a lion by Alison and John, as well as impala, anteaters, terrapins and a puff adder.

Trapping, observation by day and night, collection and preservation of bird and beast continued with renewed vigour; the routine of camp life revolved on well-oiled wheels, everyone knowing their designated tasks and carrying them out with brisk efficiency. John, as deputy commandant, bolstered his military hankerings by erecting an imposing camp entrance which provoked some incredulity from those of less martial temperament. But perhaps Mulanjo's most spectacular accomplishment was the coaxing into life, if only for a limited period, of the rebellious jet boat.

It was immediately utilised for the tasks to which it had been assigned, the craft coming into its own as a reconnaissance vessel and, where the need arose, a fetch-and-carry ferry, making a fine sight hissing through the murky brown waters. And it was at Mulanjo too that we acquired two Johnson outboard motors for our more humble inflatables.

Ralph himself became the hero of the hour while on board one of his jetting missions to Garissa. Near the township was the Sakuri irrigation scheme, ten acres of land cultivated for the

Sakuri irrigation scheme, ten acres of land cultivated for the growing of bananas, tomatoes, chillies, aubergines and maize: a sort of cooperative project set up to aid destitute Somali farmers in the area. The general reduction of water had been trouble enough for these people, but the breakdown of their pump some months before spelt disaster. Government mechanics had inspected the damage but no repairs had been attempted, with the result that many of the farmers were giving up and returning to their pastoral life. Then Ralph appeared on the scene and for two days worked to identify the fault and effect the repair. He even found time to instruct the villagers in the pump's operation and maintenance of the system. Ralph's good deed earned him a mention in Nairobi's *Daily Nation,* which quoted him as saying: 'It was great to see the happiness in the people's faces as the water flowed'. The gruff New Zealander was not given to flowery phrases but in this instance I knew he meant every word.

If Ralph and Mona had something of a roving commission with the jet boat while at base camps, even more so did John Axford and his Tana Pox Team. We saw little of John, Sue Hall and Gilbert Wangabe, their African assistant, during the subsequent section of the expedition except for occasional reunions – sometimes by chance – but it was from Mulanjo that the trio set out on their medical survey.

I am not going to pretend I have more than the sketchiest notion of what Tana Pox and the other nectar-born diseases the team had come to investigate are all about. For a long time even the basic facts of the oddly titled Tana Pox escaped me, for it was an infection about which nobody seemed to have heard. Not surprisingly, perhaps, since it was a disease that had not fully blossomed – though I could appreciate the logic of going for a cure before it did.

Ours was not the first survey of its kind. Five years earlier one had been carried out to establish the levels of this smallpox-like virus exclusive to the population of the Tana. It was noticed that the disease was confined to the Pokoma tribe. Now John and his helpers, lavishly equipped with a white-painted Land Rover supplied by the Kenyan Ministry of Health, were all set to descend upon the local Pokomo population, whose villages were spread between Garissa and Garsen, to take blood samples and to ascertain to what extent the disease had been prevalent since then. Malaria, filariasis, cholera and other such unpleasant afflictions were present in the area, with malaria endemic throughout the Tana basin; so the team, notwithstanding additional ailments and woes their survey would assuredly uncover, had their hands full.

John projected more of a playboy than a doctor image. Twenty-three years of age, another B.Sc., and about to take his Ph.D. in immunology, he did not seem at the time certain where his future lay. His hobbies of parachuting and yachting intensified the playboy image, as did his ability to be elsewhere when there was manual work to be done. However, there was no doubting his high intelligence, and he carried out his job with a maximum of efficiency.

His associate was Sue Hall, SRN. About John's age, she had worked in both America and Switzerland and was a proficient cook. A gentle girl, she was always ready to help with anything, and it wasn't only for her culinary expertise that I wished we could have seen more of her on the expedition proper. As it was, I am certain it was she who carried out most of the donkey work on the Tana Pox survey.

Gilbert Wangabe one could best describe as a barrack-room lawyer; his favourite topic was politics, which he expounded with vigour, logic and fanaticism. Dark, educated, endowed with a pair of piercing eyes, he could be a useful person – and a dangerous one – if he chose to be.

For several days the team operated in and around Mulanjo village, being received with much hospitality and appreciation. Whilst their work was initially hampered by the remoteness of the communities, John would to go to any lengths to get through the thick bush to them. Advised by the medical authorities and 'bush telegraph' of the team's imminent arrival at a particular village, a large throng of its citizens would invariably be awaiting them. In spite of some hesitation at the start of proceedings when the first blood samples had to be taken, an issue of coloured vitamin tablets and sweets for everyone soon overcame any serious resistance. Later, I was to attend one of these village 'medicals'.

As at Kora, my stay at Mulanjo was of brief duration. I was

offered a trip to the Nairobi Base House, outward by Land Rover and back by local bus, a journey that offered some promise and would occupy much of the week. But a home, wherever it may be and for whatever duration, turns into a place of sacred memories stored away for ever, becoming dim with the passage of time and jumbled with the intake of fresher memories. 'What,' we may be asked in years to come, 'were your impressions of Mulanjo?' Those who were there will hesitate a few moments while the computer of the mind delves back into the past. No great drama notched a milestone of recollection, but Mulanjo would spell a serene content, true solitude – when the most restless part of a person relaxes and listens in a kind of agreed peace. It will be a place where the full expeditionary complement came to live together in a wilderness; for me, it was where I learnt the lesson that you can never truly know another person, or be known by them, but that the pleasure of life is in the trying. Mulanjo was a place far from our real homes, where we tried to bring the little comforts and courtesies of what we knew as civilisation to a savage acre of a foreign field. Here we entertained the local chieftain to tea, searching out the unchipped mugs in which to serve it; here we welcomed like relatives for the weekend strangers who were not strangers from the planet London. Mulanjo will be a shaft of memory where crocodiles basked on a sandbank just below the camp, a place with an entrance arch and a volleyball court, each serving as someone's idea of what makes a home.

My temporary return to Nairobi was something of a culture shock. Three of us – Nigel, Andrew and myself – left Mulanjo one steamy midday, with Andy driving the Land Rover. Crammed in the back with the cargo of the overloaded vehicle, it was one hell of a ride. At Mwingi we stopped for a beer, bread and pilchards; one of the African clients of the bar was despatched by the proprietor to purchase the bread, which we tore apart and ravenously devoured.

Darkness had fallen, and abruptly the night was so cold that the four of us were forced, somehow, into the less draughty front of the Land Rover. The un-African bitterness of that cold was, of course, Nairobi and its altitude, and I was glad that the grating hardness of a city was softened by the late hour of our arrival.

6. Korokora and Beyond

The risk with a return to Nairobi was that back at Base House one was liable to get stuck for longer than intended. There was always so much going on; so much to do that, once a returned expeditioner had come in from the field and passed through the delicious process of being bathed and pampered, he or she was straightaway embroiled in all that was happening at the expedition's tail.

The first 24 hours back in Nairobi was a treat. To sleep between linen sheets in a real bed (if the limited number available allowed it) and to eat electrically cooked food from china plates made a most pleasant change. Thereafter I was hankering to be back in the bush again. However, the daily events of Base House formed an integral part of the expedition, so to observe and be involved in what went on there was by no means a waste of time.

Susie Richardson reigned supreme. Her word was law. At our first encounters my heart had sunk. Here, I thought, was one of those frighteningly efficient women. And her previous expeditionary record supported the notion, since (with John), she had covered herself in glory with the British Trans-Americas Expedition a year or two earlier. London-born, twenty-nine and good-looking, she exuded capability from every pore. That she loved her work was patently obvious. Yet she was handicapped in this not only by two small and demanding offspring she had brought with her but with the knowledge that hers was the least melodramatic job of the expedition. That she got paid for some of it was neither here nor there. Mere money could not have turned anyone on as it did Susie. Swiftly I was to discover her human qualities and the same frailties as all of us. On several occasions I was to see her holding herself together on the verge of going to pieces when thoughtless members of her flock had undone hours of sheer hard work. She covered her confusion by an ability to admonish, and this she could do devastatingly. Down with a severe attack of dysentery at the end of the expedition, I was rash enough to be caught out of my sickbed and to suffer the backlash of her tongue. By then, however, I was well aware that her concern was human, not disciplinary.

The telephone rang incessantly. The press, a sponsor, the military at Kahawa, a local tradesman, the High Commissioner's Office, the museum, the health authorities about snake-bite serum; they all wanted something, or to set something in motion which involved *doing* something about it. Once again I found myself back in the rat race, driving errands around a city suddenly stranger than it was at the beginning of the expedition. To compound the nightmare we were now in a new Base House half a mile away from the old one. The previous owner had returned unexpectedly and wanted his house back, so added to the problems was a constant search for property. And before the expedition was over, Base House would be back where it was again. For me, though, there were advantages. At least I was able to bring my despatches up to date and visit various press agencies in the city, thus carrying out the less exotic side of my own duties.

Nigel and I were to return to the Tana – and base camp number three – alone and vehicle-less. The new camp was called Korokora and was somewhere within a few miles of a speck of a village of that name. The idea was to attempt to reach it by public transport, since the Land Rover we had brought with us was required to remain at Base House, as were Andrew and Andy.

From a decrepit Nairobi suburb we caught the overnight bus bound for Garissa with no idea how we were going to reach the camp, which was 20 miles or more from the town. The bus was a British Leyland (as most public service vehicles were in Kenya) and, for its age and conditions of operating, surprisingly roadworthy. The fare for the 200-odd miles was ridiculously low to our way of thinking, yet the bus was not overcrowded.

At Thika we turned off the main highway into the town centre and promptly knocked a cyclist off his bicycle. The chap was more indignant than hurt but his downfall caused the police to pursue us to impound both bus and passengers at the police station. We were there more than an hour while driver, cyclist and police thrashed matters out between them. To pass the time Nigel and I explored the town, which is a sizeable place possessing a modern industrial estate brandishing many English-sounding names. Thika is, of course, famous for its flame trees, which were everywhere, growing tall and thick with dark green foliage from which blossomed dozens of reddish-orange flowers, vivid as shell-bursts. Back on the bus and in spite of it still being in police custody, vendors were allowed on board with trays of cakes and armfuls of pineapples and bananas to sell to a captive market.

Thika too, of course, was where the tarmac ran out. Resuming the interrupted journey, the driver made not the slightest attempt to slacken speed when we hit the dirt, and the noise of tortured metal and rubber was heartrending. A layer of dust turned us all into ghostly figures – the source of the dust being not only that which ascended from the chassis but also what descended from bags of flour on the roof. At intervals we would halt to allow male passengers to relieve themselves against the wheels and consume replacement liquid in the form of hot, sweet tea from ever-open char-houses along the way. At Kangoni, where there was a permanent police control, the bus refused to start, resulting in an all-out-and-push operation. With the vehicle in first gear the engine fired on the fourth heave and trundled independently off down the road with everyone piling into it as it accelerated. Thereupon, the chickens belonging to a passenger on the seat behind me succeeded in escaping, resulting in a search-and-recapture operation both inside and outside the bus. I began to wonder if the good Lord meant us to reach Garissa.

Thankfully he did, and we crossed the single-track girder bridge into the town at about four o'clock in the morning. Since the bus was going no further, Nigel and I utilised a row of seats each as a hotel for a couple of hours, leaving at daybreak to breakfast on tea and chapatis provided by a dirty little cafe afflicted with flies and strident pop music.

The problem of getting ourselves to Korokora now presented itself. We made enquiries about camel hire but nothing in that line was available. From an informant in a bazaar we learnt that John

Axford and his band had been in town yesterday, which meant it
would be extremely unlikely they would be there today. Both of us
were carrying heavy packs and camp beds, which made the
prospect of walking to Korokora not particularly attractive.

Garissa was the administrative headquarters of the North-
Eastern Province and exuded a certain last frontier spirit. It had
been the main military base during the border dispute with
Somalia and seemed increasingly likely to become so again. The
centre of the township reminded me of one of those Texan
outposts one sees in the movies, but I couldn't think what was
lacking until I remembered cowboys.

Though still early, we decided to make our way to the District
Commissioner's compound. For Nigel this presented an objective
of particular interest, since years before, his father had been
provincial commissioner for this very region. Nigel had never
been allowed to join him there because Garissa was considered too
remote for colonial families, so more than a decade later, here was
god-sent chance to satisfy a long-held curiosity. On the way, we
called at the police station to see if we could raise any transport,
but to no avail. However, prospects improved at the DC's office.
Yes, of course they remembered Provincial Commissioner
Winser; he'd been popular enough to have had a square named
after him, and we were promptly rushed there by car to see it.
More to the point, they would be happy to drive us to Korokora;
but in the meantime would the distinguished leader of the Tana
River Expedition, about which they'd heard so much on the radio,
and its chronicler do the present holder of the Provincial
Commissioner's office the honour of calling on him? Unable to
decline the summons, we were taken by the District Officer to the
new section of Garissa – which reminded me a little of a suburb of
Welwyn Garden City – and in an imposing council chamber
presented to the great man. He too remembered PC Winser and
indicated the name inscribed for posterity on the Garissa roll of
fame hanging on the chamber wall. We were also presented to the
current District Commissioner, with whom we took tea, and it was
through his office that the ponderous machinery of officialdom
was cranked into motion, eventually to exude a powder-blue Land
Rover and driver for our onward conveyance to camp three. In

return for this service Nigel gravely bestowed invitations to all
three functionaries to come and 'dine' at Korokora a few days
hence and received equally grave acceptances, though for
different nights because of the problem of protocol (seemingly a
PC cannot dine with a mere DC or DO).

The rest of the day was our own and we spent the hours at the
Government Rest House ('reserved for civil servants only' read
the notice at the entrance) where we prodded the cook into
producing a scrawny chicken and rice lunch. Back at the DC's
compound we hung around again, reading the official
governmental notices on the official governmental notice board.
('Citizens of Garissa', read one of them, 'are reminded that
disposal of their dead is the duty of the authorities' – a regulation
memo that conjured up for me a macabre vision of corpses in
municipal litter bins.) By late afternoon our presence was clearly
bothering the DO, and it was partly I'm sure to get us out of his
hair that he finally summoned the vehicle to remove us from the
scene.

Assuredly the driver knew the way to Korokora. He had been
chosen for his knowledge, since he would be repeating the journey
at least twice again with the PC and the others, so it was absolutely
imperative he knew the way. We crossed the Tana (nice to see the
old river again), drove a mile down the road and then simply
turned into the bush, where there was not the slightest indication of
a track or path so far as I could see. Did he *really* know the way?
The driver smiled confidently. He was a tall Somali, seemingly
more intent on giving us a course of Somali for beginners than
involving himself in details of navigation. *Of course* he knew,
which was how we ended up in a wadi.

It was a crazy, ridiculous journey, something only the Keystone
Cops or the Goon Show could have dreamt up. In quick succession
we found ourselves in three more wadis. It wasn't as if we got into
them by mistake, for to descend their steep banks required a lot of
reversing and four-wheel drive expertise. It was just that the driver
liked driving in wadis. And when we were in we could never get
out again – except, in final desperation, by the well-tried method
of foot-down-and-charge. Twice we nearly had the Land Rover on
its back. I say 'we', but what the hell had Nigel and I to do with it?

Every time we suggested one direction Moses would take the other to prove his superior knowledge, and bang, crash, we were in another bloody wadi. And then, out of a clear blue sky, it rained: a violent inexplicable downpour that defied the season – and we all know what rain does to wadis.

Fortunately neither the rain nor the wadis persisted, and we trundled on through the bush traversing (not following) a spaghetti junction of tracks that might have led us somewhere. By merciful providence we came upon a series of goatherds and shepherds all dressed like Jesus Christ, who told us they knew Korokora and asked if they could come along for the ride. Mongooses, wart hogs, baboons, gerenuk and dik-dik fled from our spinning wheels as we flattened the razor-sharp undergrowth under about a ton of human cargo.

The bush. I have alluded to it many times, and except on Mount Kenya, it was with us all through the expedition. Yet normally one hardly notices it. Today we did. The 'bush' is one of those blanket terms covering a wide range of landscape. Some of it is rock; some – as here – is sand. It is the characteristic backdrop to Kenya. It is so unspectacular in anything but size that, after the first sight, it becomes unnoticeable. Whether broken on the horizon by hills or ruptured by lumps of rock or grazing game, its ultimate effect is of a uniform barrenness, a vast plain of scrubby grass – endless, useless: something to be driven through as fast as possible. It is beautiful, hypnotic and, finally, irritating. I read a story somewhere about a man mapping a certain region. He was helped by a sketch plan prepared by an earlier traveller, which seemed pretty accurate until he came to a vast plain. His predecessor had written boldly on his sketch the name Mamoba, but when the cartographer tried to verify this all the locals shook their heads. So the puzzled map-maker checked back to discover Mamoba to be more of a comment than a name; it stood for 'miles and miles of bloody Africa'.

At long last we came into sight of Korokora village, the usual collection of straw and mud huts, to be joined by one of the village elders who *emphatically* knew where the camp was. And the surprising thing was he did, he really did. Down an atrocious track, through a battleground of dead trees and tangled skeins of high thorn and creeper, and there it was: all laid out in line, Butlins on a sandy beach, clear of bush and close to the Tana. Everyone, including the 'know the way' throng, the village elder, the driver, Nigel and I, received a great welcome augmented by mugs of hot, steaming tea, and it came to me that if the PC, DC or DO took up their options they'd *earn* their dinner.

The voyage from Mulanjo, we were told, had been uneventful – which is a way of saying that nothing of disastrous proportions occurred. Two small and temperamental motors to four boats do not add up to the perfect ratio for utilising horse power, and inflatables are not designed with sleek streamlining in mind. In spite of this, progress was made; the popular verdict being 'Look, no hands!' (i.e., no paddling).

The river had narrowed in the vicinity of Garissa, with a lot of driftwood accumulated on the bends. Cultivation around the villages and townships gave way to forest – more like jungle – overflowing to the water's edge in a solid wall of verdure. Getting ashore was impossible, the only opportunity being where the game had forced a path when coming to drink.

Mainly on account of the fact that it *was* possible to land at Garissa, the first of the overnight sites was raised close by; it was either that or the possibility that one or two of the bachelors in the crews had envisaged another party. Whatever the reason it was a mistake, for not only was the encampment quickly overrun by inquisitive citizenry but departure next morning was accompanied by multiple hangovers. Suffice it to say, subsequent encampments were made in more rural neighbourhoods offering fewer temptations.

Again the vehicle support group had worked wonders to establish a new base prior to the mass arrival of its inmates, and that of Korokora could hardly have been more perfectly sited. Situated, as at Kora, on a spit of sand alongside the river, backed by the bush and the jungle, it even possessed a two-tier living arrangement of grassy banks on which one could go 'upstairs' to bed. There were few flies or mosquitoes, though the Tana itself was pronounced 'untouchable', which gave Mary a chance to shine with her water-purifying apparatus. Though there were no flies to speak of, a rise in the number of creepy-crawlies did not go unnoticed: the very first day young Sandy was bitten by a full-grown scorpion of the brown – and most deadly – variety, which was to lay him low for a good 24 hours.

Our newest attachment, Karen Ross, was at Korokora, having joined the Scientific Team straight from her Kenyan home. Being a budding zoologist and knowing her stuff, she was a valuable addition to the team. Furthermore, she was an extremely nice person: full of good humour and commonsense.

Nigel and I had arrived conveniently in time for supper, and although its chief constituent was naturally stew, there were fresh potatoes to go with it. To follow was fresh fruit-salad made up of luscious pineapples, bitter oranges and, because we were nearing the plantations, bananas. A dialogue had been established with the inhabitants of Korokora village, so our larder began to include items such as eggs and maize flour which, since they came out of no tin, were classed as luxuries. Before going to bed I went crocodile-observing with Ralph, Mona, Mary and Nigel as an appropriate termination to a long day. The observation post had been set up several hundred yards from the camp, overlooking a sandbank surrounded by shallow water – the perfect pad for lazy crocs. It was pitch dark of course but we could pick out, in the beams of our torches, as many as a dozen of the reptiles on the still-warm sand. Abruptly aware of our presence, most of them slunk into the water to disappear, but one large specimen thought he could get away with it by 'freezing'. Somebody, not very kindly, aimed a clod of earth at him, which landed on his head. Thereupon the creature slid into the shallow water, but finding it not deep enough, panicked and ran for it faster than I thought crocodiles could run. Its speed took the animal half-way up our bank before his centrifugal force ran out and he fell back to the river again. We fell back too, and in some alarm, a little chastened at causing such indignity to so fine a beast.

I slept like the proverbial log that first night at Korokora, with only one interruption when my camp bed tipped over. In the morning there was great excitement when one of the observation groups reported seeing signs of the presence of elephants in large numbers coming down to drink on the bank opposite our own.

Straightaway five of us – Nigel, Mary, Alison, Ken and myself – crossed the river to investigate further.

The elephants had been there all right: huge footprints and gigantic droppings on the sand and mud confirmed it. We followed a trail of broken bush, locating many signs of their activity. But the only sight of elephant we came across that morning was the saddest one of all: that of elephant remains, and in daunting proportions. Some had lain there for months and were no more than greying skeletons, but other corpses were of more recent origin and the smell was sickening. These carcasses of putrefying skin crawled with millions of the most revolting maggots, so that the whole mass of rotten flesh heaved. Of course, the tusks were nowhere to be seen, which made the reason for this slaughter painfully obvious. I love and understand animals to a degree no greater than the average Britisher, but I felt a monstrous anger at the crime of greed that had been committed at this peaceful spot.

High among the factors threatening game is poaching. Some of this is on a large scale for profit. However, it must be borne in mind that a fair amount of killing is carried out by people who are tired of having their *shambas* and cultivated plots damaged by animals. An even greater amount results from hunting for the pot. This is a particular problem; hunting is, after all, the oldest human method of obtaining food and is in itself entirely respectable. An uneducated man with an empty stomach cannot be expected to understand either the economic or the moral aspects of game protection. This kind of poacher is perhaps the hardest to stop because his conscience is clear. Yet here at Korokora the poachers had come across an elephant trail to an established drinking place and had simply lain in wait to commit this most despicable brand of murder. The recent remains had been thinly covered with branches, for elephants have a touching habit of shrouding their own dead, and even those of other beasts. The story goes that a young girl once fainted in the jungle and in the morning found herself covered in undergrowth. If true, I doubt very much if mankind deserves this privilege.

As at Mulanjo I was struck by the peacefulness of the camp and its community. Everything was so far from the man-caused dramas of the adventure teams and the clashes resulting from overstretched nerves. Here, it was like living with a different race. The big event of the day was, for instance, the proposed entertainment of the PC, and the preparations included the purchase and killing of a local goat. Of course, the PC never appeared, which meant more goat for us and no need for the trappings of an unaccustomed etiquette. We even found some lukewarm beer to go with our blow-out.

Korokora was not entirely without its drawbacks, however, in particular what resulted from that phenomenon of the river, the Tana wind. Dry sand was forever being blown in our faces, and at night, whether one slept outside or under canvas, our sleeping bags would become full of the stuff. It was no good being clever and sweating it out in a virtually sealed tent. That wind could find you anywhere.

Part of the scientific objective of the Korokora base camp and others along the Tana could be summed up, drily but to the point, as the understanding of basic ecological relationships between the small mammals, insects and plants of the riverine vegetation. Our resulting findings were to be utilised as a yardstick for future surveys, which meant that knowledge gained over different sections of the Tana was of considerable value. And it was with immense pleasure that, by now, I was beginning to form the rudiments of a picture. Take trees, for example, for I suppose they come under the scientific heading of plants. One of Tony's reports reflected his rising concern for a dearth of dead and dying trees. At Kora this was not much more than the waste product of their normal cycle of life. At Mulanjo the situation was noticeably worse, and here at Korokora things were very bad indeed. The cause (besides the year's drought, which could be conveniently blamed for everything) was that the trees were being cut down by human agency in increasing numbers the further we progressed into what, for the remote Tana, could be described as populated areas. And *why* were the trees being chopped down? There across the river lay one answer, bold as brass, as a goatherd went by surrounded by upwards of a hundred bobbing goats on their way to a patch of saplings and young trees already part-decimated so that the animals could eat their fill of crisp, tender foliage.

However, some of the side-effects were not so obvious. Not

only were the goats eating the foliage but they were also destroying the larvae hatching therein. This would result in a shortage of butterflies that, in turn, meant a reduction or glut of something else – nearly always to the detriment of the balance of nature.

My own non-scientific interests lay in less problematical matters, and my daytime incursions into the forests with Tony on his butterfly and bug hunts gave me additional insight into the ways of butterflies. Hadn't I already noted the 'mimicry' of certain species, by which they rest in such a position as to look uninviting to the passing bird. In the same manner I had seen caterpillars making themselves resemble dead twigs. And it had been revealed to me how the beautiful patterns and colours of butterfly wings were simply window-dressing; the bright coloration was, in reality, a warning to potential predators that they were not palatable. Birds would learn to associate such colours with disagreeable flavours and so would not attack or eat the butterflies. The brighter and more conspicuous the pattern, the greater the protection achieved.

Now I was to discover a second kind of 'mimicry'. In this, one conspicuously marked, distasteful species resembled another similarly marked distasteful species. The theory here was that young birds had to learn by experience which butterflies were distasteful and which were not, and therefore it was of advantage to have as few warning patterns as possible. It was all very involved but completely fascinating, as was Tony's staccato commentary on the subject of individual butterflies. One of them, the Emperor, exhibits two short tails on each hind wing. These are 'target marks' and are not infrequently snipped off by attacking lizards and other enemies. When an Emperor butterfly alights, it quickly turns about so that the head is downward and the tails uppermost. This is a safeguard, the predator attacking the tails instead of the head.

Some mornings I crossed the river to accompany mammal-trap inspection groups or, with Sandy, to see what his mist nets had caught. Likewise I would go with Charles to view the results of his Tana fish-traps; his fish collection and notes of fish seen was reaching impressive proportions. Once we attempted to catch some fish, not in the interests of high-flown scientific data but, prosaically, for the cooking pot. A dozen of us, risking the infections, strode into the Tana with a trawl net and made a great sweep of the river; the sum total of two such sweeps was four tiddlers. A young crocodile watched these antics from a mud flat with a tolerant smile on its face.

Korokora became memorable too for some exciting night observation prowls into the jungle. On one of these I accompanied Sandy and Mary; our special task was to shoot and bring back a bushbaby required by Nairobi Museum. Attractive little animals, they are a nocturnal relative of the monkey and are to be found at the tops of trees. Their huge eyes glow like cat's-eyes when the beam of a torch is directed on them, and so they are easy targets. We had seen them many times on occasions when we had no firearms, but now we were equipped with the elderly shotgun not a single bushbaby put in an appearance. Instead, we got very close to a beast that has the distinction of being the first animal in the dictionary, the aardvark, or ant-bar, a grotesque, massively-built, short-legged creature as large as a medium-sized pig, with long pointed ears, a narrow head and rounded snout. Being extremely nocturnal they are rarely seen, and ours made sure he wasn't seen for long. Following it excitedly we got ourselves hopelessly lost, which was exceedingly careless of us. I suppose it could have been an alarming experience, but for some unaccountable reason it turned out to be no more than a rather novel one. Distant sounds of lion, leopard and hyena made an eerie background to our nocturnal meanderings and the frequent consultations of the compass that eventually brought us back to the river. Here, movement among the thick, clinging undergrowth was very difficult, while there was also the underlying menace of hippos out of water. Still, all in one piece, we made it back to a somewhat perturbed camp, to receive a deserved rocket from Nigel.

As easy as getting lost in the jungle by night was losing one's sense of direction in the bush by day. Taking a stroll to Korokora village I mistook one of the tracks, and though I possess reasonable navigational ability, I found myself at least a mile upstream of the camp. The village was a typically dilapidated affair, with the mud-walled, wattle-thatched houses all higgledy-piggledy anywhere. My curiosity led me to a hut a cut above the others in that it possessed a little vestibule, in which stood a cluster of spears in the manner of gumboots and raincoats in a British country house. Taking a Cheshire-cat smile gleaming from the dark interior as an invitation to enter, I ducked under the five-foot-high lintel. Inside I could just make out the figure of an unbelievably old-looking woman (though she was probably younger than I was) sitting on the floor. But the smile belonged to a spritely young damsel who came forward to show me a fat little two-month-old baby, ensuring that I was aware of his fine healthy little balls. I felt like a vicar being offered hash by one of his parishioners – not quite knowing how to express my appreciation. The lady was laden with beads which tinkled merrily whenever she moved. 'Jambo!' I exclaimed fatuously, utilizing one-third of my Swahili vocabulary, and was rewarded by the brilliant whiteness of another smile against a jet-black face.

We still had not made real contact with the locals on the journey so far, though this was chiefly because there had been so few locals around. Only in the small number of townships through which we had passed did we come across fellow-humans in any quantity, and these were of urban communities. At Korokora, however, we were placed close to the hub of a Bantu tribe of the same name, living in tiny villages along or close to the Tana. These were agricultural people, though their land was too dry for the growing of crops on rainfall alone, a fact that entailed their dependence on the river as a means of livelihood. These were the very people we wanted to study, and on our subsequent journey south we would be meeting more of the Tana's human dependents.

It is impossible to specify the exact number of tribes there are in Kenya. Take just one species of peoples closely related by language and culture, the Buluhya, who are divided into groups such as the Bakusu and the Maragoli, with a dozen or so other major units. So is the tribe the Baluhya? Are the Bakusu a tribe or a sub-tribe or what? Similarly, the question of whether the Chuka, who live near Mount Kenya, are a tribe or a sub-tribe of some sort is, in factual terms, unanswerable. This being the case, one can only estimate that there are something under fifty tribes in Kenya. Each of these has a strong sense of communal separateness. Groups which, seen from a distance, are very similar in origin, traditions, social and political structure, language and so on – such as the Kikuyu and the Kamba – largely see themselves as entirely distinct.

The Tana, in its infancy, passes through Kikuyuland, as those of us in the Mountain Team were aware. The Kikuyu arrived with their tribal cousins, the Embu and Meru, and the Bantu immigrants who penetrated up the Tana River to occupy Fort Hall district. Originally they were in constant battle with the Masai but are now settled and growing crops in the fertile lands north of Nairobi. Avid for education, they take advantage of the innumerable government and mission schools that have sprouted in their territory, which has contributed to their becoming the leading tribe in Kenya.

East of Kikuyuland is Masailand, and though their territory does not border the Tana, some of us had passed and were to pass through the domain of the Masai *en route* to or from Nairobi. These days, tribal boundaries are vague and ill-defined by intermarriage and a lowering of tribal standards, so that it is difficult to designate territories with complete accuracy. The Masai have a nobility of character and an openness which is striking. When you meet them, no matter how much you have hardened your heart to accept every form of change and progress, you cannot help sighing for the old East Africa, where men like the Masai mattered more in that vast waste of bush than a thousand technicians. The emergence of the Kikuyu as a power, the abrupt withdrawal of the British, who protected the old Masai way of living, has left the Masai stunned. Suddenly they found themselves under a new government – a government of Africans over whom the Masai once lorded it by right of their long, slender spears. And the Masai have no education, no leaders; they are, all at once, a museum-piece, dressed as they were a thousand and more years ago, plastered with red ochre, tall and leanly handsome with ancient Egyptian features, standing in the hot silence, their long spears in their hands, wondering what has happened. Today the Masai own little of the land they conquered. All breed cattle; crops have no value for them, and their staple food remains milk, cattle meat and blood tapped from the jugular vein of the cow and drunk while it is still warm. Physically they are a strong people, superbly brave in their own and in other people's battles, but their grasslands have declined and the health of their cattle has deteriorated.

Adjoining both Kikuyuland and Masailand, north of the latter and bordering the Tana, is the territory of the Kamba, whose villagers of Kathini had so enthusiastically entertained the White Water Team. The Kamba are Kenya's third largest tribe and are noted for being fine soldiers and dancers; their spectacular dancing is spiced with fantastic, gyrating leaps in the air and double somersaults. Their warrior instincts turn them into fine hunters.

From Kora onward we had come upon the nomadic Somali and were now beginning to understand the basic reason for their nomadism. In the endless dry bush the puddles produced by the brief wet season soon dry up and the river becomes increasingly the focus of both man and beast. Thus both the Somali and the Orma peoples have adapted to the necessity of short-lived grazing. But where they are settled there is often over-grazing and soil erosion as had been sadly in evidence around Garissa. It must be said, however, that in this parched wilderness, the camels and goats looked surprisingly healthy; in light condition but strong and carrying a bloom on their coats. A camel's need for water is dependent upon whether it has green bush or dry browsing; maybe it can go ten days without watering, maybe only four or five. Milk camel, of course, and milk cattle need more water more often than the dry herd and cannot go as far for it. Cattle normally water every second day – half a day walking to water, half a day walking back, and a full day's grazing within the vicinity of the watering place. These details may seem of little consequence, but they assume vital importance to a Somali – and are most emphatically worthy of note by any survey team such as ourselves reporting back to an agency bent upon altering the course of nature.

The Somalis are Muslims and belong to the Hamitic race which includes among its north-east African members the Beja, the Afar, the Agaw of Ethiopia, the Galla and the Sidama peoples. Tribal rights over water and grazing, as can be appreciated, are likewise of vital importance and are strictly regulated. They are intelligent adaptable people; fiercely independent and proud.

Before long we would be entering the provinces of the

Ormagala and the Pokomo, and it was going to be through their eyes that we saw the human dependence upon the Lower Tana and its environment. In the meantime we had our own tribal customs to enact. By courtesy of Mary and her water management we partook of a mammoth clothes washing operation. In the ensuing free-for-all every garment emerged a tender blue when the dye ran from our non-fast, navy-blue expedition sweatshirts. Things would have been more successful had we 'gone native' and slapped our shirts and underwear against a Tana boulder. Under the not-very-deftly wielded scissors of Sandy, some of us had our flowing manes shorn so that we could see where we were going, and I had my beard trimmed for the first time since its birth. If we were not to be honoured by a visitation from the PC, DC or DO, at least we were able to play host for a couple of days to Susie and her brood, released for a while from Base House chores. With tiny Clare and Kate dashing around naked, the camp was in danger of being taken for a nudist resort. Such antics were interwoven with the serious business of expeditioning as our week at Korokora lurched towards the end.

I was awoken on the day of departure by the plaintive bark of a baboon with a sore throat, and I being duty cook, we enjoyed a hearty breakfast of burnt and lumpy porridge. A new bird for the Korokora animal book soared over us as we took to the boats; even I was able to identify it as a pelican. Education is a rewarding experience in Africa.

The resumption of the voyage was characterised, for me, not only by the novelty of powered propulsion but also by frequent switches of boats and crew. I started with Tony, Charles and Joseph in *Charity*, towing the motorless *East Midlander* containing Nigel and Mona atop a pile of cargo. *Habari* had the jet boat (crewless and once more out of action) and contained Sandy, Mary, Alison, Karen, Ralph and Ken. The remainder of the expedition members had elected to stay with the vehicle support group for various reasons, the most practical one being the undesirability of overloading the newly acquired outboard motors more than necessary.

Probably the real reason for the sudden popularity of the vehicle support group was vested in the simple monotony of motorised voyaging. Hard work though it was, constant paddling had precluded idleness and also offered – at the end of the day – a sense of achievement. In contrast, under powered propulsion, true idleness could have been a pleasure, but circumstances didn't allow this. Frequent stalling of the motors as well as the incessant grounding on shallows scotched any serious relaxation that might have been possible otherwise. Only Nigel managed a few crafty snoozes in the bottom of his vessel, but we allowed this as a privilege of leadership.

We judged our progress to be something in the region of five miles an hour – less when the wind was against us and slightly more than we could have hoped for by hand. A forfeit was the fearful racket kicked up by the motors, plus the constant whiff of petrol they exuded. Once an hour the tanks required filling, an operation that had the smelly stuff all over the place.

The first day out we saw only one hippo though numerous crocodiles – one getting so close that it nearly rammed our boat. Ashore were plenty of baboons, monkeys and impala to keep us amused. Impala are timid antelope who leap elegantly when alarmed – as they were when they saw us. Moving in a herd, they performed leaps into the air with exultant kangaroo-springs to disappear among the trees.

The Tana is a restless river, persistently changing its course, breaking its banks and generally misbehaving. One of its tricks was to undermine the bank, particularly on a curve, where the deep channel applies the pressure. An eroded bank is interesting to look at for it offers a lesson in geology – neatly displaying, in well-ordered layers, the age of its soils. Revealed too are roots of trees, coiling down towards water level blissfully unaware that the tree they feed will soon be no more than driftwood in the river.

Because of this habit of changing course – a habit accentuated during the periods of the annual flood – even present-day maps are extremely inaccurate, and as we voyaged deeper into a more inhabited zone, we were incessantly enquiring of local citizenry the distance to the next village. In view of these course changes it is hardly surprising that maps drawn by early Tana explorers are very different from those of the second half of the 20th century.

Few original place-names persist, and even when they do the place itself has probably shifted in location due to the threat of the floods. An example of very recent origin had been the village of Sarka at which we had dallied earlier, though in this case the reason for its movement to a new location had been human rather than natural causes.

Explorers of the Middle and Lower Tana included Clemens and Gustav Denhardt and Dr G.A. Fischer, whose 1879 map remains the most accurate. A subsequent explorer was the notorious Carl Peters, whose travels up river were accompanied, we are told, by 'much flogging, burning and terrorising'. Piggott's map simply confirmed the Denhardt brothers' observations, while Gregory's brief and abortive visit was plagued by illness, death and Somali raids in 1896. Captain Dundas and Hobley were another early couple who risked life and limb to plot an errant river's course and assess its possibilities.

Forty years were to pass before further specific exploration is reported in the chronicles of history. In 1935 there came another curious visitor to the inhospitable Tana, one Michael Sampson. His map showed Baomo and Garsen and also Garissa, this last a name derived from a corruption of 'garrison', since a detachment of the King's African Rifles had at one time been stationed nearby. Many moves of location and re-foundation of new communities occurred throughout the mid-1950s and up to 1961-2, when, in one of its angriest-ever moods, the Tana washed away many villages in the great flood of the period.

Now, as we throbbed like angry wasps down the more placid stream, the face of the Tana began to change. People were more in evidence on the banks, their faces alive with curiosity and excitement. Children ran chattering, their shrill voices sounding above the clatter of the pistons, while small *manyattas* – the beehive-shaped huts covered with hides, mats and foliage – showed among occasional patchwork squares of cultivation. The shiny green of banana plantations took over where the forest had been before.

It was opposite one of these villages, nestling in a clearing of bananas, that we camped that first night. Many eyes watched us as we disembarked and struggled up the steep embankment to carry out our well-practised chores. Within half an hour we were receiving visitors in the guise of the boldest of the village salesmen, who crossed the river in their lean canoes in an attempt to sell us straw mats of beautiful design.

The site of our encampment was plainly a favourite place for elephant, the sandy plateau, backed by a group of trees, being liberally sprinkled with their telltale droppings. As we settled down to sleep we heard them crashing around in the undergrowth nearby, sending each of us edging surreptitiously nearer the fire. At Korokora we had heard elephant on the *other* side of the river, which made us feel much more secure.

But what made that night memorable was a remarkable incident that occurred in the village about midnight. We were awakened from a fitful sleep by a terrific commotion in the river as a herd of hippo thrashed about in the water, grunting and gurgling. This in turn seemed to trigger another commotion, this time in the village. Within seconds, scores of fires made an eerie, flickering spectacle against which the villagers could be seen rushing madly about, accompanied by a crescendo of shouting and wailing. Gradually the flames died and the hullabaloo subsided into uneasy silence. In the morning we learnt that the two commotions were entirely unconnected. Apparently, elephant and buffalo entering the plantation had touched off the alarm of the villagers, who, with their bananas the sole means of the community's livelihood, had reacted dramatically to the arrival of their unwelcome guests.

Tinned bacon steak made a welcome change of breakfast diet, but Tony's early morning premonition that 'today was going to be one of those days' proved all-too correct.

A snapped shear-pin in *Charity*'s engine offered the first misfortune just after we had set out. This proved no great problem in itself since we carried spares, but it takes time – especially if you drop the only adjustable spanner into the Tana as Nigel did. Next we experienced another of those hippo turns. Nobody saw the big male until too late, and apparently he too had been looking the other way. Panic reigned in all directions as we caught sight of one another. Smashing towards deep water, the great beast loomed over us and we froze, paralysed with terror. Nigel recovered first and made a grab for the siren, but it is doubtful if the hippo heard the warning blast as the waters closed over the massive pink-brown body.

Zigzagging from one side of the river to the other, our flotilla continued to be dogged by misfortune, *Charity*'s shear-pin snapping twice more that morning as we failed to dodge the many logs that lay in wait just below the surface. The township of Burra was a preliminary destination, for we were to take on petrol supplies there. Informants on the banks, in reply to our repeated 'How far?' enquiries in schoolboy Swahili, invariably offered the standard reply 'Not far', which in Africa can mean any distance at all. Charles and Joseph were pressed into service to help out with these exchanges and a long quickfire conversation in fluent Swahili would ensue. 'What did they say? How far is it?' we would ask at the end of it all. Our Africans looked shamefaced. 'Not far,' they confirmed.

Burra, so big on the map, hardly measured up to metropolis proportions when, eventually, we did set eyes on it. The usual collection of African hutments was, however, enhanced by a corrugated-iron-roofed dispensary, a shop (marked as such on the 1:250 000 map) and a former airstrip. And to us, unaccustomed to so much urbanity, the place, with its concentration of forever curious bystanders, did arouse notions akin to driving into the centre of Birmingham.

Our two-hour visit coincided with a longer one by the Tana Pox Team, and John Axford and Sue were brought across the river by dugout ferry to meet us. A late lunch of biscuits and treacle was consumed to an audience of about two hundred before, refuelled with petrol from the vehicle support group, we gratefully escaped.

With Tony transferred to the vehicles, I moved to *Habari*, now crewed by Mary, Karen, Sandy and Raj. Hardly clear of Burra and we broke a shear-pin, a misfortune promptly laid at my door, though my Jonah-like presence was not to frighten away from a treetop perch what some of us identified as a rare species of owl thought to be nearing extinction in these parts. The Pels owl was later to become the subject of a prolonged jungle search by the ornithologists, and this first sighting – Pels or not – caused some excitement among them.

More about the Pels owl in due course, but its mention here

offers opportunity to report on the further activities of our birdmen and what they had been up to both at and between camps. The bird population, or avifauna, of the Tana had a strong endemic element, many of its species having flying ranges centred upon the river. Our survey, based upon observations, mist-netting and other techniques of bird-capture, hoped to produce a clearer picture of the distribution and population densities of the different types of birds found along the Tana. Already, many birds and bats had been captured, identified and released, their details such as weight, vital statistics, moult and sex noted. A few had been killed and sent to the Nairobi Museum. Also included in the survey was a programme of sound recordings of birds, especially those of uncommon parentage such as the fishing owl, *Scotopelici peli*, now causing so much anticipatory excitement. An attempt to capture such an owl by playing back a recording of its call had been discussed but finally discarded.

Almost as exciting as a glimpse of an earless owl had been that of the first coconut palm of the journey, which provoked a feeling akin to 'crossing the line' as we entered the section of the river looked upon as the 'Lower Tana'. Close to the lone palm we set up our second night's encampment, which was to become infamous by virtue of our first experience of multitudes of mosquitoes. However, both palm tree and mosquitoes signified entry into the humid zone and a step nearer the Indian Ocean.

The night was also notable for buffalo and lion that came very close, causing us to take pains to pretend that our retreat almost into the fire was because of the mosquitoes' dislike of smoke. And, of course, it was the mosquitoes that had kept us awake in the first place; otherwise we would not have heard the grunt of the buffaloes and the coughing of the lions.

A prolonged repair to *Charity*'s motor ensured little progress next morning, though while ashore effecting it, we managed to buy a hand of bananas to reinforce our midday snack. Groups of kindly, friendly people were invariably on view on the river's banks; these were the Pokomo,who would be with us now for many miles. The tribe probably left the coast ahead of the invading Galla around AD 1200, led by a sub-tribe called the Buu. They have been in their present area (centred on the township of Hola) ever since; like other Bantu, their agricultural pursuits revolved around the growing of maize and millet – entirely at the mercy of the Tana. There was once a secret society – Wakiji – whose wives formed their own women's club. Since only Pokomo males are initiated into society, this surely must have been the ultimate in early Woman's Lib.

The basis of existence is the *shamba*, the smallholding which feeds the family. Certain foods such as sugar and tea are bought, but most are grown at home in little allotments, much on the lines of those to be seen on the outskirts of towns in Britain. But in Africa they have a greater sense of purpose, since failure of a *shamba* crop means virtual starvation, and in summer, families often live in their little 'summer houses' and lean-tos to be close to their work. All this makes for a certain freedom – at least in good growing years – from the need for money.

Our good deed for the day was the saving of a wart hog. We came upon the wounded animal by the water's edge, where it had fallen from the sheer bank and trapped itself. With a badly lacerated leg, it was unable to climb the overhang and was in danger of dying of starvation. Wart hogs are courageous when cornered and this one made ominous play with its wicked tusks as we approached. Eventually Nigel and Sandy managed to lasso the beast and drag it up the bank to an unappreciative outpouring of angry grunts interspersed with vicious jabs. At the top we removed the rope and watched it hobble away, though whether we prolonged its life for long was debatable since our action had been watched from the opposite bank by several spear-carrying and hungry-looking Pokomo. A flock of expectant vultures and marabou storks, assembled on a sandbank, formed another audience – one not at all pleased with our deed. The vultures took off in disgust to float upward on invisible thermals rising towards the clear blue sky.

Back in *Charity* with Nigel and Mary, I took over the steering, to discover how quickly one gets the 'feel' of a river and an instinct for the deep channel – which occasionally plays a joke by not being where it has every right to be.

The locating of overnight camping sites was becoming increasingly difficult because of the high cultivated banks on either side of the river. And with dusk, the wind would rise to fleck the waters with wavelets which, hitting our rounded prow, deluged us in spray. The third evening's attempted landfall was more difficult than ever, but eventually we sought refuge close to a banana plantation. Wet enough already, I promptly distinguished myself by missing my footing when going ashore and falling backwards into the river. Otherwise, the night was remarkable for an absence of elephants, lion, buffalo, hippo, mosquitoes and village upheavals.

The township of Hola, which we expected to reached by late morning next day, was a landmark we all looked forward to as a break from the monotony. Circular beehive-shaped houses of straw and wattle appeared among further coconut palms and, new to us, a sprinkling of mango trees.

Every tribe builds its own houses, and though often quite simple in structure, they serve adequately in a climate which is seldom harsh. Weather-proofing is achieved by the use of materials that come readily to hand: the trees of the forests, the grasses of the savannah and the earth of ant-hills. To a large extent the shape of a house is dictated by tradition and controlled by what materials are accessible. Generations of experience have resulted in a wide number of distinctive tribal styles. The ones we had seen, and were to see, might have differed in shape and materials but, more often than not, consisted of a space where food was prepared, a sleeping room containing a low, hard-mud bed or straw matting on the floor, and a cooking room from which smoke escaped through small vents. Sometimes there was a second sleeping room, and occasionally a pen in which animals – chiefly goats – were kept. Inside the houses, apart from the glowing embers of the fire, it was pitch dark, and because of a lack of ventilation, the heat and smoke is all but unbearable for European visitors. But though uncomfortable, these dwellings have the advantage of repelling insects. The cow dung wards off the ticks while the smoke deflects the flies and mosquitoes.

At the approaches to Hola we noticed an increase in communication along and across the river by means of the inevitable dugout canoe. It needs one whole mature tree to make a dugout, the trunk being laboriously chipped out by hand, a job taking perhaps a year or more to complete. Sizes vary and, being a man's prize possession, canoes are handed down from father to son. In every village through which we passed, at least one and often more of these craft were to be seen under construction amid a carpet of chippings. A further threat to the trees indeed, and the threat increases as the population grows.

Hola is well known for its irrigation scheme, originally started by Mau Mau internees of the local prison and now a flourishing source of rice, cotton and other crops. Subsequently, another and even larger scheme was opened near Burra. Unlike Burra, however, Hola is more of a town, with identifiable streets and the very beginnings of a traffic problem. It is here that a second dam complex was envisaged by the Tana River Development Authority.

We spent a couple of hours in the ramshackle town, topping ourselves up with beer and Coke, and our water cans with what purported to be pure water from the irrigation scheme. There were a number of badly constructed concrete buildings in Hola, plus quite a selection of bars, drapery stores and 'butcheries', the last displaying unlovely carcasses of meat crawling with flies. People were everywhere, drawn from their usual pastime of doing nothing to watch us working. They congregated at the 'quayside', where we had drawn up the boats, and some of us had to act as a rearguard to keep an eye on the contents and boats. Light-fingered they may have been but the citizens of Hola made a colourful bunch, all chattering animatedly about the queer tribe that had arrived in town. As Mary and I staggered along holding a five-gallon drum of water between us, my pride suffered grievously as we lurched past two women each carrying even larger containers of water on their heads. And they almost dropped them for laughing, not because their loads were heavier, but at the sight of a man helping a woman!

Another swift dose of urbanity and we were off again, pleased to be out of the stifling concentration of brown mud houses and fly-blown commerce. The countryside was abruptly greener; the undergrowth more lush. River birds called thick-knees flitted ahead of us then froze on twigs, to speed away once more uttering plaintive cries. Two crocodiles slid, soundlessly, into the water from the bank. A fish leapt out of the water straight into *Habari*, and a weaver streaked, in orange and yellow brilliance, across our bow. Banana plantations, some of their stalks clasping green fingers of fruit and small red tassels, alternated with sentinel ranks of maize to clothe the shore, while the perpendicular earthen banks bared their tree-root teeth in fixed grins.

We made our last overnight encampment beneath a copse of mango trees close to the village of Handampia. We never saw the village, but were visited by the headman and his family, who bade us an official welcome. His wife and children helped us carry our provisions ashore and collect firewood, so we invited them all back for supper. It was pleasant to be able to entertain an African woman, since they were customarily left out of such social affairs.

In all our Tana voyages so far we had underestimated distances and taken little account of the inevitable hold-ups along the way. For this the maps, though detailed, must take their share of blame: the blue squiggles are but a fraction of the number of the Tana's actual coils. We were over-optimistic, finding it hard to allow for engine-failure; on the other hand, time was not an enemy: we had no train to catch. And anyway, had we arrived too early we would have been embroiled in the task of raising base camp, surely the prerogative of the sissies of the vehicle support group. Though we had expected to reach our final destination, Kipendi, today, it would again have to be tomorrow.

We made good progress the fourth day in spite of a faulty spark plug in *Charity* and Karen falling out of *Habari*, but it was still late afternoon before we passed the village of Wenje, a mile or two below Kipendi. The open country abruptly contracted and thick jungle closed in to the river's edge. We killed our motors and took to long-rested paddles, gliding through mirror-glass water. A flight of pelicans sailed purposefully towards a dying sun.

Our silent approach paid a dividend. There in a clearing by the Tana's edge was a herd of elephant including young – the first we had seen. They made a superb sight and a curtain-raiser for all that Kipendi was to offer.

7. A Walk in the Forest

If those elephants were an omen, then Kipendi was to prove it to
be no false one. We found a campsite besieged by baboon and
wart hog, alive with the evocative cry of the fish eagle and the
chatter of monkeys. Situated on a double bend of the river, within
sight of Kipendi village, the only eyesore – and that only
temporary – was the huge carcass of a recently dead elephant in
mid-stream, upon which hordes of crocodiles feasted.

Even after only four days of being on the move, to be back to
an organised camp equipped with more-or-less civilised amenities
like earth closets, simple washing facilities and tents pitched in a
straight line came once more as not at all an unpleasant shock.
This was a yearning of which I was secretly beginning to feel
ashamed. Are we never satisfied, we humans? Yet life is made the
fuller by contrasts of living and, without doubt, we would be
experiencing more contrasts and raising the same yearnings over
the weeks ahead. For the first time I began sleeping under canvas
for the sole reason that a tent frame provides support for mosquito
netting – and the Kipendi breed of mosquito was ravenous; our
bare legs were devoured by these pests which, when swatted,
squashed with great smears of our own blood. I suppose the
African outback would not be the African outback without such
torments. Another new affliction was an unfortunate tendency for
the smallest cut or thorn puncture to develop into a suppurating
sore.

I know I speak for all members of the expedition when I say
that Kipendi will be remembered not only as the camp of the wild
animals but of the Pokomo people.Even before we had arrived,
John Richardson and the support group had built a relationship
between themselves and the villagers. They came each morning

not simply to look at us but to help with the camp duties and offer us their friendship. We began to know their names, their activities and their prospects. Whenever Richard went into the thickets to build a hide, he would be accompanied by a retinue of earnest youngsters; when I made a wood-collecting sortie I would find a bevy of kids at my heels, and it was sometimes even difficult to go to the lavatory without a hand-maiden.

Morning greetings between our new-found friends and ourselves developed into a ritual, one that was repeated a thousandfold on jungle tracks, on river banks and wherever a new contact or re-contact was made. 'Jambo!' would come the hearty greeting to evoke an equally cordial reply, 'Habari!', and then we were all into a quickfire question-and-answer game concerning each other's health, affairs and destinations. Many of the Berber peoples of the desert have the same custom, and it is one I find intensely attractive, for in our modern world there is little time or even inclination for such courtesies between strangers.

It was exceedingly clear that the Tana, and in particular the state of the Tana, was a chief local concern. That the river was at its lowest level ever by virtue of the lack of rain and the action of the dams at Kinderamu proposed a direct threat to tribal livelihood and, indeed, lives. This concern is reflected in the songs and dances of the Pokomo, the manner in which they bless their canoes before commencement of a journey, as well as many other features of their natural affinity with the Tana's waters. Even the government irrigation schemes at Burra and Hola were then at risk. It seemed at the time that the solution may have lain in a question of priorities, or perhaps that something could have been achieved by the harnessing of more watersheds to the river in its upper reaches. However, the point of our survey was to lay bare the problems for man and beast, not to solve them.

I would have thought that another problem would have arisen from the nature of the *ingredients* of the Tana, for from Garissa onward the river's contamination was fast increasing. Some would have said that it was surprising that no major epidemic had yet occurred, since many people along the banks drank directly from the river. Though Tana Pox was probably not attributable to this factor alone, the contamination of the water clearly contributed to poor health, and part of John Axford's survey incorporated the location of the host factor of all riverborne diseases.

As well as Kipendi villagers, we were also to meet the good citizens of Wenje, the district centre for the area. They must have known of our close proximity on their own account, but the fact that John Axford, Sue and Gilbert happened to be 'processing' that centre prior to our arrival ensured it. The chief and his son invited themselves to dinner the first evening, though they finally arrived in time for breakfast next morning – with the explanation that elephants had barred their path at dusk forcing them to turn back. This excuse was not as crazy as it sounds, for the footpath to Wenje led through thick scrubland, well populated by elephant, buffalo and rhino, as we were to discover for ourselves. Attacks on lone travellers, particularly by the wily buffalo, were not infrequent and a number of Wenje inhabitants had met their end in this manner. It was noticeable that from here onward African foot travellers were never to venture far without a spear in hand.

The following afternoon we received a mass visitation from the Christian choir of Wenje, who, unheralded, rendered for our benefit a selection of religious and tribal songs of a standard that would not have disgraced an Albert Hall concert. I did not much approve of the missionary zeal of its leader, a young man bearing the crazed stare of a fanatic, who appeared to believe himself to be chief public relations executive for the Good Lord. But the singing itself was sweet and tuneful. It issued from some two dozen children of ages ranging from five to fifteen, and their faces and poses were a picture. The girls wore cotton dresses of vivid colour, and their dark faces made a study in ultra-serious concentration as they went through their repertoire. Some of the songs called for rhythmic stamping and swaying, which was executed with a high degree of precision greatly appreciated by an audience that included a large percentage of the mothers and children of Kipendi as well as ourselves. In the forest the other side of the Tana the fish eagles concluded the grand finale with their own haunting amens.

Not knowing quite how to show our appreciation of this impromptu performance, we invited the choir and the Kipendi section of the audience to lemonade and biscuits and made an appropriate donation to the mission. This must have been the correct gesture, for we in turn were invited to a social evening in Wenje that night.

Because of the danger of aggressive wildlife, we had to make our way to Wenje in bunches as dusk fell and, though unarmed, we raised enough din to scare away the most ferocious of beasts. The chief of Wenje was owner of the only bar in town, and it was to this we were directed following a three-mile perambulation that was to make my future forays to the 'local' a very tame business. The greatest risk in this instance came not from buffalo but from elephant which, though not normally particularly aggressive, had been poached liberally in the area – so that there might well be the odd tusker 'who remembered'. An elephant charges with serious intent only occasionally; more frequently, he will make a false charge or feint at a human. The problem is to decide how serious an elephant bearing down on you really is!

Together with the regular customers of the little bar, we consumed cool Tusker lager laced, all too often, with gifts of palm 'wine' – foul-tasting but potent. The African clientele made us most welcome, and a party developed that spilt over into the village square – to warm up to such a degree that most of the population became involved. As the night wore on, the rhythm of the drums (mostly upturned oil drums) grew wilder and the dancing transcended the pseudo-Western to become primeval tribal, into which we were drawn in a fever of mounting excitement. A full moon bathed the orgy in a phantom-like radiance, while torch beams picked out the star performers. Sweat gleamed on black and white skins, and on the brows of young girls as women and youths each vied to out-perform the other in a mêlée of repetitive contortions and gyrations.

The music of tribal dances is primarily based on percussive rhythms. For thousands of years the African has fulfilled his need for music with the throbbing drum. Today the need is just as great, and skilful drummers can achieve just the tempo to take people out of the normal conscious state so that their actions are, instead, controlled by beat. The dancers give the impression of having inexhaustible energy, becoming lost to themselves in a world where the subconscious rules. They dance like souls possessed, the fluidity of their limb movements seemingly activated by an imponderable vigour. The music, often bound up with religion, may be composed as a prayer to bring rain, to bless a hunting expedition, to cure an illness, to ensure that a young girl will bear children or, more likely in Wenje, to encourage a resumption of the Tana's full blessings.

One such animated prayer was the Circumcision Dance performed by the older women, who in a frenzy of swaying bodies, flowing garments and wild laughter shook their ample extremities in a ferment of expressive movement. Like Christians being flung to hungry lions, we white visitors were pushed into the pulsating, swaying circle to prance haplessly around a corral of grinning faces in a fetid atmosphere of sweat and stale palm wine. What we were supposed to be dancing we had not the faintest idea. Returning to camp in the early hours of the morning, our group, supporting a well-sloshed Joseph and Charles, spared little thought for prowling terrors of the jungle, though a more temperate group, home-bound earlier under John Richardson, had allegedly met a pride of lions and beat a hasty retreat.

Fascinating though these first contacts with our Pokomo brethren had been, it was our first real contact with big game that excited us. Our very first night we were to see some fourteen elephants tiptoe down to the drinking place on the river close to where our boats were drawn up. Most of us were asleep at the time but the two zoologists were as nocturnal as some of the animals they had come to study, and they woke us up. Before long, a score of eyes were watching the great beasts quenching their mighty thirsts.

The African elephant is larger than the Indian species. A bull weighs up to six tons and stands twelve feet at the shoulder, yet they can move unbelievable quietly. They are highly intelligent creatures and have a life span – if allowed it – of about sixty years. It is not universally realized that when an elephant has lost its last set of teeth or they have grown too worn to chew, a young bull will often keep fierce guard over its older kin. When it drinks, the elephant sucks water into the trunk and then blows it into its mouth and down its throat. The babies use their mouths, quite often lying on their sides in the water to do this. All elephants are inordinately fond of water. They bathe every day if they can, and are very noisy bathers in contrast to their uncannily silent movements on land. It must be admitted that they are frequently destructive in their eating habits. They will push over small trees, eat a few leaves and wander on.

Another night we were able to observe, by the light of a full moon and through the image intensifier, a herd of forty zebras working their way slowly and with infinite caution down to the river. It was an incredibly beautiful sight, but we had to lie very still, since one sound would have caused them to disappear in the twinkling of an eye. The zebra is, together with the giraffe, a distant relative of the hippo, though unlike either is known to suffer heart attacks if abruptly frightened. In East Africa there is the common variety and a species known as Grevy's, slightly taller with larger ears and narrower stripes. As we watched each animal quench its thirst, it would raise its head, listen and then saunter off, so that for more than half an hour there was a constant coming and going at the watering place.

I participated in a number of night observation stalks in the dense forest behind the camp. On one we caught a glimpse of an elephant in a thicket and waited, hopefully, for the animal to emerge. To go in after it would have been dangerous, particularly as we had been told that a family of buffaloes lived there. A dozen bushbuck flitting across a clearing rewarded us for our pains, however, their beautifully marked bodies flowing with a movement that was a joy to behold. Bushbabies we saw too, but not for the shooting on this occasion, and a civet, a long-bodied, wiry-coated animal as large as a medium-size dog – though looking more like a cat.

Returning to camp, we froze at the sound of snapping twigs, expecting something of the calibre at least of a black rhino to emerge. Instead, a tiny dik-dik, barely a foot high, stood in the middle of the path as though hypnotized, then raced into the cover of the trees followed by its mate. They never go singly, these dik-dik; perhaps because they are so small and defenceless each acts as sentinel for the other. Richard, accompanying us with his inquisitive camera, managed a fine flash photograph of a nightjar on its ground-floor nest of dead leaves. Mesmerized by our the bird simply sat there allowing us to tiptoe right up to it.

We were now in the territory of the mangabey and of the colobus monkey, two primates of the monkey family, the observation of which was one of the zoological quests of the expedition. Another, of course, was a sighting of the Pels owl, which some of us had optimistically reported seeing. However, Ken was too fastidious a person to go in for half-measures, so he spent a whole night across the river, lying up alone in his tent watching activity in the thick undergrowth. One such night he found quite enough: he returned with the dawn somewhat white around the gills, for it had been an unnerving experience. But he reported the sighting of a mangabey. This crested, grey monkey is found only along the Tana River, and resembles the long-tailed, more general variety, except for the pointed tuft on the top of the head. It feeds on fruit in the trees or on insects at ground level and alters its habits accordingly. The colobus – while we are on the subject – is another uncommon monkey, or at least the breed that lives along part of the Tana is uncommon. The common variety is jet-black in colour with a magnificent white mantle, white face and white-tipped bushy tail. All their lives they seldom descend from the trees. However, it is the red variety that is the rarer one, and this was the subject of our quest.

Tony too spent much of his time hidden deep in the undergrowth at all hours of the day and night examining snakes and beetles. He once found himself surrounded by eight elephants, his only concern being that he might be late for supper. He spoke of crickets as big as man's fist, but I refused to believe him until I found two of these harmless creatures in my rucksack while repacking it one evening.

The day came when I left Kipendi after yet another incomplete sojourn at a base camp. The diversion this time was an 80-mile foot safari in the company of John Richardson and Sandy to the subsequent base camp at Hewani. Originally it was to have been a larger party but volunteers were hard to come by – an 80-mile plod, unarmed, through game-infested bush and jungle beneath a burning sun not being everyone's cup of tea. Our brief was a multiple one. We were to observe the crested mangabey and red colobus primates and report their locations. We were to track down and observe the elusive Pels and report its location. We were to look for a species of butterfly – a gold-banded forester – which changes its hue the further south it lives, and report on the colour change and its location. Finally, we were to leave messages of the cleft stick variety along the river indicating anything of profound interest on either bank which could be investigated further by the boat contingent during the onward voyage from Kipendi a couple of days hence.

Being independent of vehicle support groups or boat party stores, we had to carry our own equipment and provisions for at least a week. I had packed my rucksack, carefully selecting only the minimum of spare clothing and necessities. The day before, I had sprained an ankle, while the opposite ankle, pierced by a thorn, had turned septic. Thus I was not in my best walking condition. John came up to me and dumped a plastic sack heavy with tinned rations at my feet. 'Yours,' he said laconically, giving me a funny look. I laughed. 'For a moment I thought you were being serious,' I responded. 'I am,' said John. Repacked, it was as much as I could do to get the whole bag of tricks onto my shoulders. It had been the same on the mountain, but there the temperatures were not in the nineties and my feet were in better trim.

Mary devotedly covered my sores in evil-smelling ointments and filled our pockets with Paludrine tablets. Yet she seemed quite pleased to see us go. I wondered why, and then remembered that John, Sandy and I were her most regular and persistent customers; full of septic sores, bites and heat rashes. And now she was sending us off on a death march!

At least we got a rousing send-off. Derek and Clive Bromhill, Andrew and Richard, all festooned with cameras, snapped away at our departing backs as we forced a path through bush and banana plantation – and a knife-edged grass from which zebra ticks had a field day transferring themselves to our bare legs. We negotiated small groups of *manyattas*, around which families of Pokomo sat cooking or relaxing and, like the Pied Piper, our followers multiplied as curious children attached themselves to the cavalcade. Stepping over pots and pans, walking between thatched 'igloo' houses, I felt something of an intruder into private lives, but everyone was exceedingly gracious, polite and helpful; some villages even offered us mangoes as we stumbled by.

With our retinue finally reduced to just Andrew and Richard, we came upon a clearing that contained the bizarre sight of a large luxury caravan, complete with dining-room exquisitely laid for dinner; silver cutlery, cut-glass decanters, lace doilies, the lot. While we were goggling through the window at the apparition, the owner arrived in a Land Rover with two African bearers carrying guns and a dead geranuk between them. I glimpsed Andrew's face contort into a mask of disapproval at the sight of the slaughtered gazelle, its delicate rufous-coloured flanks streaked with dried blood. But the impending storm abated with an invitation to partake of a cold beer. The hunter, it transpired, was one Franz Lang, a German organiser of up-market safaris, who was doing very-nicely-thank-you conducting prosperous businessmen on trophy-hunting expeditions so that millionaire drawing rooms could be decorated with antelope heads between the Rembrandts. The iced beer was nectar and Herr Lang an interesting conversationalist. We could hardly criticise his vocation following his promise to bring to the camp an animal for the pot – and he was as good as his word.

We left, hugely refreshed, and continued along a track, to come upon an elephant graveyard – a sort of Stonehenge of bones in which John was soon in his element sorting out and identifying the bits and pieces of the skeletal jigsaw puzzle. It was here that the final members of our sending-off party left us, a boneyard being, I suppose, as good a place as any from which to bid us farewell.

The moment our erstwhile companions disappeared, I cut a new notch in the yardstick of my African experiences. Here we were, just the three of us, alone, unarmed, uncertain, in the savage African outback. All around us, unseen but undeniably present, were the beasts of the jungle, river and bush. Here was the most abundant and varied life still existing on earth; we were surrounded by the imminence of death: the horns of rhino and buffalo and elephant, the teeth and fangs of crocodile and snake, the claws of the great cats. Varied emotions licked the pit of my stomach: excitement, insecurity, alarm and sheer dread.

Yet the track that was to lead us to the village of Maroni, an outpost and last habitation, we imagined, before the lush jungle of a newly designated but yet 'untamed' game reserve, showed us no more than baboons, Sykes monkeys, jackals and dik-dik. The jackals we were surprised to see, for they are mainly nocturnal animals. On John's recommendation we walked in single file, keeping a sharp eye open for movement and marking the position of climbable trees. Those initial hours every bush held menace; each sigh of the breeze in dead foliage was a lion tensed to spring. Bulbuls flickered in the branches of trees agitating the leaves, to cause me involuntary gasps, and snake tracks in the sandy soil kept my eyes darting everywhere. A bird called a tauraco flew up close to my feet – to give me near heart failure, the afternoon sun glinting through its blood-red wings.

Maroni was a near-dead village, a community of deserted mud houses dilapidated or collapsed. A prosperous-looking Christian church topped by a golden cross on its stubby tower made an incongruous impact as well as shade for a goat chewing firewood in the imposing portal. But Maroni was still kicking. As we halted in the square beneath the canopy of a tree, we were aware of a family staring at us from an aperture in a mud wall, and could feel other inquisitive eyes boring into our backs. Using sticks of dead wood, we made a small fire on which to brew a cup of tea to go with our biscuit and squirt of greengage jam. Whilst we were doing so a handsome young African, spear in hand, materialised to give us instruction on how to get to Makere Ya Gwano, some four miles distant, where the game warden lived. There lay our destination for the first day's walk.

I felt vaguely annoyed. Here we were, getting to grips with Africa, and along comes someone not the least surprised to see us and able to converse amicably in near-Harrovian English. This, plus afternoon tea in the village square. All we needed now was a silver teapot, cucumber sandwiches and a Maroni First Eleven cricket side to wreck everything.

I was in this bolshie mood when we bumped into the elephants. It was quite obvious that none of us had been observing properly, for, abruptly, the great beasts were all around us. Eight of them, with two babies, were over on the left, a couple of tuskers were munching the scrub on the right; only the track ahead and behind was empty. Personally I was all for minding our own business and pretending we hadn't seen them, but John and Sandy, of course, had other ideas. John, aware of his responsibilities as leader of the patrol, only wanted to take photographs, but young Sandy, off the leash from the more staid members of his team, was up to no good. The family group of elephants over on the left offered the greatest photographic attraction, and we zigzagged from bush to bush to get near. John took a few shots, then Sandy performed a kind of jig before the brutes, attempting presumably to alter their docile expressions for the camera. That they didn't much approve of Sandy's performance was made quite plain, and a charge, feint or in earnest, became all too likely. Then they seemed to have second thoughts, turned tail and disdainfully stalked away. My relief was profound.

The track led straight towards a dense patch of jungle that promised all manner of surprises, but to reach it we had to run the gauntlet of more elephants. They were everywhere. Some were close to the path, half-hidden behind clusters of scrub, and we had to veer away to keep our distance from them. As long as elephant can see you everything is plain sailing. They don't like being caught off guard.

A gazelle got up suddenly and sped towards the horizon. Peter's, Thomson's or whatever, there is an elegance and dignity in all gazelles and antelopes and this one was no exception. But we were not going his way. Somewhere behind the thick belt of jungle was the abode of the warden and a European or two we wanted to contact. One of them was Jim Alloway, who was undertaking an elephant survey, and we were eager to tap some of his knowledge. We entered the gloom of enveloping foliage.

At once we were aware of the birds. The trees were alive with their screech, trill and song. Something with iridescent green feathers and a breast that flashed into flame caught my eye, but mostly it was just noise. Rounding a substantial mound of undergrowth that looked like over-indulgent rhododendron, we walked into the rump of another elephant. It never saw us. Or if it did it gave no sign. An enormous beast, its form loomed over us as we crept away. There were others among the thick scrubwood and we had the very devil of a job avoiding them. One did catch sight of us, trumpeted loudly and made towards me, but stopped in its tracks wildly flapping tattered leather ears as if in anger. A baboon screamed and hyenas wailed like fog-bound ships. All through this tableau of sound, the other elephants noisily ripped off branches and toppled young trees as they devoured the stalks and leaves.

The sun lay low in the sky as we came into a clearing, where two bungalows made up the sum total of Nakere Ya Gwano. A herd of frightened impala streamed by within a few feet, almost knocking us over in their flight, and we peered uneasily into the dusk, wondering what it was that had frightened them. The bungalows proved to be unoccupied though plainly in use. While we waited to see if anyone would turn up, we ambled down to the river bank to renew our acquaintance with the Tana and found a herd of five hippo, four crocodiles and half a dozen zebra close to the water's edge. In a welter of stampeding hooves and farts they took off at our approach.

The first humans to appear were Jim Alloway's two servants and the brother of the game warden, who spoke good English. He confirmed that Alloway would in fact be returning shortly with a couple of guests from an elephant observation stalk. (We didn't think he'd have to go far for this since one specimen was grazing noisily just yards from his front door.)

Jim Alloway turned out to be a lean young American when he eventually arrived in an ancient Toyota. He was also not at all pleased to see us. The guests – both Englishmen – showed more amiability, though it was the game-warden's brother who offered us the use of a tent, situated 200 yards away and reserved for official game conservation visitors.

We made a fire and cooked ourselves a substantial tinned meal for the dual purpose of assuaging an appetite and lightening our rucksacks. The mosquitoes were equally hungry, whilst to add to the discomfort, my inflamed ankles throbbed and ached in unison. We must have been in a breeding ground of those monster crickets too, for they were everywhere; one even managed to join me in my sleeping bag. And if all this hadn't contributed to keeping me awake, the night noises of the enveloping jungle and river would certainly have done so. Hippos burping, lions sighing, elephants grazing, small mammals squeaking and night birds creating such a racket that they set off most of the day birds as well. It was all something like Disneyland on the fourth of July.

The next day we sallied forth to see Jim Alloway and friends again. He must have slept better than I had, for he was more disposed towards us than he had been earlier. It was arranged that he should drive John back to Kipendi later in the day to report the attractions of the reserve, so that Derek Bromhall and a photographic team could stop off as they came by in the boats. Alloway rather reluctantly agreed to this on condition that he and his guests could attend supper at the camp. This business transacted, we decided to spend the rest of the day investigating some of the livestock that had contributed to the night's sound effects.

At first we followed the shore of the river, enjoying – in my case at any rate – a certain security in the knowledge that the steep bank could offer some protection in the event of sudden attack by something of the calibre of buffalo or rhino – particularly buffalo, for which, I don't mind admitting, I held a healthy respect. Experienced hunters will smile at my alarm, but then hunters have guns and know what they are about. Of course, if a land animal failed to get you on the bank then a croc might do something about it under the bank. But things don't happen quite like this, though one's imagination in these circumstances works overtime.

Turning away from the river, we entered an eerie world of shadow: tall trees rejecting the strong sunlight. We began noting each trunk in earnest, assessing the branches as a ladder upwards and away from some fanciful pair of viciously wielded horns. But every cluster of undergrowth we passed yielded nothing more deadly than dik-dik, to become just one more empty chamber in a game of zoological Russian roulette. A rustle of leaves would jerk us into fleeing in different directions, but it would be only a stirring of monkeys as they leapt from branch to branch, twittering as they did so. Forest guinea fowl, chortling fiendishly as they ran across the path made us jump. What had frightened them? Baboon, wart hog, elephant, lion, *buffalo*? We stood at the base of our chosen tree refuge, waiting and listening for something to emerge before sheepishly regrouping.

A putrid smell led us to a dead elephant in a clearing. This one had met his end but a few days earlier; the corpse was revolting in death – blown up with gas, crawling with maggots, a turgid liquid emanating from the bowels. Sickened, we turned away to re-enter the twilight, a patch of jungle dense with grey-green lichen festooning the trees. Again, the strange, mournful call of a hyena arose. The call may have been part of its mating ritual or an announcement that it was being stalked by a lion. The king of the beasts is thought to loathe the hyena, perhaps because the lion is haunted by the presentiment that, in old age, those same hyena who fear him now will pull him to the ground and tear him to pieces as they sometimes do his cubs. The spotted hyena is, however, not the coward it is reported to be; it hunts in a pack and will drag down a wildebeest. Spotted hyenas have the strongest jaws of all mammals, and their boldness grows with the night: then they will even bite a piece from the limb of a sleeping man.

There came another kerfuffle in the tree tops. A pack of monkeys leapt across a gap between two branches, then another and another. We stared up at them, shading our eyes from the sun that pierced the shield with daggers of light. Without a shadow of doubt these were colobus, the shyest and most acrobatic of the tree dwellers, moving with great rapidity and skill. They travel through the forest, venturing out to the furthest extremities of branches and hurling themselves into the air to land with a great curtsying and swishing of boughs twenty or thirty feet away. Black with a white fringe draped low across the back like an academic hood, tails a long bush of pure white thicker than a fox's brush, and black faces severely framed in white as though they wore the closest fitting of a nun's coif. Yes, these were certainly colobus, though still not the red ones.

They were gone in an instant, so we sat down on a log to see if more would come along. Idly I watched a butterfly hover on a twig then flutter a few inches off the ground to another perch. A beautiful insect, the wings were ... I looked again with a more analytical eye and, glory be, there before us was the golden-banded forester! The three of us dashed about trying to catch it, and in the process disturbed two more. All that was wanted now was a mangabey and a Pels owl to parade themselves and we could go home and put our feet up. Then a wart hog dashed by, grunting indignantly, and I was surprised to see John half-way up a tree – more surprised still that I hadn't beaten him to it.

We came out of the gloom into the sunshine again, marvelling how a little brilliance can restore one's equilibrium. It was a clearing of dead trees, stark skeletons of rotting wood that could have offered morbid fancies but for the midday sun. A maniacal snicker did have us imagining shapes again but the elusive hyena was not to be seen. This one may have been the more timorous striped variety, which local people say changes its sex every year. If true (which I doubt) it may or may not have something to snicker about. Sandy climbed a tree – voluntarily – to look for elephants that had advertised their presence by leaving visiting cards of still-steaming droppings (which, incidentally, when dry make good fuel for camp fires) but, again, nothing was in sight.

A tornado of vultures led us to the river and along it to a sandbank alive with marabous, wooly-necked storks, two crocodiles and more vultures. In their midst lay a pathetic grey mound that was another not-long-dead elephant. Squabbling and squawking, the birds were tearing at the main carcass, except for the marabou storks, which cannot tear the meat off but have to wait for the crumbs, and which stood quietly by with beady, frustrated eyes. The biggest vultures had taken command and were chasing intruders away, stalking in Prussian-style goose-step fashion towards them, the big capes of their wings spread out menacingly. The air was filled with the noise of gluttony. It was horrible, macabre, yet engrossing to watch, and when one thought about it not ferocious at all – simply using as food whatever had died, leaving the earth clean and fresh. All the same, we shooed them away to give them indigestion for their pains; but the moment we walked off they were back, minus the crocodiles, who played it more coolly.

To the croon of a distant lion we crossed one of the Tana's tributaries and, at the edge of the river, beheld a mighty crocodile – the daddy of them all – fast asleep beneath an overhang of the bank. John crept forward, intent upon obtaining a photographic close-up. In this he succeeded brilliantly, barely managing to get its full eighteen feet in the viewfinder. Unable to resist it, John uttered a low 'Boo!' and the croc had the rudest awakening of its life. It lifted into the air, all four feet frantically paddling, and was gone. A moment later the overhang gave way and, in a shower of sand, John found himself where the reptile had been seconds before.

Returning the way we had come, we glimpsed more colobus. They gave us little chance to identify them but the afternoon sun had shown up the ginger-red crown on their heads before the monkeys had thrown themselves out of sight: red colobus. Our day's perambulation had not been in vain.

The game warden had returned during our absence and we were able to call on him at his office. And here, to our chagrin, was another initially hostile character. Suspicion appeared to be at the root of his unfriendliness. He was displeased to learn that we were occupying the visitor's tent, and when John came to the bit about the expedition's desire to film in the reserve he exploded. Expounding regulation after regulation concerning governmental permission, which we were quite certain Derek had obtained, he found every reason to forbid probing cameras onto his patch. What with the unsociability of the few authoritative humans we had so far come across in the reserve, combined with the number of dead elephants, I began to think nasty thoughts. I was to later meet the warden in happier circumstances and find him quite charming. But that was on neutral territory outside the game reserve.

At dusk the warden, Jim Alloway and his two guests, plus John and Sandy crammed in the old Toyota and whirled away towards Kipendi in an angry storm of dust. I volunteered to stay behind since someone had to. They'd be back before nightfall, they said.

Left to my own devices, I built up the fire and prepared to chalk up yet another experience in my life. From three in the jungle, here was I by my own sweet self. And never have I felt so alone in all my days. Lonely no, alone yes. And there is a difference. Loneliness is a gradual melancholic emotion; being alone in such circumstances can build up into something approaching stark terror. Tripping down to the Tana to refill a bucket with water, I found a monster crocodile leering at me, together with a quartet of hippos blowing raspberries. And before they disappeared, more reluctantly than usual, I noticed the expressions on their faces were quite different: a sort of there's-only-one-of-you-now-isn't-there look. I retired, chastened, to the tent and attempted to cheer myself up with the prospect of three tinned treacle puddings for supper and a bottle of beer that John and Sandy promised they would bring back with them later.

Throughout the hot day the elephants had been musing and swaying in some cool recess of the forest, but now they began to rouse themselves and drift to their night-time feeding grounds like great grey shadows, their bodies moving through the undergrowth so gently that the only sound was the faintest whisper of leaves rustled by a tiny breeze. Sometimes a herd of elephants will move so silently through the tangled undergrowth that you are only aware of their presence by the one noise over which they have no control – the prolonged, often-sonorous rumblings of their stomachs.

A herd of the great beasts began grazing their way in line abreast, moving in the manner of a fleet of battleships, slowly but relentlessly towards me, munching raucously, pulling great chunks out of the vegetation. As the line approached, the nocturnal noises of the jungle abruptly turned to full volume, each howl, squawk and scream a drumbeat of menace. The hairs on my neck rose to attention. From the direction of the Tana my riverine companions got into the act with a chorus of belches that defy description.

The trouble was I couldn't *see* anything. I am something of a man of action: let me see the foe and I'll have a go at him. I searched the night shadows till my eyes ached, but nothing moved. The fire shrank to a glow; to replenish it would mean a lone walk towards those evil noises, which was out of the question. Frantically I blew on the dying embers and raised a tiny flame to kindle a spark of courage within my breast. A military maxim arose in my mind, offering a clarion call to action: *To attack is the best form of defence*.

The nearest of the elephants loomed out of the darkness; a shadowy outline as big as a house against the greater darkness. I picked up a faggot that had burst into feeble flame, wielded it about my head, uttered a banshee war cry last employed in my one and only World War Two bayonet charge, and hurled myself at the foe. I felt better now. My tormentors were phantoms no longer.

I knew where I was going.

The big tusker was too intent upon stuffing its face with trunkfulls of fodder to notice me at first. Then it looked round, perceived a miniature ape-like figure fast approaching emitting strange noises, opened wide its eyes in disbelief, turned and bolted. A thunder of hooves, a smashing of undergrowth and, what was more, the whole herd was routed. To consolidate my triumph I flung my smouldering faggot at the retreating elephantine rear, and had to spend the next half-hour extinguishing the forest fire I'd started.

I would say here and now that my actions are not to be recommended to anyone getting into a similar situation. Remaining quite still would have been a wiser course. But you live and learn in this jungle business.

My foes never moved far away. I heard them resume their interrupted feasting over at the other side of the warden's house. They were still there close on midnight when I heard the Toyota returning and realized that an unsuspecting John and Sandy would walk right into the middle of the herd *en route* to the tent. I crept along the path, moving from bush to bush with sounds of munching all around me, to gain Alloway's house. In this way I managed to guide the two back by a circuitous but less risky route.

We sat round the recharged embers of the fire sipping the beer they had brought, and I was to learn with some chagrin that the visit to the camp had coincided with the consuming of a buffalo donated by the German, Lang, and that I was the only one to have missed the party. (I subsequently obtained some satisfaction from the number of consumers who went down with the 'runs' following this overindulgence!) But John had reported our findings, and arrangements had been amicably made for the proposed incursion into the reserve by a photo team of expedition members. To the usual renderings we crept into our mosquito netting and sleeping bags.

Again it was elephants that wrecked any hopes of a peaceful night. We listened uneasily to them tiptoeing about, right up to the guy-ropes of the tent, and any moment I expected a great foot to descend through the canvas – which goes to show how little I knew about elephants. In the morning we discovered that one of them had sucked dry a whole bucket of water positioned by the tent flap in readiness for our morning tea. There had been two bucketfuls there, the other untreated, and as luck would have it the animal had consumed the treated one, which meant we had to go through the whole purifying performance again. And to make matters worse I drank a whole mugful of the *wrong* stuff – straight from the disease-ridden Tana – before we had worked out which was which.

We left following a delayed breakfast and a session of first aid in which John had the odious task of extracting about a pint of pus from my poisoned ankle. We moved south via an oxbow – where the river had changed course – and across the territory of the game reserve with commendable rapidity but still considerable caution. Here and there were tiny communities of Pokomo living in stockaded acres of cultivation and *shambas*. In a sandy hollow we came upon the spore of what Sandy took to be a leopard. These cats are rarely seen, being frequently nocturnal. Their favourite food is baboon and there were plenty of those about, yapping at us at intervals. Another cat we kept our eyes peeled for was the cheetah, for these, though elusive and fast, hunt by day. Nearing the village of Baomo, a confusion of tracks nearly led us astray, but a charming lady stoically undertaking a man's job of reroofing a house, directed us with much graceful gesticulation.

Baomo was an interesting little place. No more than a compact group of mud and wattle-daub houses, it exuded the atmosphere of true African tribal village more than most. We were at once the centre of attraction for a host of children, their shy, wide-eyed faces radiant with excitement. To the eldest we gave a 'to whom it may concern' letter requesting that it be delivered 'in person' to any of our compatriots who might be stopping off in the village. This was more for the boy's benefit than anything else, and it was a joy to see the look of pride suffuse his face with the sudden shouldering of responsibility. Beneath a huge mango tree lay a massive dug-out canoe under construction among a thick carpet of wood chippings: the co-operative effort of the village males. We decided that Baomo would make a good subject for Derek's camera so, out of sight of the children, placed a message on a stick and poised it on the bank of the river. But either the message fell into the wrong hands or it simply fell, for the boats never did see it and Baomo was denied its hour of fame.

In spite of steadily eating our way through the tinned rations, our packs remained consistently heavy, our sweaty backs indelibly staining the fabric. On the credit side, we were seldom without the reassuring presence of a tribesman, who would appear in the most unlikely of places and always as we were having trouble deciphering our outdated map. From dense jungle to banana plantation, from riverbank to bushland we trudged, my ankles standing up well to the heavy punishment. Twice we were provided with an armed escort by fellow-travellers who would insist upon accompanying us carrying a spear at the ready, appalled at our own lack of weaponry. These courteous fellows guided and protected us through many a hostile strip of forest to put us on the right path to a neighbouring village. They asked for nothing in return but were appreciative of the cigarettes and few boiled sweets we were able to offer them.

We would have been more than appreciative ourselves of their protective measures during early afternoon when we made the brief but dramatic acquaintance of an injured rhino. The meeting occurred in a dense portion of jungle bordering the Tana. The thicker the undergrowth the more care we applied, and we were dutifully marking our respective climbable trees in the forbidding gloom when it happened. We were walking parallel to the river some fifty yards from it, when Sandy, in the lead, raised his hand to bring us to a halt and an instant state of readiness. I saw the animal first: simply a large hindquarters behind a palm clump. 'I think it's an aardvark, I'm not sure,' I whispered in a voice not my own. John and Sandy were better at the animal backside recognition business. 'It's a bloody rhino!' they exclaimed in unison. 'Quick, Drop your rucksacks and up your trees. Hurry!' This put the wind up me to such an extent that I was unable to disentangle myself from my harness, and while struggling to do so failed to make the silent getaway intended. The cymbals of a military band could hardly have made more din as the tin mug and mess-tin strapped to various buckles clashed together, and, hardly surprisingly, the rhino turned about in some concern. As I finally shook free of my harness I glimpsed the beast's head lower for a charge, and it came to me, even in that instant, that for the rhino caught between the river and a trio of dithering humans, the humans were the line of least resistance. I saw the great horn point straight at me: I turned and ran.

The smash of trampled undergrowth, coupled with a series of low-pitched snorts, drove me forward on winged feet. My chosen tree became the single goal at the further end of a vortex of my life. Nor was I alone in my fleeing, for in the next instant, all three of us were struggling up the same tree. In spite of my advanced age I had beaten John to it by a short head, to scramble up the slender boughs neck and neck with the agile young Sandy.

From a safe height we peered down to see the bewildered rhino hurtle by beneath us and glimpsed a spear wound in its flank. The Black Rhinoceros is a solitary animal and a vegetarian, but will charge and overrun anything – even a train – that its poor eyesight is able to make out.

The danger seemingly passed, we descended shakily from our eyrie and re-shouldered our discarded loads. But hardly had we ventured more than a hundred yards when we found ourselves cheek-by-jowl with the same iron-clad bottom. Recognition was mutual and instantaneous, and once more we took off, this time in all directions. But climbable trees had abruptly become scarce, and I had to run back to the river bank before I could find one. Behind me the rhino hesitated, unable to fathom what was going on. It remained stationary, ears cocked and grotesque head raised, nostrils dilated as it searched the wind. Uttering a couple of blast-like snorts, looping a stringy tail over its rump, the beast trotted away at a slinging, zigzag pace through the trees, to wheel round and stare once more. Then it gave us up as a bad job and lumbered off.

The path led out of the trees to a patch of bush. In it we brewed a cup of tea, which, with a couple of biscuits liberally spread with marmalade, went some way to restoring our shattered morale. A herd of more than forty oryx and waterbuck occupied our attention in the late afternoon and as the sun ripened and lost its sting we performed a little stalking of our own. Oryx are powerful and fierce. They are beautiful beasts, reddish-brown in colour with black-and-white face markings. Their companions in this instance were waterbuck, which wear friendlier expressions, shaggier coats of brownish-grey and a tail their creator forgot to complete. The herd had smelt our presence but could not see us as we crawled towards them intent on getting as near as possible for a photograph. Only when we could see the whites of their eyes did they catch on. Promptly the herd wheeled and thundered off to less disturbed pasture.

Pressing on, we forged a way through some dingy pine and palm forestry, walking at speed, conscious of the fast approaching night. According to the map Mnazini was a village of a stature that might rise to spare accommodation for the weary traveller. But we were fast losing confidence in the map, though the absence of big stretches of green were no fault of the cartographer. Instead, it was another sign of the times and evidence of the Pokomo's destruction of his forest. Close to the river again, we finally managed to obtain our bearings and strode on with new-found confidence.

Mnazini was, in fact, something of a Wild West village, complete with one main street, a beer house and a couple of shops with colourful façades in compensation for the drabness behind them. Interspersed between the mud huts were an occasional plaster wall and rash of corrugated iron sheets that raised the village from a rural community to an urban one. At the end of the street was the faithful Tana, tolerating a fleet of dug-out ferries, open-air laundering facilities and, upon its scarred banks, a sort of village riviera in which everybody sat around in cheerful inactivity. Placed at a strategic position betwixt beer house and river was the public loo which, I was to discover, produced cockroaches of such size as to constipate a European for life.

For our next few days' hiking we would no longer be in an inadequately protected game reserve, though this fact would make little difference to events. In a way it was no more than a case of moving from a frying pan into a fire.

8. The Search for an Earless Owl

The warden said: 'Our reserve has only recently been gazetted but, one day, we expect big things. We shall be more wild than Meru and the other long-established game parks. We want people to come and see the wildlife and environment of the riverine forest, which will be faithfully preserved and protected from our own people; but the reasons are conservation more than display – which will make us different from the well-patronised parks. Nevertheless, we *want* publicity.' He sounded enthusiastic – quite different from the negative tone displayed earlier – as he warmed to his subject. As if aware of his previous sullenness, the chap had taken the trouble to catch up with us at Mnazini. 'The reserve occupies 170 square kilometres astride the Tana,' he went on, 'and is likely to be included in UNESCO's Man and the Biosphere Programme for the conservation of representative and unique ecosystems.' He looked hard at me as though a point had been made, so I nodded sagely. We were sitting in the dark on hard chairs on the pavement outside our temporary abode in the high street, as everyone else was doing in Mnazini.

'The forests are the home of a number of rare animals, including the Tana River varieties of red colobus and crested mangabey. The reserve is also estimated to contain about 55 per cent of the remaining population of both primates.' I was on safer ground here, for the subject was one upon which I had carried out my homework. To hear people talk, one would think the country was one vast game reserve cluttered in places with annoying humans. In fact, both the bush and its game (not to mention the humans) are a nuisance as well as an asset.

In economic terms, big game is big business. But wild animals pose a number of problems for Kenya. As already made clear, they can be a great nuisance to the people who live near them. The loss of a few cattle or the laying waste of a field or two may not be very serious to a reasonably prosperous farmer; to a poor man relying for six months' food on a small *shamba*, one night's incursion by game can spell disaster. Fencing is far too expensive for all except a few.

Both farmers and game have their rights and they can be mutually exclusive on a large as well as a small scale. The Tana River irrigation schemes are a case in point. On the one hand, enclosed farmland along the river would stop game getting at water. On the other, a whole new source of food – and increased water supplies – might attract enough game to overrun and wreck the whole scheme.

Game reserves are, by themselves, no answer. Kenya's wildlife population had been safeguarded less by sufficient wildlife sanctuary than by a reasonable degree of safety outside the reserves and parks. However, this safeguard may be a fleeting one, and it will be necessary to increase the number and area of the sanctuaries. This may merely clash with farming interests, though should the animals be allotted areas too poor for farmers – and thus the animals themselves – in which to flourish, there would be no advantage to man nor beast. More important – though again not a complete answer – is the education of the public to regard game as a possession of which they should feel proud. This is being done through schools and on television; but the Pokomo, one feels, will take a lot of convincing. The problems loomed again, spreading to territories beyond just that of the Tana; in fact, progress solves one problem only to reveal two more – and here was a multiple one to add to the investigative role of our humble expedition.

I asked about the communities within the reserve and how they fitted into the scheme of things. The warden's reply smacked of oil on troubled waters. 'We are transferring some,' he admitted. 'Many families have, in fact, been allocated new homes in this very village. But for the others we are relying on education; teaching them not to spoil the environment that is their fortune.' I guessed – rightly as it turned out – that I would be hearing more on this topic.

Inevitably, the subject of poaching arose. The warden could recollect the time when this activity was carried out with spears and traps alone, the procurement of meat being the sole object. All that changed in the 1970s as a fresh wave of poaching swept through African parks. The greed for ivory was nothing new, of course. In North Africa it led to the disappearance of elephants during the Middle Ages. And this century has seen their extinction in Somalia, Gambia, Guinea-Bissau and other African countries.

What prompted a new demand for ivory, though, was the uncertainty of international finance when the dollar's relationship to gold was broken in 1972. On top of this, Africa was suffering from political instability, and whereas you could buy a kilo of ivory for $7 or $8 in 1969, by the mid-70s the price had shot up to $100. Since a good tusk can weigh a hundred kilos, the inevitable occurred. And not all countries have yet joined the more recent ivory importation ban.

In the massacres that followed, the World Wildlife Fund has estimated that between 50,000 and 100,000 elephants were slaughtered annually. Poachers took half the entire elephant population of Kenya. In Uganda, numbers fell from 30,000 in 1970 to a tiny fraction of that figure. And with the increase in poaching has come a new breed of poacher, hunting with automatic weapons which he is equally willing to turn upon those engaged in protecting the animals. Thus, pitched battles to the death are not uncommon.

The wind that forever sighs across the bush intensified the vastness of it and gave a sinister edge to the subject of man's fanatical greed. Early afternoon's brilliant quality of light, filtered by thin cloud, brought an un-African irradiance to the landscape.

Upon arrival at Mnazini, John, Sandy and I had been received by the chief. He was a fat little man with a cheap ballpoint sheathed in his curly black hair. He owned the local stores and was plainly a man of substance judging by the hangers-on engaged upon menial tasks in his backyard. He was also boss of the small bar, but, being Ramadan and most of his flock being of the Muslim faith, he had allowed his beer stocks to fall to zero, which resulted for us in a diet of Seven-Up. In mysterious dark outhouses and recesses a fever of cooking, baking and washing was going on, which at least provided us with an intermittent source of hot water during our stay. The chief graciously provided a storage room in which to sleep: a bare concrete chamber adequate for our needs, for which he declined payment. An elderly man had been in occupation, but was consigned elsewhere.

So for two days we became temporary citizens of Mnazini. The chief's son, an intelligent youngster, was a constant visitor, who arranged for a supply of his friends to sit and chat with us over the evening social hour. From them and others we began to accumulate facts and figures concerning kings, sealing wax and Pels owls, and it was our quest for the Pels that was the reason for our remaining at Mnazini so long. Willing as he is, an African so often exhibits that annoying habit of replying to a question with an answer he thinks the questioner *wants* to hear, whether it is accurate or not. Many of our informants had a smattering of English, and from them we learnt of an old man who lived in the forest, who could lead us straight to this owl. The difficulty was to get through to them the correct *species* of owl we wished to observe. The fact that it had no ears hardly made the bird a universally popular subject for study. Yet everyone claimed to know it.

From owls the conversation switched to buffaloes, for in the African world of the bush this was the animal that had the most effect on their lives. That we had walked all the way from Kipendi unarmed and mostly unescorted raised many eyebrows in Mnazini since, allegedly, we had passed through very dangerous country thoroughly infested with these vicious brutes. In a manner reminiscent of World War Two bomb stories, these people had a nice line in buffalo anecdotes, and we were treated to some pretty grizzly tales of attacks on humans by wily bulls who anticipated every effort to escape them. In the woods supposedly harbouring our precious Pels would be many buffalo, we were energetically informed, particularly in the wood named Katherine Homeward (after a lady who had studied mangebys in the area) and in others across the river. In fact, according to popular opinion, worse terrors lurked on the east bank than on the west.

In spite of mosquito netting, everyone except myself was bitten that first night in the village. John's attackers were a brand of tree lice emanating from a timber store adjacent to his bed space, while Sandy sustained his usual working over by ants, to which he seemed particularly susceptible. Breakfast was the inevitable porridge, bacon roll and tea, cooked on a small fire in the main street. In place of the eight o'clock news we were treated to the views of the local political agitator, a forceful character in smart European dress, with a strong line of English patter. His wrath centred upon those who had forcibly evicted innocent families from the new reserve without, according to him, offering any compensation. He waxed bitter on the subject of the primates that had lived there for centuries (as if it were all their fault) in harmony with the Pokomo villagers, and could see no reason for the sudden uprooting of the human populations. If there had to be an uprooting, why not the monkeys? To him it was a simple case of *Homo sapiens* v *Colobus bardius* and the rest. And with the threat of an importation of urban communities to Pokomoland it could be that the Pokomo themselves were becoming the real endangered species. He had a point.

We crossed the Tana by dug-out, I willing myself to remain absolutely still to prevent capsizing the boat, and, climbing the opposite bank, we promptly walked into the very man we had set out to find. He was a 50-year-old African named Komora Bashova, of gamekeeper-like appearance, who had once been a companion of Katherine Homeward. He spoke a little English, knew the woods like the back of his hand and, of course, recognised the brand of owl we were searching for. With us too had come a youngster who had designated himself as general dogsbody and hanger-on. The *Msee*, as the older man was respectfully titled, immediately dropped whatever he had been doing to lead us to the elusive bird, which, he vouchsafed could often be seen asleep atop the highest trees.

The whole morning was spent combing woods and thickets, seeing several red colobus monkeys and mangabey but no Pels. At every isolated *shamba* enquiries were made of its whereabouts, and we were led to places where the bird would surely be – but wasn't. Ever sensitive to the presence of buffalo, my eyes wavered between possible owl perches and climbable trees. I got the shock of my life when, crawling about in a thicket, I looked round to find myself staring between the eyes of a mournful light brown face. Buffalo! The message flashed to my brain, but, as I lay prostrate under an entanglement of brambles, the normal reaction got short-circuited and I remained glued to the spot. The same kind of reactive hang-up must have afflicted the waterbuck – for that is what the animal was – and five long seconds were to pass before it took to its heels.

With one of my ankles swollen to twice its normal size, I was glad to return to Mnazini shortly after midday, we having arranged with Komora to institute another search at dawn next day. Meanwhile John and Sandy, full of vigour, took themselves off to Katherine's Wood. When they had gone I attempted an overdue wash in a biscuit tin of water, but a bevy of local lovelies came to watch the performance. 'Why not you wash everywhere?' one of them asked, and I had to look hard at her to find out if she was being serious.

I suppose I should have rested my ankle for the rest of the afternoon, but, being what I am, I found more worthwhile activities to pursue. The construction of a mud villa was in progress next door and I was allowed inside to watch the creation of the interior walls. Rough and ready construction it may have been, but inside the house was beautifully cool. Once the framework of wood had been erected, interior work consisted of little more than the throwing of fistfuls of mud at it. Someone took me to see the interior of his *manyatta* at the rear of the village and, again, I was able to marvel at the coolness of its dark interior – even though, in this case, the roof was but straw and wattle. Furniture was home-made, right down to an ingenious article I eventually recognised as a washstand of the sort my Victorian grandparents used.

Back in the high street, I visited the two shops which were, of course, the meeting places of those in the village with nothing to do, i.e., the men. In one of them I was invited to join a 'sit-in', during which community affairs were aired. Probably for my benefit the subject of the game reserve arose, and very soon I was made aware of how unpopular the concept was. But though the accusation hung heavy in the air I could obtain no concrete evidence of families being ejected without compensation.

Our dawn awakening next morning was a belated one, with all three of us oversleeping. Komora had nearly given us up as we met at the ferry landing under a weak sun, and together proceeded to a wood we had christened 'Hell's Pels Park'. We observed many owls, including some intriguing breeds of considerable size, but they all sported ears and so were not for us. From wood to wood we went, coming upon monkeys, waterbuck, and a leopard which we were fortunate to glimpse if only for an instant. This cat hunts by night, but is otherwise more doglike in its habits. It is wary and extremely dangerous when cornered or wounded; in company with the cheetah, it is the fastest animal on earth. As we returned to the river an impala watched us, head raised alertly, a fine tautness in its glossy flanks and slender neck. But of Pels there was no sign.

The inevitable happened as we re-crossed the Tana, this time at a lesser ferry point upstream of Mnazini. Our dug-out was a smaller and narrower craft than before, and in mid-river a ferocious horsefly settled on my naked back. Forced to knock it away, my impulsive movement upset the boat, tipping everyone into a couple of feet of water. An audience of Africans – as well as a ferryman grievously scarred from a hippo attack – thought it all extremely funny, but John and Sandy were not amused.

We partook of a late and very public breakfast, providing an hour's entertainment for a sizable portion of the community full of unhelpful suggestions about what to do with baked beans. Then we were off again to the west bank forests on a last-ditch search. Once more colobus and mangabey of all hues exhibited themselves in profusion, but the confounded owl wasn't caring a hoot. It was not until late afternoon that a wildly excited Komora made a dramatic gesture towards the sky as if he were Abraham beholding a miracle. 'There, look! On that furtherest bough!' he shouted so loudly that he woke the thing from its slumbers. But it wasn't a Pels, and we all returned crestfallen to the village aware, as we had half-suspected all along, that we had been led on a wild-goose chase.

Next morning, consigning the wretched bird to its ancestors, we loaded ourselves up and struck southwards, escorted by a platoon of children who slowly dropped away at the 'outer suburbs' of

Mnazini. The last house of the village displayed the following
'Trespassers will be prosecuted' notice:

> A Bad notice to everybody. Please make sure that, if you acoming in my
> cotage you get permission or you will be killed mind you. My instinct is to
> kill whoever comes in here without any permission. Please do not try
> because you will regret why you've done. By order of Sheik Zubeir Bin
> Oman.

We asked one of the last remaining boys if the writer was a
hostile character. 'He is my uncle,' came the reply and we left it at
that.

At a hamlet – Bubesa – we rested beneath a mango tree.
Finding the way out of a village invariably involved a high
percentage of guesswork, owing to the multiplicity of tracks
running in all directions. However, in Bubesa we were lucky, for a
tall Somali was on the verge of leaving for Mwina, about 18 miles
distant and on our route. He graciously allowed us to accompany
him.

He set a gruelling pace, taking no account of our heavy loads,
but we appreciated the fact that it was vital we reached a
habitation before nightfall so uttered no complaint. The way, too,
was composed of long flat stretches of bush and thicket – perfect
buffalo territory – and the Somali's spear was a comfort not to be
spurned; the chap himself looked the type able to use it.

We reached Mwina exhausted but unassailed. While we were
resting weary feet on the edge of the village the young chief
arrived, greeted us cordially and showed us to his house, which he
handed over for the night. We had made no request, asked no
favours, but there he was assuming us to be travellers needing a
bed. We were deeply touched by this act of spontaneous
hospitality. The house was of neat, mud-and-wattle construction,
our 'front room' containing a number of straw mats, which to a
village African is all the furniture deemed necessary in a bedroom.
The one concession to high living was a decoration of painted
palm leaves serving as a picture on the brown mud wall.

Though dusk was settling upon the sky, the sun was still warm
and my longing for a swim in the forbidden waters of the Tana
was not lost upon John. He had mentioned earlier that he had seen

the locals bathing at the point where the river came nearest the village, and the pleading in my eyes overcame his medical strictures. 'It's moving water,' he opined and, glancing at the ingrained filth on my body, added 'if I save you from bilharzia you'll only catch typhus,' which was assent enough for me. I dashed for the river and caught the other bathers completely by surprise. They were the ladies of the village, about two dozen of them and all in the nude. Pandemonium broke out, and I was able to turn my back while they emerged with much shrieking. But one lady was too slow, so took cover by ducking into the water. And there she remained, too frightened to go deeper because of the crocodiles and too embarrassed to emerge because of me.

John plus any number of helpers had our supper well in hand. All sorts of offerings kept appearing – from bananas through plates of cooked peas to chicken paté. These gifts were shyly presented by the women of the village, who were extremely curious to discover how and what the white man ate, though I fear they took away with them some pretty poor impressions. Sandy was busy playing with a squad of kids, and judging by the squeals of merriment, making a good job of it.

The men with a smattering of English joined us over tea for a chat and general airing of their linguistic abilities, an area in which, rather naturally, the local schoolmaster shone the brightest. As I expected, the way we had come was pronounced very dangerous: a sort of 'black spot' for buffalo, and nobody went there at night. There followed the routine crop of buffalo stories and those resulting from the *shifta* troubles, when the village had picked itself up and moved westwards across the river – an event that explained a hitherto unaccountable deficiency in our outdated map.

It was my turn for a bad night, though it resulted less from attack by creepy-crawlies than from anticipation thereof. By the light of my torch I found one aircraft-carrier of a bug – all masts and antennae – and a vivid imagination did the rest. John was not going to get it all his own way either: the secret of his medical prowess out, a patient came wandering in during the small hours intent upon being first in the morning surgery queue.

And morning surgery it became with a vengeance. While I

made breakfast in the house next door (which was, in fact, the chief's kitchen) John dealt as best he could with the onslaught, Sandy acting as receptionist and nurse. The villagers of Mwina seemed, in general, quite a healthy lot. However, treatment by a *hakimi* – the first, probably, ever to practise in Mwina – was an experience to be enjoyed even by the healthy. Genuine ills, of course, there were too: malaria, venereal diseases, liver complaints, open sores, scabies, a host of eye-disorders and an assortment of ailments resulting form dietary deficiency.

While John ministered to the sick, I fed him mugs of porridge made in a series of mess tins over a smoky fire. My assistant was the chief's father, a gentle, charming man who controlled the fire, the smoke from which was supposed to exit through the roof. But for virtually the first time on the expedition it rained solidly, and the smoke was as reluctant as we were to go anywhere. Outside, everything turned to sticky mud.

Leaving John to repay our debt to society, Sandy and I returned to the forest in company with one of the village hunters in a desperate bid for the Pels. Instead we came across the usual plague of red mangabeys, twittering and flinging themselves about in the trees, and when we were back in the village, a boy brought us one which he had caught. The poor thing was tied up like a dog, but, with the cord out of sight, made a fine photograph.

The sky was black and ominous, but the rain had slackened as we evacuated Mwina. The chief accompanied us to the ferry-crossing point, downstream of my lido of yesterday, and his personal ferryman poled us across the browner-than-normal Tana to the east bank. There he proudly showed us his *shamba* and 'workhouse' of palm leaves, from which emerged his mother and two sisters to be solemnly introduced. As a farewell gift he presented us with six eggs, for which we could repay him with but a few boiled sweets and a book of matches. The four of them stood watching us go, waving all the time; we hoped the messages addressed to our compatriots would result in a beneficial visit to Mwina by the boat party as it came by. The most pleasant and hospitable people, these villagers possessed yet another virtue: honesty. Earlier John had dropped his compass, though the first he knew of it was when a man came running to return it.

The rain held off just long enough for us to get far out into open countryside; then it came down in cascades. In moments we were soaked through, which in my case meant little since I wore only shorts and a singlet. John and Sandy, however, sported more conventional attire: bush shirts, khaki denim trousers and a sun hat in lieu of a helmet. All of us wore safari boots. Ignoring the rain, we pushed on, the river to our right swinging towards and away from us as we cut across its corners. The countryside changed gear from bushland to open savannah.

Even without an escort to set the pace we walked hard and fast. The plain, dead flat, would have made monotonous though easy walking at the best of times, but the rain had turned it into a quagmire, the water and clay-based soil producing a glutinous mixture of mud, known – and dreaded – by the motor-rallying fraternity as 'black cotton'. And what this substance can do to tyres it can, on a modified scale, do to boots. Within minutes, the weight of our footwear had doubled and trebled as the sticky solid adhered to the soles and spread outwards to form snowshoes of packed mud. To attempt to kick the stuff off was tantamount to tearing a leg from its socket; yet to ignore the build-up not only anchored feet to the ground but caused blisters from contortions of the canvas uppers. Thus, to add to the afflictions of my ankles came blisters as big as acorns on toes and heels.

Gradually I fell back, halting every now and again to wrap agonised toes in fresh strips of sticking plaster that refused to stick. Blood stained my filthy socks while boots, once off, exhibited a marked reluctance to go on again. Sandy likewise was showing signs of wear, but solved *his* problems by removing his footwear altogether and walking barefoot. It was a sensible move, but my feet were in such a poisonous mess already I felt it would do more harm than good if I followed suit. Only John seemed impervious to the conditions, striding on towards the limitless horizon. Imperceptibly, the distance between us lengthened.

With the onset of the savannah we had noticed the spoor of lion, and their presence in the clumps of undergrowth that clung to the plain was periodically confirmed by their coughing grunts, low and muted. That they were close added to my unease, though lions are indolent, lazy creatures, preferring as little exertion as possible in the attainment of their food. Nevertheless, I felt myself to be a sitting duck. A lion will eat anything, no matter how 'high' or maggot-infested – which offered me no comfort either! When really hungry, lions become extremely bold and determined, stopping at nothing to bring down a victim. Normally they prey upon the larger antelopes and zebra, ostriches and buffalo, and occasionally giraffe, but, when pushed, nothing is too small or insignificant for them to catch and devour, and man himself may fall a victim under such circumstances. And once a lion has tasted human flesh, and found how easily man can be stalked and killed, it very quickly becomes a confirmed man-eater. Me, I had not the slightest desire of leading lions into bad habits.

More dead than alive we staggered into a hamlet. The place had about it an air of decrepitude, but a track led out of the cluster of silent mud dwellings scarred by tyre-marks, which offered the notion that we were back on some sort of channel of communication. There were people on the route, too, seemingly intent on getting somewhere: presumably Kulesa, a larger community we could make out in the far distance. Gritting our teeth, we battled on.

A sizable school complex characterised the new village, which showed more life about it than the previous one. As we sprawled, licking our wounds, beneath a tree, we were subjected to a barrage of questions concerning our mission and destination. Most of the questions came from off-duty local schoolmasters, and we were to learn from them that Weme, the district centre close to our final destination, was 'just down the road'. We asked the reason for a lack of children in so scholarly a community and were told, with some surprise, that they were working on the *shambas*. By a combined effort of will we worked out the day to be Sunday.

'Just down the road' represented two miles on the map and nearer six on the ground. The savannah had surreptitiously given way to forested country, well cultivated and inhabited. And Weme, when we reached it, showed us a general store, a tractor depot and a missionary church. It was the store that satisfied our immediate cravings with the provision of Fanta orange squash and thick, creamy goat's milk unearthed from a damp cellar.

We debated the option of spending the night in Weme, which to our individualistic minds promised more interest than a regulated camp, but the Church intervened. Its representative was a forceful Irish Methodist priest who insisted upon running us the last couple of miles in the back of his van. And just as well perhaps, for, alone, we would never have found the site. The boats had not arrived, so only Robert, Raj and Tony witnessed our ignominious arrival on wheels.

The boat party had left Kipendi in high spirits. Again, a whole week in camp had created an urge to see what the Tana had to offer around the next bend.

And round not so many bends lay, of course, the game reserve where, below Ya Gwano, they made their first landfall. And once more it was elephants that provided the chief subjects for study and photography, with Karen, transfixed, being playfully charged by a baby – one of two probable orphans since no mother intervened.

Derek had a field-day filming multiple groups of the great beasts drinking and at play in the river. At one time he counted upwards of fifty, which must have been quite a spectacle. His most intriguing sequence of shots was of a female with her baby coming down to the water to bathe. Fascinated, Derek watched the mother step into the shallows, musing to herself as if testing the temperature before wading out with assurance to deeper waters. The baby arrived at the bank, gave a ridiculous squeak, then hurled itself into the stream towards where the parent lay placidly squirting water over her shoulders. To the adult, of course, the water was not deep, but the baby was well out of its depth. Not that this was the slightest deterrent: Junior simply disappeared beneath the surface, using its trunk like a periscope. Reaching his mother's side, the baby scrambled out onto her wet flank, giving out little squeals of pleasure.

The motor boats behaved themselves better than previously and progress began actually running to schedule. Missing the Pels Quest Team's message at Baomo, a second night's encampment was made above Mnazini, which was visited the third morning. Thereafter the main preoccupation became that of sticking it out under prolonged torrents of rain.

A halt was made at the ferry-crossing close to Mwina where, it was learnt, the Pels Team had spent the night in the dry. John, Sandy and Chris Portway had, in fact, only recently left, which provoked the sardonic comment: 'They must have seen us coming.' In such weather conditions, walking takes on a certain attraction when set against huddled inactivity, soaked and miserable, in a rubber boat with water both above and below. Some hours were spent ashore, which at least gave an opportunity to stretch cramped limbs, dry out bedding and meet the overwhelmingly hospitable villagers.

African weather is fickle in the extreme, and a few hours later a warm sun had dried everyone out. The final night's encampment was as if nothing disagreeable had occurred; just a lot of steaming undergrowth as a reminder.

Water – and not only that emanating from the sky – played a not unnatural but exaggerated part on the voyage to Hewani. Even the activities of the wildlife seemed to be dictated by it. Rhino are solitary and silent creatures, but at the water's edge they foregathered with their neighbours: there were bathing parties, flirtations, and fights accompanied by weird, high-pitched screams and long drawn-out groans – not the sort of sounds one would expect from such massive beasts. Heard but not seen, they were very close that night. Buffalo herds also came in the dark to drink, though the oryx and zebra, on this occasion, preferred the heat of the day during which to slake their thirst. Elephants drink at any hour of the day or night, and many were seen spending the day under the shade or shelter of the few trees or bathing in the river. Rain. We humans hated it; the wildlife of the Tana revelled in it.

The humans, for their different reasons, were gratified beyond measure to reach the creature-comforts expected of Hewani.

Yet Hewani, too, had its scourges. Mosquitoes: in spite of elaborate precautions and all manner of Heath Robinson defences, their attacks struck home. Snakes: the only really dangerous species we came across appeared in my tent then disappeared, an action that sent the human occupants out to sleep in the open at the mercy of the mosquitoes. (Of course, it rained, so we took what seemed the lesser of two evil alternatives and returned to the tent.)

A lavatory beside the Tana: romantic perhaps but perilous if you were in a hurry at night and missed the cliff path leading to it.

Hewani was also a clump of mango trees among a bristling sea of palms, their trunks grey and straight like factory chimneys. The evening cry of a bird that sounded as though it had swallowed a lawnmower and left the engine running, and the morning throb of frogs expanding and deflating amongst the dew. Best of all was the prospect of sparse but interesting game and the close proximity of a new Tana tribe – the Orma Galla.

Waterbuck were our first visitors. They took a wrong turning and a herd of them found themselves surrounded by tents. Realising their mistake they leapt the slop pits and vanished. A more regular visitor was the Catholic priest, who on his second visitation brought a baboon-ravaged dog, upon which John was persuaded to operate. Otherwise, our visitors were black and two-legged, emanating from Hewani village, round the bend of the river, and the Orma village, two miles distant.

The Orma, a branch of the Galla, live intermingled among the three Pokomo sub-tribes. They are tall and slender, with narrow faces, long noses, long, narrow skulls and narrow shoulders – all vertical dimensions it will be noticed – which description fits, of course, the Masai, to whom they are related. Whereas the Pokomo men basically dress in Western-style shirt and trousers, or perhaps a brightly-coloured *kikoi* (a cloth wrapped about the waist), Orma men favour gaudy, toga-like apparel, often a strikingly self-coloured blue. In the case of women it is the Pokomo who favour bright cloths (vivid-coloured body wraps called *kanga*), while the beautiful Orma women wear mostly black – embellished, however, by hand-beaten aluminium bangles on the upper arm.

Tribal policy dictates a practice of cattle-raising instead of cultivation. The Orma are less nomadic than formerly: at some places they inhabit separate villages (such as near Hewani), though they also occupy special 'wards' of Pokomo villages.

I was the first member of the expedition to visit the Orma village. I went there by tractor at the invitation of an African plant engineer from Weme who was reinforcing the village well. The community had given up their nomadic habits ten years before, finding the district to their liking, but chose to stick firmly to themselves. The village was an intriguing sight, the houses contrasting strongly with the mud-daub of the Pokomo. These were tall and round, beehive-shaped, built of grass thatch laid over a series of frames made of withy bundles bent over and fixed at either end. They were beautifully constructed: veritable little cathedrals of straw – and the interiors were even more remarkable.

Invited into a couple of them, I struggled through the slit of a doorway of the first (and I do cut something of an Orma figure myself) to behold the intricately woven frame lashed at the joints by thin vines. There is very much more room in these houses than their exteriors suggest, and the floor was spotlessly clean. A double bed, raised off the floor and of almost four-poster construction, took up a third of the space, its 'springs' the leaves of the phoenix palm. Animal skins formed the mattress. Various items of 'furniture' and ornaments, such as raffia gourd holders and shelves holding curling photographs of respected relatives or ancestors, gave the house a home-like quality. The second house I saw was similarly fitted, though its entry slit was even narrower and protected by a curtain of dried grass. I was told that each house lasted for five or six years, after which a replacement would be commenced close to the old one.

I watched one under construction – by the women, of course – and was informed that it was being built for a couple not yet married. My informant gleefully explained that the wretched bride and groom would have to remain indoors until they could produce proof of the consummation of the marriage, all food and the necessities of life being passed to them through the narrow door.

From a group of Orma warriors I purchased a spear to take home for my young son, and quickly raised the commercial instincts of the village. Within half an hour of my return to camp the first of the spear-and-bangle sales persons arrived, and thereafter there were seldom less than half a dozen Orma around our tents. With everyone short of money, we devised a system of barter: spears and bangles in return for lemonade powder and bars of soap, with which we were plentifully endowed. Palm wine was easily procurable too. The best 'brew' came from the phoenix palm, the sap of which is fed into gourds, where it is allowed to ferment as a milky fluid. It must be drunk fresh – if drunk at all –

for after very few hours the stuff goes sour. Here was another scourge of the forest, for the removal of sap eventually kills the tree; in this case the fine, long-stemmed phoenix palm – so called because it is invariably the first tree to grow following a bush or forest fire.

Being the penultimate base camp of the expedition and the last to be supported by vehicles with luxuries such as laboratory tents and dissection benches, investigatory work went ahead with renewed vigour. In the zoological field Andrew, Karen, Sandy, Raj and Ken were out in the forests or on the Tana all hours of the day and night. I joined one night observation voyage on the river, half a dozen of us drifting downstream in complete silence, equipped only with head-torches and the image intensifier. A moon, wearing a yashmak of cloud, was only one of many eyes that dolefully gleamed from everywhere as we listened for tell-tale noises of the creatures of darkness. Some pinpricks of light were spider's eyes, some were those of crocodiles and others we knew not what. Andrew had learnt his lesson with eyes in the night when he mistook a crocodile for a spider, so henceforth he treated every pinpoint of light with caution. Most of the river eyes this night were crocodiles, many quite small, and by the end of our nocturnal drift we had caught five of them. Baby crocodiles have all the attributes of their elders and betters but scaled down to size. The largest specimen we caught was about two feet long and its snapping ability was considerable, as an embarrassing rent in Andrew's trousers was to testify. A few inches to the left and the occupier would have forever lost his manhood. When caught, they make pathetic little cries which are intended to call their parents to their aid. We allowed three of the objecting offspring to go and held onto two for further study.

With a great clatter of sound a flock of ibis flew out of a bunch of ghostly trees, which in turn set off a drumbeat of hooves from a hidden herd of buffalo who suffered even more of a fright than we did.

All these sounds were faithfully recorded by Derek with his tape recorder, as were those of numerous daytime incursions in the forests. A safari was made to Lake Biliso, ten miles to the west, where drinking buffalo were observed; later, Sandy and Andrew were to come face to face with one at point blank range – each backing away from the other in a prolonged moment of pure drama. A huge concentration of hippo were seen and counted near Mziwa on a 'dead' bend of the Tana that still contained water. My dug-out-capsizing disgrace at Mnazini was avenged when John and Robert upset their vessel in much deeper water; each was trying to out-balance the other, including the ferryman, whose responsibility it is to maintain equilibrium.

We had noted the extent of the croppings of vegetation as we proceeded down the Tana, but I have made small mention of more specific botanical tasks that formed part of the general survey. With the help of Samuel Paul Kibua, a bright young Kenyan from the East African Herbarium in Nairobi who was with the expedition for this period, we continued to identify species of plants and classified the predominant types of trees, bushes and grasses. Even the analysis of hippo dung came into it for the establishment of their food pattern in different regions. At Hewani the vegetation showed a marked difference in texture and type, with the proximity of the Indian Ocean now making its influence felt.

Bats were either more numerous at Hewani or blinder than elsewhere, for our nets caught many of them. Most flew into captivity at dawn or dusk; because bats are rabies-carriers Sandy and Ken had to take precautions when handling live specimens. Distribution and density of all birds was painstakingly maintained, though Hewani was to be the last base camp where Lorio and Joseph were able to mount specimens in the field. This was also the 'camp of the millipedes', and one in particular, a character known as 'Harold', who was as long and as thick as a slow-worm, made himself at home in the 'kitchen' throughout our stay. Small-mammal collecting was a disappointment as far as numbers were concerned, though one specimen could not be identified, which raised hopes of the discovery of an unknown breed. Charles determinedly continued searching the Tana for differing strains of fish, and some unexpectedly interesting species were caught. All were of the smaller variety, the Tana not being a 'big fish' river. Charles was a fish-fancier in more ways than one, frequently having to be restrained from consuming his samples!

It was from Hewani camp, however, that I was able to spend a day with the Tana Pox trio to see how they operated. Their survey had commenced at Garissa and was to end at Garsen, the two largest 'towns' on the middle and lower Tana. Garsen was, in fact, just six miles downstream, so my investigation of John Axford's activities took place just in time. The district centre of Weme was the location for the day's blood-taking and I was given a lift there, with Sue and Gilbert, on the bonnet of the medical Land Rover laden with supplies.

One sees the strangest sights in these tiny African communities – strange to our eyes at any rate. Often the most bizarre activities are carried out so naturally that it is not until later that the penny drops, so to speak, and the event is savoured against a European notion of behaviour. Where in a respectable English village could you see, for instance, a woman sitting in the dust of the roadside, happily extracting *jigga* flea eggs from the nail of her grandfather's big toe? (These fleas are picked up by walking barefoot in sand, and the eggs are deposited in crevices behind the toe–nails. I was to unearth at least two from my own feet, and Tony ended the expedition with a half a dozen.) And where in Britain would you find the local barber shop and beauty parlour installed beneath a tree? Two women, hammering away with a pestle and mortar, were having their hair plaited in rows across their scalps while another young lady – remarkably beautiful, extremely pregnant and wearing a kind of shortie nightie of brilliant orange and pink – was having hers turned into a tight pagoda on the back of her head.

Because of pre-consultation with the district health authorities the team were expected, and upwards of two hundred souls were awaiting our arrival in the village square. The chief was among them, and he greeted us gravely. He then announced to his flock – most of whom were no more than onlookers – the sequence of events, the reasons for them and the benefits, including the pot of gold at the end of the rainbow: the issue of a vitamin tablet. A queue formed and Gilbert took names and particulars of all donors. Between them John and Sue syringed out the blood, applied a plaster (which became a status symbol), popped a tablet into expectant mouths and the job was done. Most of the donors were children. Many rural Africans are kids at heart, and among the adults I could see expressions of indecision crossing many a face as both men and women wrestled with temptation. Some surrendered, to come forward sheepishly for treatment and the pill.

While we packed up the open-air surgery, John told me of some of his earlier experiences. A number of the village dispensaries and clinics were, relatively speaking, of a high order. Others were not, but Kenya is progressing fast in the treatment of health in its more backward territories. I have already alluded to types of diseases and afflictions revealed in our survey, and the Tana Pox Team spent a lot of time dealing with ailments far removed from Tana Pox. As with all the poorer countries of the world, a hard core of prejudice is present that only education can eradicate.

The saddest sight in Weme was an albino woman, strangely white yet negroid in feature, who crossed the road as we were returning to camp. Like all albinos – and we had seen a number of afflicted children from time to time – she was semi-blind and seemingly unbalanced. However, such unfortunate people are unhesitatingly accepted by the community, which speaks volumes for one aspect of African life.

My initial lone visit to the Orma village had developed into a two-way affair as our people made courtesy calls on the inhabitants who supplied us with eggs, bananas and coconuts. Neither were the Pokomo of Hewani village ignored: Raj and others were, on several occasions, invited to dinner in their simple homes in return for the small services we had been able to undertake for them.

John Richardson had never quite come to terms with the one disappointment of the Pels quest safari, our failure to locate the chief object of our search. What ensued was to affix the seal of success to our week at Hewani and to send John, Sandy and myself into paroxysms of frustration. One morning, Alison, hungry as always, was staring up into the big trees that roofed the camp-site, her eyes searching for late mangoes. Instead she found herself looking at a specimen of earless owl – a Pels no less – oblivious to the world as it slumbered on an upper branch.

9. Via Ozi Swamp to Kipini

The one aspect of the expedition I had not yet experienced was that from the point of view of the vehicle support group, but I was to rectify this omission upon departure from Hewani. The sole permanent member of the group was Andy Winspeare, his accomplices stemming from the ranks of volunteers at each successive camp. However, our last base camp was to be unattainable by wheeled transport, which would offer me a somewhat distorted picture since the Bedford was to form its own base at the mouth of the Tana, downstream of the main camp. Here it would await the arrival of the scientific team on completion of their final sojourn.

A week of idleness on the shores of the Indian Ocean was not an unattractive proposition, and the three expedition members selected to spend it thus were Nigel himself, Alison and I; a selection no doubt based upon a high degree of uselessness so far as Alison and I were concerned and a brief period of reflection for Nigel as expedition leader. The thought came to me at the time that there must be a catch somewhere and Andy must have come up with the same idea for, without a murmur, he relinquished his driving seat for the rubber thwart of an inflatable. With John Richardson and Robert having to return to Nairobi, Andrew took over command of the shrinking boat party.

In our different ways we all left Hewani at the same time. The two motorless boats – towed by the others – were heavily overloaded to the point at which navigation was both difficult and dangerous. It took time for the captains of each craft to accustom themselves to new techniques needed to overcome a tendency for the cargo boats, low in the water, to swing round and drift ahead of their tows. After an abortive start – one filmed from the air by

Derek esconced in Karen Ross's father's private aeroplane – some delay was incurred while the heavy cans of petrol and water were rearranged to give better handling control.

In the meantime Nigel, Alison and I drove to the ferry at Garsen, there to await arrival of the boats and to check that all was well. A so-called main road crossed the Tana there, and though Kenyan economics had not risen to a bridge, a picturesque vehicle ferry existed. This contraption was something of a do-it-yourself affair, in which the foot passengers and drivers lent a hand at the ropes to drag the flat-ended vessel along its guide cable from shore to shore. There was no toll, except of effort.

A pitiless sun beat down from a clear sky and shade was at a premium as Alison and I walked into the small town to buy samosas and kebabs for our midday meal. The township was a typical African one: a 'Wild West' façade mainstreet and the usual conglomeration of mud-daub houses interspersed with a few ugly concrete structures that had never been completed. The existence of shops made the place an attraction for miles around and the streets hummed with people: idle Orma, Pokomo and Somali bodies strewn about the steps and broken-down verandahs of the 'general stores' and other emporia waiting for something to happen. Alison, more than I, provided the source of the current happening that day, she being barely covered by a flimsy item from a bottomless wardrobe of bikini-type apparel that formed the bulk of her baggage. Buying our samosas became not unlike walking onto the stage of the London Palladium

The boats arrived as we returned to the ferry, and all appeared shipshape and bristol fashion; Andrew was in command of the situation.

We remained on the east bank of the Tana for the drive to Kipini, the journey commencing with a fanfare of screeching gears as Nigel, unaccustomed to heavy truck driving, went into reverse instead of first. Thereafter we bowled merrily along the Lamu road, a highway of dust but endowed with good shoulders and a reasonable surface. How strange is was to be travelling at 40 miles per hour! It had been estimated the boats would take five days to reach Saidbabo, the scheduled but unreconnoitred site of the final base camp. From there to Kipini and the Tana's mouth would be at least another one. Yet in our fine motor vehicle we expected to be in Kipini with no effort at all within three hours.

At Witu we turned off the Lamu road. Its overgrown mango plantations gave hint of a prosperous past, but few would guess this sleepy village was once the centre of an important sultanate and, briefly, capital of the short-lived state of 'Swahililand'. The area was also a German protectorate until the Treaty of Berlin brought the whole of modern Kenya under British jurisdiction.

Witu additionally heralded an entirely new texture of countryside. The road took us across lush grasslands spiked with candelabra-like palms before turning to marshland and embryo mangrove swamps as we neared the sea.

Our first sight of the Indian Ocean was through a frame of palms. I viewed it with mixed feelings. Guilt was the initial emotion – guilt about not having physically earned the vision of this leg of the journey. Disappointment too, for it was not the way I had for so long imagined I would first see the sea. But there it was: a preview of the end of the voyage. We rattled into Kipini and braked outside the cracked concrete building of the police station. We expected to be in or around Kipini for at least ten days so felt it expedient to have good relations with the law.

Finally we put down roots on a sandbank between the village and the shore. Empty, the back of the lorry made a roomy bed-sit for the three of us, and with the erection of a canvas awning, we had a dining-room-cum-kitchen as well. We fashioned a fireplace adjacent to the covered area, and the whole complex rejoiced in the unregistered address of 'The Bedford Hotel, Lone Palm, Kipini', the tall slender palm tree beside our front door being a landmark for miles around.

The sea claimed us even before commencement of our home-making operations. Kipini is situated at the spot where the river emerges into the ocean, which it does at an angle since a promontory gives the coast a forty-five degree bend. The closest water to us was that of the brown Tana, but mixed with sea-water it was tolerably disinfected. Half a mile downstream, deserted golden sands sprinkled with exotic shells, was the sea proper, though its blue-green waters were stained by the river. Depending upon the tide there were potentially dangerous currents together with a profusion of underwater reefs and the unwelcome presence of sharks. Even these detractions were deemed acceptable conditions for our first unhurried swim in the Tana and subsequent immersion in the cleaner, gentle rollers of the Indian Ocean. Crocodiles were presumed to disapprove of salt water.

Kipini itself could be described as a fishing village, since a percentage of its inhabitants were occupied with the sea and that which could be extracted from it. Some half-dozen small fishing vessels and dhows, paint-starved and primitive, lay beached around a tangle of driftwood. Among them was the decaying wreck of the last British DC's launch, the *Pelican*, to add fuel to stories we were to hear of the haunting of the old DC's house. As the district headquarters, Kipini had acquired some notoriety through the suicides there of three administrators, and the village continues to exude a sultry and vaguely sinister atmosphere. Most of its denizens are Moslem, and they live in an assortment of mud and stone-walled houses with coconut-thatch roofing. A small hospital was one of the more recent amenities, and Alison was to learn that the greatest scourge of its patients was bilharzia. A couple of 'general stores' made up the rest of the small community that both history and progress had bypassed on the march to the renowned Lamu beyond.

Our first night we turned in early, to lie with the sound of the sea pounding the beach in our ears. A warm wind blew in our faces to deter all but the most persistent mosquitoes. It was strong enough to blow down part of our verandah in the middle of the night but there was nothing vital to do next morning beyond raising the energy to replace the toppled supports.

Right from the start our sojourn at Kipini was enlivened by village visitors, who arrived at intervals to discuss their affairs, learn of ours and to undertake small chores for us. The customs official was one such visitor, a jovial fellow who lived in one of the 'better' houses (his description) and whose wife was persuaded to provide us with African meals in place of the tinned concoctions of which we were heartily sick. In return, we kept her in porridge oats, stew and corned beef. Another visitor was the one-and-only policeman, who periodically dropped in for a chat and to see that we were behaving ourselves. There were also two students,

Marxists both, who never missed an evening of political discussion over a cup of Bournvita. One of them – Omar – exhibited a schoolboy crush on Alison, who would accompany him on daytime strolls along the beach, thereby raising his hopes the more. The current DO and his retinue we met too, as we did the local fisheries officer, another genial civil servant whose ebony face was permanently creased in laughter. He would look in on us daily for a cup of tea and a joke, as if to compensate for another 'regular', the mournful old fisherman with tales of woe to unfold as well as the occasional, very welcome, freshly caught crab for breakfast. The appearance, one day, of a rich German hunter with a millionaire's plaything of a cabin cruiser was not so welcome, but he did not find much to hold him in Kipini. More rewarding was a conversation we had with two Belgian agriculturalists who were deeply concerned with the population growth along the Tana; a growth, they affirmed, that could only increase the wasteful 'slash and burn' methods of agriculture practised for centuries. The only satisfaction we could raise from this exchange was that our own findings agreed with theirs. Thus, the cast of Kipini: its stars and the chorus line.

In all we remained at this pleasant spot for eleven days, though this was not to say that Nigel and I idled there the whole time. After only two days our commitment to the expedition reached out to draw us back into its orbit. Guarded by the doting Omar, Alison held the fort while we set off for Saidbabo to make contact with our compatriots. We left in the cool of early morning, for we held expectations of a tough 25-mile hike across difficult country with no roads. We carried a map, compass, water bottles, iron-ration biscuits, the rifle and a few rounds of ammunition.

Nine miles out and we reached the hamlet of Mwoga Hakai, where we were directed to Kau. Both of us were bathed in sweat, but at Mwoga Hakai it rained to wash the salt out of our eyes. A complicated irrigation system led us astray, the raised paths alongside the jigsaws of cultivation making navigation difficult. The rain brought out the giant millipedes in strength; some almost nine inches long. The steaming mangroves reminded me of Dutch polder country with trees, for we were now in an area that formed part of the flood basin of the Tana. Annual flooding covers land on

either side of the river about a mile across, the water breaking
through the banks to form broad discharge channels. Some of
these channels follow the lines of old river courses; others empty
into permanent lakes such as those of Bilisa or Shakababo. Very
occasionally the floods reach dramatic proportions. The last time
this happened – indeed the only time within living memory – was
during 1961-2 when the triangle of Kurawa-Garson-Kipini and a
strip ten miles wide on either side of the Tana from Garsen to near
Hola was under water.

A substantial tributary of the river blocked our route. A log that
looked as if it had been intentionally placed in the brackish,
stationary water to provide a fording place indicated a method of
crossing. The water was deep and the mud the abode of millions of
bilharzia-bearing snails; in fact, the location simply reeked of the
disease. Twice we tried to negotiate the obstacle dry-legged but
muffed it, the muddy water rising to our thighs as we sloshed
through the tributary. On the further bank we hastily wiped dry our
legs with our shirts.

By enquiring the way to Kau at every *shamba* in sight we
finally attained the township, the standard collection of mud
dwellings but on a slightly larger scale than Mwoga Hakai. Here
we came across the mayor, who introduced himself as Mohammed
Juma Esq. He would, he told us, be happy to offer us food if they
had any. Or bananas if there were any. But it was *Ramadan* so we
got nothing anyway. Saidbabo? You'll *never* find Saidbabo, we
were told. It was a village no more,and there was not even the
track marked on our map leading to where the village had been. So
an elderly guide was fetched who, they said, intended going there
anyhow. So why did he want five shillings from each of us for this
hardly sacrificial service? Because he was going tomorrow but
because of us he would now have to go today. Said Nigel: 'OK,
we'll go tomorrow,' which produced a stalemate. The truth was
we possessed not a brass farthing between us.

The Tana at Kau would make a fine picture postcard. The river
here executes a sharp curve as it flows into the village and is
joined by a sizeable tributary. The banks were bushy with rich,
green foliage and raised umbrellas of trees. While we were
appreciating the view, a young man approached with an offer to

guide us to Saidbabo. He wanted to go to his village beyond and would be happy to have our company – irrespective of the deficiency of finances. He would be ready when we were. We accepted the offer with alacrity, and while he was away packing his bag we sat down on the porch of a house and tried to eat some hard-tack biscuits without anyone seeing. That's the trouble with *Ramadan*. Even an infidel is shamed into starvation.

To cross the tributary involved the use of a dug-out canoe ferry, and to reach the vessel a passage through glutinous, evil Tana mud extending to the knee. Barefoot – for a shoe would be lost for ever in a moment under such conditions – we forged our way to the canoe, each of us overbalancing in the process and gracefully sinking backwards into what felt like a deeply upholstered sofa. Instinctively one put out a hand to push the body upright again, whereupon the arm disappeared into the morass right up to the shoulder. Since the other arm, Excalibur-like, was holding rifle, shoes and assorted provisions, progress came to a standstill. But aid was at hand, and half a dozen villagers began wallowing about extracting us and themselves to a symphony of glutinous glollops. It was a schoolboy's delight.

The ferry crossing and ancillary attentions cost us our complement of boiled sweets, and the other side was an encore of the mud game with only ourselves to extract one another from the quagmire. Weighing considerably more with the adhesion of mud about our bodies, we bade a none-too-reluctant farewell to Kau and set off over open country trying to shake the worst of the mire from our feet. The afternoon sun was gruelling, drying the stuff on our skin to the consistency of a cracked suit of armour. Our companion, whose name was Odha, turned out to be another of those Zatopek cross-country fanatics, so the pace was excruciating.

We had barely covered a mile when we heard the motors. The sound was indistinct but we would have recognised it anywhere. We could hardly believe our ears, but what other powered vessel could possibly be in so remote an area? I fired off a round from the rifle as a signal to the crews, and Nigel struck a thunderflash, but it was wet and refused to explode. We then rushed towards where the river seemed likely to be and Nigel managed to detonate the last thunderflash, which went off with an ear-shattering roar. Odha followed us, perplexed – not understanding the reason for our strange behaviour. There had been no answering fusillades or shouts from the river so, despairing of losing contact and missing the boat party, we dashed over a *shamba* and into thick ranks of ten-foot-high reeds that indicated the proximity of water. They also indicated something else, and I heard Odha shout a warning, but its import was not immediately apparent. Then, as I struggled through the tall, sharp rushes I heard the snorting and grunting that could mean but one thing: we had blundered into the midst of a colony of hippo! The noise of our own progress through the unyielding vegetation was promptly eclipsed by that of much heavier bodies as the disturbed creatures panicked and bolted for the river. But the boats – whoever they belonged to – would be there blocking their escape route and deflecting the great four-legged steamrollers back to us. And when frightened and aroused the hippo could be as savage as any buffalo. All this came to me as I ran, but my own momentum and desire to keep up with Nigel propelled me onwards. From every direction came battering-ram noises of disturbed leviathans, and to my right, I perceived the reeds flatten abruptly in a most disquieting fashion. At any moment I expected to be confronted by a great bulk and was ready to fling myself from its path.

Suddenly we found ourselves on the river bank and face to face with Andrew and Sandy. They had heard our signals shortly after observing one of the largest concentrations of hippo seen, realised our peril and came ashore to warn us. Together we descended to the anchored boats.

But why, Nigel wanted to know, were the boat party so far down-river? Didn't they know they were well past Saidbabo and the designated site of the new base camp? But Saidbabo, it appeared, was not the heavily forested location that showed so enticingly green on the map. Instead, all that remained were a few copses and tangled undergrowth, offering little promise of worthwhile game. Even the surrounding bush was dry and devoid of life. Therefore they had pushed on through a revitalised Tana that, as we had painfully discovered, teemed with hippo. The mangrove swamps below Kau were likely to support far more abundant river wildlife and an ecological change of scene of much greater interest than anything Saidbabo had to offer. Nigel saw their point. But the two of us nevertheless pondered upon what our fate would have been had we failed to make this lucky contact and had staggered on to Saidbabo. Virtually foodless, we could have found it more than inconvenient.

Odha happily joined us when Nigel and I took to the boats for the return journey towards Kipini. The attraction of riding with us in an inflatable was obviously more powerful than a simple return to his village – even if that had been the reason he came with us in the first place.

The approach to the delta region and swamps of the Tana's mouth by water was far more dramatic than it had been by road. The river widened perceptibly and took on the haughty grandeur of a wise old man, while its shores – they could no longer be described as mere banks – were overhung with a botanical fever of bloated shrubbery. Kipini is not the 'natural' mouth, but simply the outlet of a small creek, the Ozi. The Tana's original mouth was 20 miles down the coast, but in the 1860s the Sultan of Witu had a canal cut from Belazoni, on the Tana, to join the Ozi, thus making the Tana itself navigable from Kipini. In 1895 the DO at Kipini had the canal widened as a famine relief project; shortly after this an unusually heavy flood carved a wider channel, and the Tana upped and henceforth entered the sea via the Belazoni Canal and the Ozi. The old mouth at Mto Tana ceased to function except as an overflow during flooding – when the whole area below Ngao takes on a delta appearance.

The first indication of the close proximity of the sea came with the realisation that we were barely moving. The reason was exciting but hardly helpful. The tide was coming in and we had reached a point where the river was actually flowing backwards. We were aware that from now on we should have to take into account the tidal flow for further progress. In the meantime it was plain that this day's voyage was nearly at an end. In the face of insistence from Odha that Ozi village was 'just around the next bend' we began searching for an overnight encampment site. Two, three, four bends later, with still no Ozi, an abortive landing had half a dozen of us up to our knees in mud again, which with a fast-approaching night and boats virtually at a standstill only added to our predicament. In some desperation we dropped anchor opposite a banana plantation and, as luck would have it, an evil-smelling and mosquito-infested backwater.

That night was not one of our more successful of wayside camps. Creepy-crawlies were legion, with biting insects as hungry as we were. A group of us remained around the mosquito-defying smoke of the fire until well after midnight; after this I finally shared the floor of a canvas shelter with Derek. And what was left of the night was one long sweat. The sea breezes of the Hotel Bedford became infinitely desirable.

Nigel must have been thinking along the same lines, for after a cooked breakfast, he was quick to propose to me a return there. His idea was to walk to Ozi along the bank and 'thumb a lift' on one of the rice-carrying canoes that (according to Odha, who volunteered to lead us to the village) plied between it and Kipini with the late morning tide. The inflatables had dropped out of sight below a bank that had now become apparent as the water level had sunk by several feet with the outgoing tide. Carpets of mud cradled the craft, now beached. As soon as deep water returned, the boat party were to continue downstream to raise their own base camp at the first suitable site beyond Ozi.

The walk to the village raised similar obstacles to those of the day before. Small backwaters and inlets interrupted our progress, while another irrigation system with its squares of cultivation deflected us from the direct route; but our reliance on Odha's local knowledge in preference to an obsolete map made the going easier.

Ozi had been one of those villages affected by the great flood of 1961-2. It had consequently transferred itself a mile back from the Tana, to repose self-confidently on a bump in the terrain. Yet close to the river, bits and pieces of old Ozi not only showed but were in process of resurrection.

Our anticipated canoe ride to Kipini seemed initially to be no more than a figment of Odha's imagination. A number of dug-outs lay at their moorings, but none appeared to be going anywhere. We sat down and waited, and half the population of the village crowded round to wait with us. After a long interval Nigel enquired with some irritation as to what we were waiting for. The boat for Kipini, said Odha in unison with his compatriots. But when was it coming, demanded Nigel, and his question was answered by a host of massive shrugs and bland expressions of indifference. At this, Nigel displayed a measure of anger that finally aroused everyone from their stupor. One of the larger dug-outs at the quayside turned out to be the vessel in question, its cargo of sacks of rice close by. What everyone had been waiting for remained a mystery, for boats don't load themselves. But it personified the African mentality to perfection: never do anything until you have to.

While the craft was being loaded our own boats arrived on the scene, the crews coming ashore to stretch their legs and investigate the village. This provided further distraction,but after the dug-out was finally loaded, Nigel and I stepped gingerly into the boat – to a barrage of gratuitous and fatuous advice from our own compatriots – to seat ourselves on the precariously balanced cargo in the stern. But there was no capsize: this dug-out was made of sterner stuff. We were joined by two paddlers, who sat in the middle of the boat, though such was the state of the tide it was the current that provided most of the momentum.

The ensuing voyage was of an hour and a half's duration, and rarely have I enjoyed a river cruise so much. Here and there were miniscule rice paddies in tiny clearings where the thick jungle relented momentarily from its embrace of the water. And rounding a bend, we came upon a giant tusker standing at the river's edge, trunk raised, ears wide, the great head poised in challenge. He stood his ground as we glided by but lost his nerve at the last moment, turned tail and crashed into the undergrowth.

The water was brackishly salt; the wavelets miniature copies of those of the sea. But the salt had not yet had time to mix with the muddy brown deluge of the river, and the result was a moving pattern of strange watery shapes and shades. There were no hippo below Kau, the villagers had assured us but, lo and behold, we counted nine pink-brown heads in our path. One by one they sank, blowing resentfully, as we approached. Birds and baboons screeched in wild cacophony, but through the din, faint and doggedly, came the sound of the ocean rollers.

Ever wilder, the Tana expanded into the Grand Waterway, abruptly pompous in its exit to the sea, with thickly clustered courtiers of trees bowing in obeisance at its passing. At each bend the trees shrank in stature, but steadfastly continued to line the royal way. Another bend and there were no more trees. Instead, the beach of Kipini provided a yellow cloth of gold prostrate upon the threshold of the estuary, a touch of faded pageantry or a shroud for a dying soul. Merging with the sky, the sea barely displayed acknowledgement as it accepted the lifeblood of the aged river.

Over on the left the lone palm pinpointed the Bedford Hotel.

Minus the amenities offered by vehicle support, the rain at Base Camp Six, downstream of Ozi, was particularly unwelcome. Whatever African weather does, it does it with a thoroughness that is disconcerting to the spoilt European. When it rains in Africa the heavens simply open and water plummets from the sky. This was not the rainy season, but we were to see a good impersonation of it.

All we had in the way of cover in the steaming mangrove swamps of Ozi was a single tent, an assortment of plastic sheets and a communal ingenuity born of necessity. Within hours, home-made bivouacs were blooming amongst the tree-trunks, root-stems and rotting logs of the twilight world beneath the dripping branches. Within days, each bivouac had become a masterpiece of inventiveness that not only kept out some of the rain, but provoked the passionate pride of its owner. Tony even went so far as a kitchen garden, fenced and gated with creepers – in lieu of roses – round the door.

With little or no scientific equipment to hand, Ozi became something of an observation-only base from which forays were made, night and day, into the swamps and jungle. In many respects the site was a more interesting than that of some of the earlier bases, in that the flora and fauna of a mangrove swamp offered a new range of subjects for study.

As with mangrove swamps along tidal estuaries the world over, that of Ozi was composed chiefly of trees and shrubs belonging to the genus *Rhizophora* of the family *Rhizophoraceae*. Their trunks and branches produced adventitious roots, which, descending in arched loops, struck at some distance from the parent stem to send up new trunks, the forest thus spreading like a banyan grove. An interesting feature of the mangrove is the air roots projecting above the ground. These are provided with minute openings into which the air diffuses and passes through passages in the soft spongy tissue to those roots underground.

Here, too, was virtually a rain forest with a dense tree canopy, the individual crowns forming two or three distinguishing layers effectively keeping out much of the sunshine. The trees themselves displayed straight and slender trunks, to give a somewhat dismal prospect of uniformity to the human eye, while the foliage held a quality of sameness giving the illusion that one was living within a massive hothouse. Contrary to popular belief, the tropical rain forest is not an impenetrable jungle of undergrowth, creepers and rotted vegetation – this description fitting no more of it than the edges of clearings and the river banks, where the sunlight could penetrate to the forest floor.

On the mangrove floor were clay mires; the deep cracks and uneven blocks are difficult enough to negotiate at dry times, but the mires become completely impassable during the rainy season. Andrew and Sandy took a whole day to fight their way on foot to and from the tall sandbanks, towering over the tree canopy in the distance, that bordered the sea south of Kipini. And even there, several miles from the mouth, they found the water was rusty with the Tana's mud.

Another observation trek undertaken was to a clearing near Ozi, where elephants were found in considerable strength, the party having to dodge from tree to tree in an effort to bypass them without provoking disturbance, flight or anger. Lion and leopard too were firmly in residence; we heard them at night and again during the daytime, and Andrew caught sight of a leopard bounding away into a tangle of undergrowth very close to our makeshift camp. For size and weight, a leopard is another dangerous animal. Normally shy and retiring, and always seeking safety by stealth, a wounded leopard will nevertheless charge as soon as its place of concealment is approached, and so determined and courageous is it that the animal can seldom be stopped except with a bullet. It moves very fast, is low to the ground, and the method of attack in such circumstances is usually to 'scalp' an aggressor with those fearsome claws.

An excursion up-river beyond Kau, spanning the hours of dusk and darkness, took a party to Kibokoni, meaning 'Place of the Hippo', where large numbers of these beasts were observed at play – entertaining one another by pushing pink rumps into brown faces, an action that, to a hippo, might have had a beautiful meaning. As darkness fell, observations were resumed using the intensifier, reinforced by an infra-red torch which acted as an invisible searchlight. Somebody then switched on an ordinary torch, and with a great welter of splashing the actors on the Tana stage disappeared from view.

Crabs of all sizes, snakes and crocodiles, all were equally at home in the mangroves. We managed to catch only one snake, a brilliant green specimen an inch thick and two feet long. However, it was the crabs that stole the show. They were everywhere, the bigger ones having an aggravating habit of creeping into a bivouac, seizing an article of equipment and scurrying off down a bolt-hole with it. Several spoons and forks were lost this way, some being recovered by digging up the burrows to reveal all manner of articles – even including an undischarged thunderflash!

But it was for the rain that Ozi camp will be remembered. Not that it spoilt the ten days spent there. It was simply an element of nature that vied with brilliant sunshine, to be sampled as yet another face to the Tana and the wild environment through which it passes. And, as I said, in Africa even rain can be an exciting experience.

Back at Kipini only Alison and I could afford to be relatively idle those last days we were on our own. For Nigel, the yoke of responsibility continued to rest upon his shoulders, the fatigue of accomplishment sustained by worry. With the expedition drawing to a close he had still to get his team back to Nairobi, thence back to Britain,and to lay to rest the many spectres that clamoured for his attention. He, Sandy, Derek and Alison would be remaining behind following the main group's departure, to dot the i's and cross the t's of the project. And that would be only so far as Kenyan involvement was concerned. In Britain a new set of post-expedition tasks would arise, with the exploitation of the scientific and other findings together with the satisfying of our many sponsors and supporting institutions. For a leader of such a mission as ours a moment of calm is essential.

In addition, there were the reports he would be required to make to the Polytechnic of Central London [now the University of Westminster], Royal Geographical Society, Medical Research Council, Ministry of Overseas Development, World Expeditionary Association and other bodies, as well as the formulation of a post-expedition programme to hold our membership together upon return to Britain. It was these obligations, with their mass of impending paperwork, that were to occupy Nigel during those few relatively quiet days we stole at Kipini.

I had only my promotional writings to worry about. A number of Kenyan publications had requested reports and articles following our return to Nairobi, and several magazines in Britain expected something within a week of us arriving home. For me the sunny hours and stormy intervals on the beach of Kipini were a time for some hectic scribbling.

And the book. How was I going to present the story of the Tana River Expedition? What had it taught me? How had it affected my fellow-members? What had three months and more of being thrown together in a milieu of rough living done to a bunch of varied individuals aged twenty to fifty-two? In effect it would be the story of *any* expedition, but told from the point of view of a participant with no expeditionary experience – for that was the only way I *could* tell it.

Ignoring the stares of a perpetual audience of dumb-struck children, I cast about for occurrences of human behaviour that shone the brightest or produced the greatest surprises. In view of the stories I had heard of fevered relationships occurring behind the scenes of bigger and more famous expeditions, ours had been a model of its kind. With a composition of military, scientific and specialist minds and attitudes there was, of course, the occasional clash of personalities and snap of temperaments. Fatigue, hunger, malaise and worry each provided platforms for bickering and heated exchange, but, in fact, such outbursts had been rare and of short duration. We – all of us – not only put up with the idiosyncrasies of our fellow men and women but grew to accept and even admire some of them. I think this aspect of the expedition was something that was of real satisfaction to everyone, particularly our team leaders, whose understanding of human weakness was put to the ultimate test.

Both before and after the expedition I was asked about the problems of mixed sexes in such close, predominantly male company, but it was only after, that I could come up with any answer, and this only a personal opinion. Experiences of members of other expeditions may differ, but, believe it or not, sex played little part within our close-knit community, in spite of what they say about it making the world go round. This is not to say we became a group of zombies completely unaware of the attributes of certain of our fellow beings. But in a strange environment of different cultures, new sights and sounds, spiced with an element of risk and danger, our relationships never became less than that of mutual understanding and respect. Man and woman lived side by side without the usual embarrassments that centuries of overemphasised decorum have prescribed, and because the preponderance of males made it more of a man's world, the women quickly learnt to tolerate the male weaknesses – which are probably female weaknesses too. There is, it could be said, a time to live and a time to love. And in the African jungle and bush living is a full and exhausting enough performance on its own. Only Alison infuriated us by managing, superbly, to look like a woman and not an explorer!

Our retreat to Kipini could not last. Nigel began to fret about how things were getting on at base camp. I fretted in case I was missing something. Again the two of us set out in an attempt to walk through the west-bank mangrove swamps to Ozi but were defeated by vicious undergrowth and bog. Hippo and elephant tracks crossed our path in alarming profusion, while the humidity brought out not only the sweat but clouds of mosquitoes. We withdrew in some disorder. Next day we caught the 'banana boat' – another cargo canoe – going upstream with the tide, to voyage in majestic silence and ease. Two herds of hippo watched us go by; their company is assuredly preferable in water than on the shore.

Reunited with the dwindling numbers of the expedition, our last night round the communal camp-fire carried an air of sadness. But with the dawn came the rain, and so began the wettest day of the expedition as well as the last. We loaded the inflatables for the final time, conscious of the fact but unable to raise much glee. And then we were off, chug-chugging down the Tana watched by our retinue of hippo and crocodile. From the trees came the plaintive aria of the fish eagle and a farewell chorus of jungle birds.

The river mouth was grey with rain and Kipini obliterated by a wall of water. I wore no more than my faithful swimming trunks and was decidedly chilly, but wet clothing is anathema to me.

We came ashore like drowned rats from a sinking ship, and it came to me that only Nigel and I had been privileged to sample the rightful splendour of an epic journey's end. It was a privilege all should have shared.

Conclusion

All things being equal, I would have chosen to return home there and then. Hardened travellers may like to pooh-pooh the comforts of civilisation, but they would hardly be human were there to be a complete absence of appreciation of the switch to the little amenities and luxuries of life long denied them. For me, 'going home' – one's *real* home – is one of the joys of travel, for it puts 20th-century life into true perspective. And this, of course, is in addition to the reunion with loved ones left behind.

An abrupt transfer from wilderness to the razzmatazz urbanity of Brighton would have been fun. As it was, we made the transformation to our home locations piecemeal, with a few days as tourists at Kilifi, and then a week in Nairobi as disciples of commerce at the city's trade fair. I cannot, in all truth, say I found the hours of swimming off the barrier reef in the Indian Ocean a hardship, and at the trade fair our expedition exhibit won both praise as well as a prize for the most original exhibit – us – which was satisfying.

We celebrated our last night in Kenya with a party at the Nairobi Hilton. Serving our every need were obeisant but contemptuous waiters, and on the garish stage leering musicians played music that had a distant relationship to that of the African bush. I watched, incredulous, a dinner-jacketed guest turn away a superbly cooked steak Diane because he had been forced to wait a hundred seconds for the accompanying vegetables. There was fluorescent, unnatural illumination and a menu that read like a book, with caviar at a hundred and five shillings – enough to keep a Tana family alive for a month. We eyed the ranks of cutlery around our sparkling plates uneasily, glancing at other diners to see how they selected the correct implements for each successive course. A virgin white napkin, artistically folded into the shape of a petulant butterfly, I hardly dared touch. The occupants of the room were mostly white but with a sprinkling of Africans, all with gleaming, greedy faces. Opposite them sat wives or girlfriends, ever-conscious of their appearance – pretending not to be comparing themselves to their over- or under-dressed counterparts at other tables.

Suddenly I was back in the jungle again, but it was a different jungle, equally ruthless, equally vicious. Already the other jungle had receded to an inner compartment of my mind, awaiting the moment to be hauled out and paraded in drawing-room and pub. I tried to catch a recollective glimpse of the sluggish, brown Tana winding through that other jungle and told myself how much I longed to be back there.

But I knew I was acting a lie, for, already, I had been ensnared into my world; back into a life I recognised and accepted as my own. Just for a moment, against the black of the velvet drapes, I saw the river, the Pokomo villagers, advancing elephants and a charging rhino, but the vision collided with that of a neat little home with a pocket-handkerchief lawn and exploded into a spray of coloured lights.

I reached for the wine.